Writing a Successful Grant Application

Writing

A SUCCESSFUL GRANT APPLICATION

Second Edition

Liane Reif-Lehrer, Ph.D.
Tech-Write Consultants/ERIMON Associates

Jones and Bartlett Publishers
Boston • Portola Valley

Editorial, Sales, and Customer Service Offices
Jones and Bartlett Publishers
20 Park Plaza
Boston, MA 02116

Printed in the United States of America
10 9 8 7 6 5 4 3

Library of Congress Cataloging-in-Publication Data

Reif-Lehrer, Liane, 1934-
    Writing a successful grant application.

    1. Proposal writing in medicine. 2. Medicine --
Research grants. I. Title. [DNLM: 1. Research Support.
2. Writing. W 20.5 R361w]
R853.P75R44   1989   808'.06661   88-13800

ISBN: 0-86720-104-5

DEDICATION

This small volume is dedicated:

*To my husband, Sam, and my children, Damon and Erica, for always
    "bearing with me;"*
*to my mother, Clara Reif, who, at great sacrifice to herself, made it
    possible for me to have the luxury of a lengthy education;*
*to my brother, Fred Reif, for taking it for granted that I would have a
    career;*
to all those who taught me, and encouraged me;
to Cho Cho San, and Pete for sharing their lives with us;

> *and, as always,*

to The Little Prince *(A. de St. Exupery).*

Foreword

- Please use the material conveyed in this book as a guide—not as a set of rules. Every study section is different, every reviewer is different, every grantee is different!

- Please do not use this book in place of reading the National Institutes of Health (NIH), or other granting agency, instructions. This book is intended as an aid. It is your responsibility to read the instructions carefully and to follow them meticulously.

- Note that the second edition of this book was started in the summer and fall of 1987. The material presented is, to the best of my knowledge, correct at the time of writing the revised edition. Although the principles presented are unlikely to change for some time, the specifics do change frequently. Always check with your potential granting agency about changes in policy and procedures before investing time in preparing a proposal.

- Although the information and examples used in this book focus primarily on NIH investigator-initiated grant applications, much of the information given can be extrapolated readily to many other types of applications for grants and fellowships.

- Please note that government documents reproduced in the body (but not appendices) of this book are indicated by a different style of type.

Table of Contents

Preface
to the Second Edition

This book primarily concerns investigator-initiated research grant applications (R01s) to the National Institutes of Health (NIH). An appendix by Dr. Bruce Trumbo (revised for the second edition by Dr. S. S. Lehrer who is currently on a National Science Foundation review panel) addresses some of the similarities and differences in grant application and review at the National Science Foundation (NSF). However, the basic principles of writing a good grant proposal can be extrapolated for writing many other types of grant proposals. Although the review process may be different at each funding agency, the sorts of things that reviewers look for in an application are not very different in essence.

The suggestions in this book are based largely on my own experience serving on an NIH Vision Study Section, Vis. A (later Vis. A ad hoc) from 1976–1978. Some information was also obtained from the various publications put out by the U.S. Department of Health and Human Services and from seminars presented by NIH administrators. In addition, since 1984, I have given numerous workshops and seminars on grant proposal writing throughout the United States. On several occasions NIH Study Section members, Executive Secretaries, or other grant administrators have attended these talks. It has been gratifying to have them concur with what I said and to get additional useful information from them. I also learned much in researching answers to questions that have come up in the course of the workshops and in discussions with scientists at universities and at the NIH who have been involved, more recently than I, in the grant process as grantees, reviewers, or administrators. I have added this newly acquired information to the second edition.

The second edition encompasses what was in the first edition but I have also incorporated much from a "handout" I developed for my workshops and have attempted to update all the information in keeping with changes in procedures and in the general funding ambiance at NIH.

Much of the information in this small volume is intentionally presented in outline form. The format stems from my conviction that the readers of this book will want the maximum amount of information in the minimum number of words. I trust the text has not lost clarity from the sparsity of words.

The new edition of the book is based on the new NIH application form (PHS-398 revised 9/86) released in June, 1987.

The application form for a grant continuation (PHS-2590) was revised at the same time (9/86).

NSF also released new grant application forms and a new instruction booklet in 1987 (*Grants For Research and Education in Science and Engineering,* Document: NSF 83–57; Revised 1/87).

Note added in second printing: Minor revisions were made to the PHS-398 form (Revised 9/86) on 10/88. The 10/88 revision was released in Spring, 1989. The major changes were to the Checklist page.

Acknowledgements

My sincere thanks go to many colleagues, friends, and associates who helped in various ways with the preparation of the new edition of this book:

- David Freifelder, Ph.D., who was instrumental in the publication of the first edition and also made helpful suggestions with the manuscript for the first edition. (Dr. Freifelder died in March, 1987.)

- Bruce Trumbo, Ph.D., Professor of Statistics and Mathematics, California State University, Hayward, who wrote Appendix VII about the review process for NSF grant applications for the first edition.

- Sherwin S. Lehrer, Ph.D., Senior Staff Scientist, Boston Biomedical Research Institute and Principal Associate, Department of Neurology, Harvard Medical School, who served on an NSF review panel from 1986 to 1988 and who made some revisions to Dr. Trumbo's appendix for this second edition, and also made suggestions about the rest of the new manuscript.

- Jack A. McLaughlin, Ph.D., Associate Director, Extramural and Collaborative Programs, National Eye Institute, who made helpful comments about the first edition at the time I was planning the revised edition.

- Mischa Friedman, Ph.D., Chief, Referral and Review Branch, Division of Research Grants, who provided me with the revised PHS-398 forms prior to their general distribution and who graciously gave of his time to discuss various NIH procedural matters with me. Dr. Friedman retired from NIH in June, 1988.

For critical reading of the manuscript for the second edition:

- Richard Pharo, Ph.D., Director of Research Administration, Eye Research Institute of Retina Foundation.

- Anita A. Suran, Ph.D., Program Director, Fundamental Retinal Processes Program, National Eye Institute.

- Arthur H. Neufeld, Ph.D., Director of Research, Eye Research Institute of Retina Foundation and Associate Professor, Department of Ophthalmology, Harvard Medical School, and currently serving on an NIH Study Section.

- Thomas M. Richardson, M.D., Assistant Clinical Professor of Ophthalmology, Harvard Medical School, and currently serving on an NIH Study Section.

- The principal investigators who graciously gave permission to publish, anonymously, their "Pink Sheets."

- The many investigators and grant administrators with whom I have had helpful discussions over the years about grants and the peer review process.

- Joshua Stayn, who, at age 13, typed much of this manuscript in the summer of 1987, with an efficiency, speed, and accuracy that would be admirable even in someone twice his age.

LIANE REIF-LEHRER

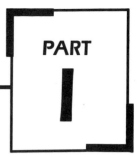

Understanding the Review Process

INTRODUCTION

A good grant proposal requires a good research idea—a unique, interesting, important, and well-defined problem for which you can suggest a sound and viable experimental approach that is likely to lead to a tangible solution, that is, an hypothesis that you can test and either prove or disprove.

The GOOD IDEA must be

- FEASIBLE
  - Do-able by you and your staff
  - Do-able at your institution
  - Acceptable to your institution
  - In conformity with human and animal welfare policies

- Conceptually significant
  The successful resolution of the research idea (solution to the problem) should result in a substantive (non-trivial) finding that will benefit the profession or the public.

The best writing cannot turn a bad idea into a good grant proposal. However, bad writing can turn a good idea into a poor grant proposal. So, planning, writing and revising the proposal are important to the development of a successful application. These are the aspects of proposal preparation that this book is intended to teach.

Aside from the primary requirement—a good idea—several things will help you end up with a proposal that will "fly," that is, one that will be approved and funded. These are

1. Having a well-focused, well-written research proposal
2. Having a long history (unless you are a new investigator) of concentration in a particular research field or problem or—if

you are a new investigator—having good training and substantive preliminary results (pilot studies)

3. Being prepared to devote a substantial effort to the proposed
   work (100% is best, 50% is OK, below 25% is "iffy" unless
   you have a very good reason!)
4. Maintaining a stable work group
5. Having ample publications in well-reviewed, competitive,
   and (if you are in a non-clinical field) preferably basic science
   journals

UNDERSTANDING THE REVIEW PROCESS

Understanding the review process will help you write a better
grant application just as understanding the requirements for a job
can put you in a better situation to prepare yourself for the job
interview. Good expository writing requires that you write for the
benefit of the reader, not the writer. What does the reader, in this
case the reviewer(s), need or want to know? Thus, you must
understand the review process, and the situation of the reviewer
within that process, to be able to write a good grant application.

NIH Has a Dual Peer Review System

THE FIRST LEVEL OF REVIEW is by an Initial Review Group
(IRG), often referred to as a **STUDY SECTION** constituted by
scientific discipline or biomedical topic.

The Study Section

- Provides initial *scientific review* of grant applications
- Assigns a priority score based on scientific merit
- Makes budget recommendations
  (but no funding decisions—funding decisions are the pre-
  rogative of each Institute, which has full discretionary
  powers)
- Does *NOT* set program priorities (Program relevance repre-
  sents Institute priorities)
- Has about 14 members, all scientists
- Is headed by an Executive Secretary from the Division of
  Research Grants (DRG) and a scientist chairperson who is a
  member of the Study Section
- *Is only advisory*

THE SECOND LEVEL OF REVIEW is by individual Institute
NATIONAL ADVISORY COUNCIL.

The Council

- Concurs with or modifies Study Section action on grant
  applications—or defers for further review
- Evaluates applications against program priorities and rele-
  vance
- Makes recommendations about funding to the Institute staff
- Advises on policy
- Has 12 or more members, both scientists and non-scientists
- *Is only advisory*

The travels of an NIH grant application

A Grant Proposal to NIH is

- Initiated by a Principal Investigator (PI)
- Submitted by her/his sponsoring institution to the NIH
- Received at NIH by the *Division of Research Grants*

The Division of Research Grants (DRG)

- Is not part of any Institute
- Is a separate body that answers to the Director of NIH
- Is advisory to the Institutes
- Sets up Study Sections (both standing and, when necessary,
  ad hoc) to review research grant proposals (R01), Research
  Career Development Awards (RCDA), First Awards, and
  fellowship applications (NRSA)
- Has about a dozen referral officers who determine to which
  Study Section proposals are assigned for review
- Uses guidelines to make assignments of grant applications to
  Study Sections and Institutes

When a grant proposal is sent to NIH, it first goes to DRG. Here the grant is assigned a number, for example: 1 R01 EY 01234–01:

1	R01	EY	01234	–01
Status of grant proposal (new, renewal, etc.)	Type of grant proposal (R = research)	Funding Institute*	Identification Number within the Institute	Year of project

[Sometimes there is a suffix, for example: A1 (means amended) or S1 (means supplement)]

Grant Application Assignment to a Study Section (SS)

At DRG, the proposal is assigned for review to one of about 68** chartered Study Sections.

- DRG Referral Officers assign the application to a Study Section. (The Referral Officer may discuss the appropriateness of a Study Section with the Executive Secretary of that Study Section.)

You may suggest an Initial Review Group and/or an NIH component that would be appropriate for your application.

- Attach such correspondence to the application at the time of submission.
- Suggestions will be considered, but the final determination will be made by the DRG.

If you think there has been a serious error in the Study Section assignment of your application, you may request corrective action by writing to the Executive Secretary of the Study Section.

---

* See **Appendix VI-A** for a list of abbreviations of funding Institutes.

**At the time this book is going to press, there are 68 chartered Study Sections. Some of these are sub-divided into two or more subcommittees; thus, there are actually 92 operative Study Sections. In addition, there are several Study Sections that are run by the Division of Research Grants (DRG) for other agencies, but are not DRG Study Sections; for example, AFL and SOH listed in Appendix VI C. Lastly, three to five new review groups are now being formed to review applications related to AIDS research. Information about Study Sections may be obtained by calling (301) 496-7534.

Grant Application Assignment to an Institute

At DRG, your proposal is assigned for review, management and possible funding to one, or in some cases two (a dual assignment), Institutes or other funding components (see Appendix VI.A.). The assignment is made

- According to the *overall mission* of the Institute
- Relating to the *specific programmatic mandates* and interests of the Institute

At the Institute, the application is assigned to a

HEALTH SCIENTIST ADMINISTRATOR (HSA) who

- Is your primary Institute contact for all matters dealing with your grant application before and after the review process;
- Is responsible for administration of the grant if the application is approved and funded;
- Attends the Study Section meeting at which the application is reviewed;
- Is prepared to defend and elucidate the recommendations of the Study Section to Council; but
- Does NOT actively participate in the review and evaluation process at the Study Section meeting.

The health scientist administrator assigned to your grant acts as an ombudsperson for the applicant with respect to procedures that affect the grant at NIH. It is the responsibility of the health scientist administrator to respond to questions by the applicant. These questions may relate to priority scores, to items within the summary statement and rebuttals to items, and may concern advice about the course of action to be taken when a proposal is not funded. In addition, the health scientist administrator can be questioned about the relevance of potential research ideas with respect to the research priorities of that Institute. The health scientist administrators are instructed to remain neutral in all grant dealings.

THE STUDY SECTION

Each Study Section is composed of about 14 scientists chosen for their competence in particular scientific areas. One of these scientists is the chairperson of the Study Section. She/he moderates the discussion of the scientific merit of the proposals during the Study Section Meeting. An administrator from the DRG serves as Executive Secretary of the Study Section.

The Executive Secretary

- Nominates Study Section members (sometimes using recommendations of retiring members)
- Performs administrative and technical review of applications
- Selects primary and secondary reviewers for each proposal
- Manages the Study Section
- Prepares Summary Statements
- Provides requested information about Study Section recommendations

CONSIDERATIONS FOR CHOICE OF STUDY SECTION MEMBERS

- Represent a wide range of expertise related to main subjects reviewed by that Study Section
- Represent different geographical areas (U.S. divided into 4 areas)
- Have only one member from a given institution
- Member may be on only 1 Study Section at a time
- Member serves 4 years (8 year maximum)
- No more than 25% of members may be federal employees
  (In practice, the DRG aims to have no more than 1 federal employee per Study Section)
- Attempt to get representation with respect to sex and ethnic status

The specific members, the chairperson, and the Executive Secretary of every NIH Study Section are listed in an NIH publication entitled **NIH Advisory Committees: Authority, Structure, Function, Members,** which is updated annually. You should be familiar with the members of the Study Section that will review your proposal.

The Executive Secretaries of Study Sections sometimes enlist ad hoc members for specific meetings when additional expertise in a particular field is necessary. The names of these ad hoc reviewers are furnished on request. The Executive Secretaries of Study Sections also may request "outside" opinions about a proposal, by mail, if there is insufficient expertise on the topic of that proposal within the Study Section.

The Executive Secretary of the Study Section assigns specific grant proposals to particular reviewers. Each grant application is assigned primary and secondary (and sometimes tertiary) reviewers who are responsible for its in-depth review. The reviewers study the proposal and the appendix material carefully and often do a great deal of homework and library work to determine the merits of the proposal. You will not be given, and should not ask for, the names of the primary and/or secondary reviewers of your proposal.

Each member of the Study Section is sent a copy of each proposal to be considered at the meeting. To enable them to participate in the discussion and rating of all proposals, all Study Section members are expected to be familiar with all the proposals. The primary reviewers are responsible for thoroughly evaluating the scientific merits of the proposals assigned to them.

The Primary reviewers come to the Study Section Meeting with a written report in which they have assessed, to the best of their ability, the

1. Scientific and technical significance of the proposed research
2. Originality of the proposed research
3. Adequacy of the outlined methodology
4. Qualifications and experience ("track record")—or potential, in the case of a new applicant—of the investigator(s) and of the staff
5. Suitability of the facilities (including availability of resources and scientific ambience)
6. Appropriateness of the requested budget
7. Appropriateness of the requested time to carry out the project (usually 3 or 5 years)
8. Other factors: ethical matters, human subjects, animal welfare, biohazards etc.

Shown below are the instruction sheets that NIH reviewers are asked to follow when they write their reports about each proposal for which they are a primary or secondary reviewer.

(Most of the italicized words are underlined in the original document. I have added a few additional italics to call attention to important points.)

Document 1

GUIDE FOR ASSIGNED REVIEWER'S PRELIMINARY COMMENTS ON RESEARCH GRANT APPLICATIONS (R01)

NIH Document, August, 1987

With the advent of the latest (9/86) revision of Form PHS 398, reviewers need to be aware of several issues that will affect the manner in which applications are evaluated. Additionally, during the period of transition to the new form, it is likely that the older form will be used by some applicants. It is important that all applications be reviewed taking into account the features or limitations of the specific form used.

The most significant change in the new form is the imposition of a 20-page limit on Sections A through D: Specific Aims, Background and Significance, Progress Report/ Preliminary Studies, and Experimental Design and Methods. The *Principal Investigator is requested to provide only an outline in the Experimental Design and Methods section.* An appendix is still allowed, but it may not include more that 10 published or accepted manuscripts. *Reviewers must take into account that these limitations preclude the level of detail requested previously, and applicants should not be penalized for failure to provide the detail to which the study sections have become accustomed.* On the other hand, investigators who use the older form should be neither advantaged nor disadvantaged by having provided a longer, more detailed application.

Total costs are requested on the new application form along with direct costs. *Indirect costs must not influence the priority score or the assessment of the budget.*

Please use the following guidelines when preparing written comments on research grant applications assigned to you for review.

DESCRIPTION: Use the abstract on page 2 of the application unless inappropriate, *making sure the objectives and procedures are clearly and concisely described.* Do not make evaluative statements as part of the description.

CRITIQUE: Do not include descriptive information in this section. Provide an analysis of the strengths and weaknesses of the research plan, which consists of Specific Aims, Background and Significance, Progress

Report/Preliminary Studies, and Experimental Design and Methods. For Deferred or revised applications, evaluate changes since the previous review.

> NOTE: The new application form requests only an *outline* of Experimental Design and Methods, and page limitations preclude the level of detail requested in the past.

INVESTIGATORS: Assess the competence of the principal investigator and key personnel to conduct the proposed research.

RESOURCES AND ENVIRONMENT: Evaluate any special attributes or deficiencies relevant to the conduct of the proposed studies.

BUDGET: Evaluate the direct costs only. Determine whether all items of the budget are *appropriate and justified.* Provide a rationale for each suggested modification in amount or duration of support. For supplemental applications, comment on the requested budget in relation to the parent grant.

OTHER CONSIDERATIONS

> *Overlap:* Identify any apparent scientific or budgetary overlap with active, pending, or planned support.

> *Foreign:* Comment on any special talents, resources, populations, or environmental conditions that are not readily available in the United States or that provide augmentation of existing United States resources. In addition, indicate whether similar research is being done in the United States and whether there is a need for such additional research. In the case of a domestic application with a significant foreign component, apply the same criteria.

> *Human Subjects*

>> *Exemptions Claimed:* Express any comments or concerns about the appropriateness of the exemption(s) claimed.

>> *No Exemptions Claimed: Express any comments or concerns about the appropriateness of the responses to the six required*

points, especially whether the *risks* to subjects are reasonable *in relation* to the anticipated *benefits* to the subject and in relation to the importance of the knowledge that may reasonably be expected to result from the research.

Vertebrate Animals: Express any comments or concerns about the appropriateness of the responses to the five required points, especially whether the procedures will be limited to those that are unavoidable in the conduct of scientifically sound research.

Biohazards: Note any material or procedures that are potentially hazardous and indicate whether the protection proposed will be adequate.

SUMMARY AND RECOMMENDATION: Summarize the strengths and weaknesses of the application and provide a recommendation of approval, disapproval, or deferral. *You may recommend a priority rating.*

Note: Your written comments will be destroyed after being incorporated into the summary statement. However, they should not bear personal identifiers because, under the Privacy Act of 1974, principal investigators may, upon request, gain access to documents relating to the review of their applications. In the rare event that your comments must be made available to a Principal Investigator, you will be notified promptly by NIH staff.

At the Study Section Meeting

The primary and secondary (and tertiary, if there is one) reviewers read their reports aloud at the meeting. This oral presentation is followed by general discussion, by all the Study Section members, of the merits and pitfalls of the proposal, the qualifications of the principal investigator (PI), and the appropriateness of the proposed staff. All members are expected to be acquainted with the general substance of all of the grant applications to be reviewed and to participate in the discussion. Administrators from the relevant NIH Institute are often present at the Study Section Meetings. They may be asked to provide administrative information, for example, about the applicant's grant history, but they do not participate in the general discussion. After the discussion, which may take anywhere from ten minutes to as long as an hour, a recommendation is made by majority vote for

1. Approval,
2. Disapproval, or
3. Deferral for additional information.

For each application recommended for approval, each Study Section member individually records by secret ballot a numerical score that reflects a personal evaluation of the scientific merit of the proposed research. This score is based on a scale of 0.1 increments* from 1.0 (the best score) to 5.0 (the worst score).

The budget is usually discussed after the vote to approve, disapprove, or defer, but it must be discussed before the numerical priority score assignment. (See page 2, paragraph 3 in NIH Document, REVIEW PROCEDURES FOR INITIAL REVIEW GROUP MEETINGS, August, 1986, shown below).

Shown on the following pages are the NIH review procedures for initial review group (Study Section) meetings. (Many, though not all, of the italics (underlines in the original document) have been added by me to call attention to important points.)

---

* As this book goes to press, NIH is doing a study about the possibility of changing the scoring system back to increments of 0.5, the system used in the 1970s. Keep track of possible changes such as this by reading the *NIH Guide for Grants and Contracts* (see Appendix XI, Resources).

Document 2

REVIEW PROCEDURES FOR INITIAL REVIEW GROUP MEETINGS

NIH Document, August, 1986

The initial review group (IRG) evaluates the scientific merit of each grant application according to specific criteria. The principal criteria for the initial review of research project grant applications[1/] based on the Public Health Service (PHS) Scientific Peer Review Regulations, include:

- scientific, technical, or medical significance and originality of the goals of the proposed research;

- appropriateness and adequacy of the experimental approach and methodology proposed to carry out the research;

- qualifications and research experience of the principal investigator and staff, particularly but not exclusively in the area of the proposed research;

- availability of resources necessary to the research;

- the proposed budget and duration in relation to the proposed research; and

- where an application involves activities that could have an adverse effect on humans, animals, or the environment, the adequacy of the proposed means for protection against or minimizing such effects. (See pages 2 to 4.)

In addition, for renewal and supplemental applications, preliminary data and/or progress to date must be evaluated. For revised applications, the changes must be appraised.

During the meeting, the Chairperson of the IRG, following an agenda prepared by the Executive Secretary, introduces each application, calls upon the individuals assigned by the Executive Secretary to present their written comments, and invites discussion. At an appropriate time, the Chairperson requests a motion on the application. The possible motions can be for approval, disapproval, or deferral. It should be noted that *only regularly appointed members may make motions, vote, and assign priority ratings.*

- *Approval:* The application is of sufficient merit to be worthy of support based on the appropriate review criteria. A vote for approval is equivalent to a recommendation that a grant be awarded *provided sufficient funds are available.* A priority rating is required.

- *Disapproval:* The application is not of sufficient merit to be worthy of support. *Disapproval may also be recommended when gravely hazardous or unethical procedures are involved,* or when no funds can be recommended, as in the case of a supplement deemed to be unnecessary. No priority rating is assigned.

(End of page 1 of NIH Document about Review Procedures: August, 1986)

Deferral: The IRG cannot make a recommendation without additional information. This information may be obtained by a project site visit or by the submission of additional material by the applicant. *Deferred applications are usually reviewed again at the next IRG meeting.*

After a motion of approval, disapproval, or deferral has been seconded, the Chairperson asks for any further discussion. The Chairperson then calls for the question, and the regularly appointed IRG members vote on the motion. The recommendation of the IRG for each application is made by majority vote.

The budget must be discussed before a priority is assigned. The budget recommendation, which can be for the time and amount requested or for an adjusted time and amount, should include not only the first year but also each subsequent year.

Split Vote

If two or more of the regularly appointed members disagree with the recommendation of the IRG, the dissenting members must prepare a written minority report. For any recommendation obtained by a split vote, the full action of the committee must be recorded: number of votes for the motion, number of votes against the motion, and the number of abstentions. Members are encouraged not to abstain. However, if a member is unable to assess the merit of an application without additional information, as evidenced by his/her prior discussion or recommendation for deferral, that member should abstain from voting on a motion for approval or disapproval.

Priority Rating

For each application that has been recommended for approval, each regularly appointed member who votes *for or against* the motion records a numerical rating that reflects the member's opinion of the merit of the application. The numerical rating ranges from 1.0 (the most meritorious) to 5.0 (the least meritorious) with increments of 0.1. *The priority rating pertains to the recommended, not the requested, budget and duration of support.* Abstaining members, i.e., those who do not vote on the motion, do not assign a numerical rating, and are not counted in calculating the average of the individual ratings.

If any member who votes *for or against* a motion for approval does not assign a priority rating, that member's action shall be recorded as an abstention.

OTHER CONSIDERATIONS

> *Overlap. Reviewers will identify any apparent scientific or budgetary overlap with active, pending, or planned support.*
>
> *Foreign Organizations.* The proposal is evaluated in terms of any special opportunities for furthering research programs through the use of special talents, resources (human subjects, animals, diseases, equipment or technologies), populations or environmental conditions in the applicant country which are not readily available in the United States or which provide augmentation of existing United States resources. In addition, notice is taken whether similar research is being done in the United States and whether there is a need for additional research in the area of the proposal. In the

----

(End of page 2 of NIH Document about Review Procedures: August, 1986)

> case of a domestic application with a significant foreign component, the same review criteria are applied.

Research Involving Human Subjects

Applicant organizations have the primary responsibility for safeguarding the rights and welfare of individuals who participate as subjects in research activities supported by the NIH. However, the NIH also relies on its IRGs and National Advisory Councils or Boards to evaluate all applications and proposals involving human subjects for compliance with the Department of Health and Human Services human subject regulations.

The regulations define "human subject" as a "living individual about whom an investigator obtains (1) data through interventions or interaction with the individual, or (2) identifiable private information." The regulations extend to the use of human organs, tissue and body fluids from individually identifiable human subjects as well as to graphic, written, or recorded information derived from individually identifiable human subjects. *The use of autopsy materials is governed by applicable state and local law and is not directly regulated by the Federal human subject regulations.*

The Department will fund research covered by these regulations only if the institution has filed an assurance with the NIH Office for Protection from Research Risks and has certified that the research has been approved by an *Institutional Review Board (IRB)* and is subject to continuing review by the IRB. When research involves only minimal risk and meets certain other conditions, the IRB may waive the requirement for obtaining informed consent. In addition, certain research that poses little or no risk to human subjects is exempt from IRB review and approval. In such cases, however, adherence to ethical standards and pertinent laws is still required.

The review by the IRG is expected to reflect existing codes adopted by disciplines relevant to the research or the collective standards of the professions represented by the membership. The evaluation by IRG members is to take into consideration any potential risks to the subjects, the procedures for protecting against and minimizing these risks, *the potential benefits of the proposed research to the subjects and in relation to the importance of the knowledge that may reasonably be expected to result.* Based on this evaluation, the IRG may recommend:

- approval without restrictions;

- approval with recorded comments or expressions of concern to be communicated to the institution and principal investigator;

- approval with limitations on the scope of the work proposed, the imposition of restrictions, or the elimination of objectionable procedures involving human subjects;

- deferral for clarification; or

- disapproval if the research risks are sufficiently serious and protection against the risks so inadequate as to consider the entire application unacceptable.

Any *comments or concerns* that IRG members may wish to express regarding the adequacy of protections afforded human subjects *will be discussed in a Special*

(End of page 3 of NIH Document about Review Procedures: August, 1986)

Note in the summary statement. No awards will be made until all expressed concerns about human subjects have been resolved to the satisfaction of the NIH. Specific concerns and policy interpretation requests may be addressed to the *Office for Protection from Research Risks,* which is responsible for the administration and interpretation of DHHS policy and regulations for the protection of human subjects of research.

Research Involving Vertebrate Animals

Although the *recipient institution and investigator bear the major responsibility for the proper care and use of animals,* NIH staff, IRGs, and Councils share this responsibility. Care and use of vertebrate animals in research must conform to applicable law and Public Health Service policy, especially the *Principles for Use of Animals.* These principles can be summarized as two broad rules.

- *The project should be worthwhile and justified on the basis of anticipated results for the good of society and the contribution to knowledge,* and the work should be *planned and performed by qualified scientists.*

- *Animals* are to *receive proper care and treatment,* and should not be confined, restrained, transported, cared for, and used in experimental procedures in a manner to cause any unnecessary discomfort, pain, or injury.

Any comments or concerns that IRG members may wish to express regarding the appropriateness of the *choice of species and numbers involved,* the justification for their use, and the care and maintenance of vertebrate animals used in the project will be discussed in a Special Note on the summary statement. Questions may be directed to the *Office for Protection from Research Risks. No award will be made unless the applicant institution has given the NIH Office for Protection from Research Risks an acceptable assurance of compliance* with the PHS policy and *all concerns or questions raised by the IRG have been resolved to the satisfaction of the NIH.*

Hazardous Research Materials and Methods

The investigator and the sponsoring institution are responsible for protecting the environment and research personnel from hazardous conditions. As with research involving human subjects, reviewers are expected to apply the collective standards of the professions represented within the IRG in identifying potential hazards, such as inappropriate handling of oncogenic viruses, chemical carcinogens, infectious agents, radioactive or explosive materials, or recombinant DNA.

If applications pose special hazards, these hazards will be identified and any concerns about the adequacy of safety procedures highlighted as a Special Note on the summary statement. *No awards will be made until all concerns about hazardous procedures or conditions have been resolved to the satisfaction of the NIH.*

AVOIDING CONFLICTS OF INTEREST DURING IRG MEETINGS

At the beginning of each meeting, the executive secretary orients the members by explaining the NIH *conflict-of-interest* policy. A member must leave the room when an application submitted by his/her own organization[2/] is being discussed or when the member, his/her immediate family, or close professional

----

(End of page 4 of NIH Document about Review Procedures: August, 1986)

----

associate(s)[3/] has a financial interest (indicated on Form 474), even if no significant involvement is apparent in the proposal being considered.

This would include the member's availability at the principal investigator's institution for discussions; being a provider of services, cell lines, reagents, or other materials; or writing of a letter of reference. *In these cases, the members must be absent from the room during the review.* Members are also urged to avoid any actions that might give the appearance that a conflict of interest exists, even though he or she believes there may not be an actual conflict of interest. Thus for example, *a member should not participate in the deliberations and actions on any application from a recent student, a recent teacher, or a close personal friend.* Judgement must be applied on the question of recency, frequency and strength of the working relationship between the member and the principal investigator as reflected for example, in publications. Another example might be *an application from a scientist with whom the member has had longstanding differences* which could reasonably be viewed as affecting the member's objectivity. However, if the executive secretary determines that the member *can* be objective, then a balanced point of view for the review is appropriate.

A reviewer must leave the room during discussion of an application if he/she *is a member of, or has a financial interest in the for-profit organization submitting the application.* This includes ownership of stock in, or being a consultant for the for-profit organization. A reviewer should also leave the room during discussion of an application if being present would give the *appearance* of a conflict of interest. Examples would be, an application from a for-profit organization that provides substantial financial funding to the reviewer's organization or laboratory, or from a for-profit organization that is in commercial competition with the reviewer's organization.

At the end of the IRG meeting, the Executive Secretary obtains written certification from all members that they have not participated in any reviews of applications when their presence would have constituted a real or apparent conflict of interest. In addition, *each study section keeps a log, prepared by the Grants Assistant and maintained in the study section office, of which members left the room and for what applications.*

CONFIDENTIALITY

All materials pertinent to the applications being reviewed are privileged communications prepared for use only by consultants and NIH staff, and should not be shown to or discussed with other individuals. *Review group members must not independently solicit opinions or reviews on particular applications or parts thereof from experts outside the pertinent initial review group.* Members may, however, suggest scientists from whom the Executive Secretary may subsequently obtain advice. Consultants are requested to leave all review materials with the Executive Secretary at the conclusion of the the review meeting.

Under no circumstances should consultants advise investigators, their organizations, or anyone else of recommendations or discuss the review proceedings with them. The investigator may be led into unwise actions on the basis of premature or erroneous information. Such advice also represents an unfair intrusion into the privileged nature of the proceedings and invades the privacy of fellow consultants serving on review committees and site visit teams. A breach of confidentiality could deter qualified consultants from serving on review committees and inhibit those who do from engaging in free and full discussion of recommendations.

(End of page 5 of NIH Document about Review Procedures: August, 1986)

COMMUNICATIONS WITH INVESTIGATORS

Except during site visits, there should be no direct communications between consultants and investigators. Consultants' requests for additional information and telephone inquiries or correspondence from investigators should be directed to the Executive Secretary, who will handle all such communications.

(End of page 6 of NIH Document about Review Procedures: August, 1986)

Footnotes:

1/ The specific review criteria will vary with other types of applications such as the National Research Service Awards (fellowships), Research Career Development awards, or Small Business Innovation Research grants.

2/ The term "own organization" includes the entire system in which the member is an employee, consultant, officer, director, or trustee or has a financial interest; or with which the member is negotiating or has any arrangement concerning prospective employment. However, it has now been determined that the interest involved is too remote or too inconsequential to affect the integrity of a special Government employee's review of a funding application or contract proposal from one campus of one of the following multi-campus institutions, where the interest consists solely of employment as a faculty member (including Department Chairman) at a separate campus of the same multi-campus institution:

The University of Alabama system consisting of the University of Alabama, the University of Alabama in Birmingham, and the University of Alabama in Huntsville.

The campuses of the University of California.

The system consisting of Colorado State University, the University of Southern Colorado, and Fort Lewis College.

The Indiana University system consisting of eight universities on nine campuses, with the exception of the system-wide schools: the School of Business; the School of Dentistry; the School of Medicine; the School of Nursing; and the School of Public and Environmental Affairs.

The University of Nebraska system consisting of the University of Nebraska-Lincoln, the University of Nebraska at Omaha, and the University of Nebraska Medical Center.

The campuses of the State University of New York.

The Oregon system of higher education consisting of the University of Oregon, Oregon State University, Oregon Health Sciences University, Portland State University, Western Oregon State College, Southern Oregon State College, Eastern Oregon State College, and the Oregon Institute of Technology.

The campuses of the University of Tennessee.

The separate universities comprising the University of Texas System.

The separate universities comprising the University of Wisconsin System.

c.f. Federal Register, April 25, 1986, Part 73 (Amended)

3/ Co-workers and other colleagues with whom members regularly co-author papers, consult, or otherwise closely relate. "Close professional associate" is the term NIH finds most appropriate to the word "partner" in the Federal conflict-of-interest laws and regulations.

(End of page 7 and of NIH Document about Review Procedures: August, 1986)

A SITE VISIT TO A PRINCIPAL INVESTIGATOR'S LABORATORY

May be recommended

- When information needed to make a recommendation about an application can be obtained only at the proposed research or training site
- Before the Study Section meeting if a primary reviewer or the Executive Secretary recognizes the need for additional information that cannot be obtained by mail or telephone
- At the Study Section meeting in conjunction with a deferral action
- When an application involves complex coordination of individuals or institutions, for example, Program Project Grants, Training Grants, etc.

The site-visit is made by a special site-visit committee. The Executive Secretary selects the members of the project site-visit team, accompanies them, and coordinates the proceedings. Typically, the site-visit team is composed of two or more members of the Study Section, representatives from the potential awarding Institute and, when necessary, ad hoc consultants who are experts in critical aspects of the proposed work. The site-visit team reports its findings and recommendations back to the Study Section in time for its next meeting.

After the Study Section meeting

- The Executive Secretary averages the scores assigned by the individual Study Section members for each approved application and multiplies by 100 to provide a three-digit rating known as a *priority score.*
- Percentile ranks are then calculated for these average priority scores. (See NIH Guide for Grants and Contracts: 17, #26, Aug. 12, 1988, page 2). The priority scores and percentile rankings are the primary, but not the only, determinants upon which funding decisions are based.
- The Executive Secretary prepares a Summary Statement—often referred to as "the pink sheets"—(later sent to the PI) based on the primary and secondary reviewers' reports and the discussion at the Study Section Meeting.
- The Grant Application is sent to COUNCIL

- The Executive Secretary of the Study Section attends the Council Meeting

  At the end of each Study Section meeting, the Executive Secretary prepares a summary statement for each grant application. The summary statement contains a description and critique of the project proposed in the grant application, an explanation of the recommendations of the Study Section, a recommended budget, and notations about any special points, such as a split vote, a potentially hazardous experimental procedure, or concerns about proposed human studies or use of vertebrate animals. The summary statement is forwarded to the appropriate Institute for review (in Council) and possible funding.

The Council

Each Institute has a National Advisory Council, which is composed of 12–16 individuals, approximately 25% of whom are lay people and the remainder scientists. An Executive Secretary of a Study Section attends the Council Meeting when a grant reviewed in her/his Study Section is discussed. The Council considers the summary statements from each Study Section and adds its own review based on judgements of both scientific merit and relevance to the program goals of the assigned Institute. In some cases, this program relevance can alter the ranking position of the proposal for funding. The Council then makes recommendations on funding. Consideration by the Council constitutes the second half of the peer review.

Overall, the AWARDS ARE BASED ON SCIENTIFIC MERIT AND PROGRAM CONSIDERATIONS.

OTHER CONSIDERATIONS

Keep Up to Date with What is Going on at NIH
(And other funding agencies)

- Get on the mailing list for the "NIH Guide for Grants and Contracts" (see Appendix XI: Resources).
- Get on the mailing list or subscribe to other pertinent newsletters (see Appendix XI: Resources).

- Visit the Office for Grants and Contracts (Sponsored Research) at your institution.
  - Get to know the people and the resources.
  - Does your Office for Grants and Contracts publish a newsletter?
- Maintain contact with—and establish a good relationship with—the administrators of your funding Institute.
- Note the revision date on the grant application form you use.
- Watch for changes in grant application instructions between revisions.
- Keep track of the funding situation—both nationally and within your NIH Institute.
- Understand current funding priorities for research relevance.

Know Your Study Section

- Study Section members rotate in a staggered fashion throughout the year. Find out whether the membership has changed since the last printing of *NIH Advisory Committees: Authority, Structure, Function, Members.*
- The approach to grant review may differ from one Study Section to another, and may change with time as the membership changes.
- Each Study Section has a different expertise and flavor which depends on the
  - Executive Secretary
  - Chairperson
  - Members (4-year staggered terms)
  - Number of grants being reviewed
- If you submit a proposal, and subsequently submit a revised proposal, the revision may or may not be reviewed by the same reviewers.

Think About the Reviewers' Workload

To be a successful grant writer, it is important to

- Think about the reviewers as real people who have many important obligations in addition to reviewing your proposal.
- Make your reviewers' jobs as easy as possible

  BEFORE—and *DURING*—the Study Section Meeting:

  - Write accurately, clearly, and briefly, and follow the instructions.

- Don't make the reviewer "guess" what you are trying to say.
  - Give all necessary information in the correct places, in logical order, according to the required format, and within the stipulated page limitations.
- Don't make the reviewer "guess" what you are trying to do.
  - Explain precisely what you plan to do.
- Don't make the reviewer search the library to find out how you plan to do your experiments.
- **Give the reviewer good cause to become your advocate rather than your adversary.**

Parts
of the
Grant Application

PARTS OF THE GRANT APPLICATION

The application form for an NIH investigator-initiated Research Grant (R01) is Public Health Service (PHS) form 398, revised 9/86 and 10/88. The packet contains application forms and instructions for Research Grants (R01) and other types of support such as Research Career Development Awards (RCDA) and Fellowships* (Institutional National Research Service Awards (NRSA)). We will discuss in detail in this book only the R01 application. However, many of the basic concepts presented can be adapted to other types of applications at NIH and other funding agencies.

You should be familiar with the different sections of the grant proposal and understand the purpose and importance of each.

Reproduced on the following pages are the parts of the R01 application from the PHS-398 (Rev 9/86) and some suggestions for filling them out. The complete NIH instructions are reproduced in Appendix I. It is important that you read the NIH instructions carefully.

SECTION 1: ADMINISTRATIVE AND FINANCIAL INFORMATION

In the first part of the grant application you are required to give various kinds of administrative and financial information, primarily on forms provided in the application kit. In addition, on form-page 2 there is a space in which to write a description (abstract) of the research plan that you present in section 2. The

---

* The Institutional NRSA should not be confused with the Individual NRSA grant. The Institutional NRSA is an Institutional Training grant (T-32) that is applied for via the PHS 398 form and a supplemental T-32 kit. The Individual NRSA fellowship application is made on form PHS 416-1 (Revised 7/88).

instructions in the kit are quite explicit about filling out most of these forms. Where I considered it important, I have reiterated some of the NIH instructions, and in some cases, have provided additional information that you may find helpful.

Form PHS-398, Page 1 (Face page) ▶

TITLE OF APPLICATION (Item 1) Less than 56 spaces
   Should be descriptive, specific, appropriate. (The title may help
   to route the application to the appropriate Study Section.)

DATES OF ENTIRE PROPOSED PROJECT PERIOD (Item 6)
   • The review process takes about 9 months.*
   • Enter the correct starting date according to the table on page
     11 of the PHS-398 instructions (Appendix I). Unless you have
     reason to do otherwise, indicate the earliest possible starting
     date for the submission deadline you plan to meet.
        For example, if you apply for the Feb. 1 deadline (new
        application), the starting date would be Dec. 1.

Application Receipt Date	Study Section Meets	Council Meets	Earliest Possible Start Date
Feb.1/Mar.1	June/July	Sept./Oct.	Dec.1
June 1/July 1	Oct./Nov.	Jan./Feb.	April 1
Oct.1/Nov.1	Feb./Mar.	May/June	July 1

DIRECT COSTS (Items 7a and 8a) and **TOTAL COSTS** (Items 7b
   and 8b) for first 12-month budget period and entire proposed
   project period. You may want to work with the Office of Sponsored Research or Office for Grant Administration at your
   institution to develop your detailed budget.

YOUR SIGNATURE (Item 17) Sign *before* you photocopy the
   application.

---

* NIH has announced expedited reviews for fellowship applications (See NIH
Guide, Vol. 17, #12, April 1, 1988, page 1) and for research grant applications
related to AIDS research (See NIH Guide, Vol. 17, #9, March 11, 1988, page 1 and
Vol. 17, #13, April 8, 1988.)
   Fellowship application processing time will be reduced to about 2 months.
Receipt dates (January 10, May 10 and September 10) remain unchanged, but
Study Sections will meet late March/April, mid-July and mid-November.
   AIDS research application processing time will be about 6 months. Receipt
dates for new and renewal applications have been changed to January 2, May 1
and September 1.

Form Approved Through 9/30/89
OMB No. 0925-0001

DEPARTMENT OF HEALTH AND HUMAN SERVICES
PUBLIC HEALTH SERVICE

GRANT APPLICATION

FOLLOW INSTRUCTIONS CAREFULLY

LEAVE BLANK		
TYPE	ACTIVITY	NUMBER
REVIEW GROUP		FORMERLY
COUNCIL/BOARD (Month, year)		DATE RECEIVED

1. TITLE OF PROJECT (Up to 56 spaces)

2. RESPONSE TO SPECIFIC PROGRAM ANNOUNCEMENT ☐ NO ☐ YES (If "YES," state RFA number and/or announcement title)

3. PRINCIPAL INVESTIGATOR/PROGRAM DIRECTOR   NEW INVESTIGATOR ☐

3a. NAME (Last, first, middle)	3b. DEGREE(S)	3c. SOCIAL SECURITY NUMBER

3d. POSITION TITLE	3e. MAILING ADDRESS (Street, city, state, zip code)

| 3f. DEPARTMENT, SERVICE, LABORATORY OR EQUIVALENT | |

3g. MAJOR SUBDIVISION	3h. TELEPHONE (Area code, number and extension)

4. HUMAN SUBJECTS	5. VERTEBRATE ANIMALS
4a. ☐ No ☐ Yes ⎰ ☐ Exemption # _____ ⎱ OR ⎰ ☐ IRB Approval Date _____	5a. ☐ No ☐ Yes . . . IACUC Approval Date _____
4b. Assurance of Compliance # _____	5b. Animal Welfare Assurance # _____

6. DATES OF ENTIRE PROPOSED PROJECT PERIOD	7. COSTS REQUESTED FOR FIRST 12-MONTH BUDGET PERIOD		8. COSTS REQUESTED FOR ENTIRE PROPOSED PROJECT PERIOD	
	7a. Direct Costs	7b. Total Costs	8a. Direct Costs	8b. Total Costs
From:				
Through:	$	$	$	$

9. PERFORMANCE SITES (Organizations and addresses)	10. INVENTIONS (Competing continuation application only)
	☐ NO ☐ YES ⎰ OR ⎱ ☐ Previously reported ☐ Not previously reported
	11. APPLICANT ORGANIZATION (Name, address, and congressional district)

12. TYPE OF ORGANIZATION ☐ Public, Specify ☐ Federal ☐ State ☐ Local ☐ Private Nonprofit ☐ For Profit (General) ☐ For Profit (Small Business)	13. ENTITY IDENTIFICATION NUMBER
	14. ORGANIZATIONAL COMPONENT TO RECEIVE CREDIT TOWARDS A BIOMEDICAL RESEARCH SUPPORT GRANT Code ☐☐ Identification _____

15. OFFICIAL IN BUSINESS OFFICE TO BE NOTIFIED IF AN AWARD IS MADE (Name, title, address and telephone number)	16. OFFICIAL SIGNING FOR APPLICANT ORGANIZATION (Name, title, address and telephone number)

17. PRINCIPAL INVESTIGATOR/PROGRAM DIRECTOR ASSURANCE: I agree to accept responsibility for the scientific conduct of the project and to provide the required progress reports if a grant is awarded as a result of this application. Willful provision of false information is a criminal offense (U.S. Code, Title 18, Section 1001).	SIGNATURE OF PERSON NAMED IN 3a (In ink. "Per" signature not acceptable.)	DATE
18. CERTIFICATION AND ACCEPTANCE: I certify that the statements herein are true and complete to the best of my knowledge, and accept the obligation to comply with Public Health Service terms and conditions if a grant is awarded as the result of this application. A willfully false certification is a criminal offense (U.S. Code, Title 18, Section 1001).	SIGNATURE OF PERSON NAMED IN 16 (In ink. "Per" signature not acceptable.)	DATE

PHS 398 (Rev. 9/86)

SIGNATURE OF OFFICIAL SIGNING FOR APPLICANT INSTITUTION (Item 18)

- Have the person sign before you photocopy the application.
- Have the person sign early; if you wait until the last minute, she/he may be out of town!

Abstract of Research Plan (Form, Page 2, Top)   ►

The abstract is used in routing the application to the proper Study Section and is used by primary reviewers to help write their reports. Note that the small print instructions above the box for the abstract ask that you

1. State the BROAD, LONG-TERM OBJECTIVES
2. State the SPECIFIC AIMS
3. Make reference to the HEALTH-RELATEDNESS of the project
4. Describe the EXPERIMENTAL DESIGN AND METHODOLOGY concisely
5. Avoid summaries of past accomplishments
6. Do NOT use the first person
7. **DO NOT EXCEED THE SPACE PROVIDED**

It is easiest to satisfy the instructions and save your own time by writing the abstract as follows:

> "The broad, long-term objectives of this proposal are . . . . . The Specific Aims are 1.) . . . 2.) . . . 3.) . . . . The health-relatedness of the project is . . . . The experimental design is . . . . The methods to be used are. . . . "

In keeping with points 5 and 6 of the instructions, do not begin the Abstract with a sentence such as "For the past 5 years I have been studying . . . ."

In keeping with point 7, do not try to fit more words into the box by changing to smaller print. Use 10 or 12 pitch letters and keep the text within the outline of the "box." Use the strategies in Appendix X to help you shorten your abstract.

Write the "Abstract of Research Plan" **AFTER** you have finished writing the rest of the grant proposal.

DESCRIPTION: State the application's broad, long-term objectives and specific aims, making reference to the health relatedness of the project. Describe concisely the experimental design and methods for achieving these goals. Avoid summaries of past accomplishments and the use of the first person. This abstract is meant to serve as a succinct and accurate description of the proposed work when separated from the application. **DO NOT EXCEED THE SPACE PROVIDED.**

KEY PERSONNEL ENGAGED ON PROJECT

NAME, DEGREE(S), SSN	POSITION TITLE AND ROLE IN PROJECT	DEPARTMENT AND ORGANIZATION

Make the ABSTRACT
1. A succinct and accurate description of the proposed work when SEPARATED from the application
2. Reflect and parallel the contents of the application

The abstract is often the first thing read by the reviewers and is used by the reviewers to help them write their reports (see Document 1, *GUIDE FOR ASSIGNED REVIEWER'S PRELIMINARY COMMENTS ON RESEARCH GRANT APPLICATIONS* in part I of this book). A well-written abstract helps the reviewers do their homework more easily, and happy reviewers are often more favorable reviewers—all other things being equal.

The abstract should be concise and perfectly clear and should realistically represent the contents of the total grant application. Underlining key words may help the reviewer to remember what your grant proposal is about at the time of the Study Section meeting (in addition to his/her own notes). Often days, or even weeks, have passed between the time the reviewer reads a grant proposal and when the Study Section meets. By the time of the meeting, the reviewer has read a large number of applications. Exceptionally good and extremely bad applications tend to be better retained in the reviewer's memory. For the remaining applications, the reviewer may rely on the abstract to help her/him recall the contents of the proposal. Help the reviewer remember the most important parts of your proposal by writing a well thought out abstract.

The abstract is also one of the major things read by members of the Study Section who are not the primary reviewers for that application. Although NIH Study Section reviewers rarely are asked to be primary or secondary reviewers on more than 10 or 20 proposals, they may be involved in the review process for as many as 100 or more grant proposals. Because reviewers also have full-time jobs, it may not be possible for them to read so many grant applications carefully in the allotted time (usually 4 to 6 weeks). Conscientious reviewers read very carefully the proposals for which they are specifically responsible, and often do many hours of homework before they write the reviews. For the remaining numerous applications, reviewers have to pick, choose, and scan so that they can be sufficiently knowledgeable about the proposal to participate in the discussion during the Study Section meeting. The abstract and the Specific Aims (section 2, item A of the application) are absolutely critical for this process. It is on the basis of these two sections that the reviewers will usually decide what other parts of the grant proposal to read more carefully.

Key Personnel (Form, Page 2, Bottom)

- Those who participate in the development and execution of the project (generally, individuals with professional degrees). At the applicant institution or elsewhere. Salaried or not salaried.
- For each individual, list name, all degrees, and (optional) social security number.

Table of Contents (Form, Page 3) ➤

Fill in the page numbers on this form in the LAST draft of the proposal.

(A separate table of contents for the Research Plan, listing all subheadings, helps the reviewer find topics quickly in an application that is long and/or complex. The stringent page limitatons of the 9/86 revision of the NIH application form will, in most cases, preclude the use of such an additional table of contents for the Research Plan of NIH applications. However, an extra table of contents for the Research Plan may be useful for other types of grant proposals.)

Type the name of the Principal Investigator/Program Director at the top of each printed page and each continuation page.

TABLE OF CONTENTS

SECTION 1.   PAGE NUMBERS

SECTION 3. Appendix (Six collated sets. No page numbering necessary for Appendix)

Number of publications and manuscripts accepted for publication (Not to exceed ten): _____
Other items (list):

Detailed Budget for First 12 Months (Form, Page 4) ➤

Read carefully the instructions for this section [Pages 17–19 of the NIH instructions (Appendix I)].

The budget should be reasonable, believable, well researched, and superbly justified.

- Develop the budget after you have planned the project and can calculate just what you will need to carry out the work.
- Be sure the budget accurately reflects the proposed research:
  Don't "underbudget."
  (Don't try to give NIH a bargain; reviewers will think you're naive.)
  Don't "overbudget."
  (Don't be an opportunist or a "thief;" reviewers spot that as well.)
- Discuss with the appropriate personnel at your institution which items are considered direct, as opposed to indirect, costs.
- Footnote budget items to correspond to the relevant explanation in the budget justification section (see example on facing page).

PERSONNEL

- List the names and roles of all applicant organization personnel to be involved in the project during the 12-month budget period.
- List the principal investigator first.
- List key personnel first; then support personnel.
- List personnel even if no salary is requested.

"Column 1" = **Type of Appointment** at the applicant organization

(Full-time or Part-time)

To calculate "Type appointment:"

- 1/2 time for 12 months $(0.5 \times 12/12) = 0.5$
- Full time for 6 months $(1.0 \times 6/12) = 0.5$
- 1/2 time for 9 months $(0.5 \times 9/12) = 0.38$ (Academic year)
- Full time for 3 months $(1.0 \times 3/12) = 0.25$ (Summer)

(If the 12-month year is divided into academic and summer periods, identify and enter ON SEPARATE LINES, the type of appointment for each period.)

DETAILED BUDGET FOR FIRST 12-MONTH BUDGET PERIOD
DIRECT COSTS ONLY

FROM	THROUGH
07/01/88	06/30/89

PERSONNEL (Applicant organization only) (1) NAME	ROLE IN PROJECT	1 TYPE APPT.	2 % OF APPT.	3 EFFORT ON PROJ.	SALARY	FRINGE BENEFITS	TOTALS
John Jones, Ph.D. (a)	Principal Investigator	1.0	100	1.0	$52,450	$15,735	$68,185
Jane Smith, Ph.D. (b) (Academic year)	Co-Investigator	0.56	75	0.42	$19,236	$5,771	$25,007
(Summer)		0.25	100	0.25	$11,450	$3,435	$14,885
Alec West, B.A. (c)	Research Ass't	1.0	100	1.0	$17,000	$5,100	$22,100
To be named, B.A. (d)	Technician	1.0	100	1.0	$12,000	$3,600	$15,600

NOTE: The numbers/letters in ( ) refer to explanations of the item in the Budget Justification Section.

	SUBTOTALS				$112,136	$33,641	$145,777

CONSULTANT COSTS   (2)

Jamie Northstar, M.D. — 0

EQUIPMENT (Itemize)   (3)

Zeiss Microscope, Model XYZ	(a)	$29,710	
Diamond Knife	(b)	$ 2,500	
Embedding oven	(c)	$ 350	
			$32,560

SUPPLIES (Itemize by category)   (4)

Rats (including maintenance)	(a)	$1,844	
Medium and serum	(b)	$1,120	
Chemicals	(c)	$ 680	
Glass and plasticware	(d)	$1,280	
Microscopy/photo supplies	(e)	$4,460	$9,384

TRAVEL   (5)
DOMESTIC One meeting for PI, ABC Assoc., Grant City, IL.;
FOREIGN one meeting for co-investigator, XYZ Assoc., Miami, FL. $1,800

PATIENT CARE COSTS
INPATIENT
OUTPATIENT

ALTERATIONS AND RENOVATIONS (Itemize by category)

CONSORTIUM/CONTRACTUAL COSTS

OTHER EXPENSES (Itemize by category) (6)

Publication costs (a)	$800	Computer fees	(b)	$1,340
Service contracts (c)	$540	Books	(d)	$ 250
				$2,930

TOTAL DIRECT COSTS FOR FIRST 12-MONTH BUDGET PERIOD (Item 7a) ——▶ $ 192,451

*Number pages consecutively at the bottom throughout the application. Do *not* use suffixes such as 5a, 5b.

"Column 2" = % of Appointment

- % of the appointment at the applicant institution to be devoted to THIS project
- Enter percentages for academic and summer periods ON SEPARATE LINES
- If you have other institutional responsibilities, e.g., teaching, the TOTAL % devoted to ALL research activities must be LESS THAN 100%.

"Column 3" = Effort on the Project

Calculate for each line: Column 3 = Column 1 x Column 2 (Express the result as a decimal.)

In the sample budget page (above), Jane Smith has an annual salary based on $45,800 for full-time.

Note that Dr. Smith has a 3/4-time appointment at the university during the academic year. She plans to devote 75% of her time to this research project during the academic year:

$(3/4 \times 9/12 = 0.56 \times 0.75 = 0.42 \times \$45,800 = \$19,236)$.

During the 3 summer months, Dr. Smith will work full time at the university and devote 100% of her time to this project:

$(1.0 \times 3/12 = 0.25 \times 1.0 = 0.25 \times \$45,800 = \$11,450)$.

Fringe benefits have been calculated at 30%.

CONSULTANT COSTS:

- Provide names and affiliations of consultants even if no costs are involved.
- Provide letters from consultants attesting to their willingness to work on the project.

EQUIPMENT:

- List separately each item requested that has a unit acquisition price of $500 or more.
- Check that requested items do not conflict with items listed under "Facilities" and "Major Equipment" on the form page, Resources and Environment.

SUPPLIES:

- For animals, give
  - Number to be used
  - Unit purchase cost
  - Unit care cost
- Itemize other supplies in categories such as glassware, chemicals, radioisotopes, etc.
- Itemize these other categories only if the category total exceeds $1000.

TRAVEL:

For each trip specify
- Person(s) who will travel
- Purpose of travel
- Destination
- Estimated cost

PATIENT CARE COSTS:

See page 18 of NIH instructions (Appendix I).

ALTERATIONS AND RENOVATIONS:

See page 18 of NIH instructions (Appendix I).

CONSORTIUM/CONTRACTUAL COSTS:

See page 19 of NIH instructions (Appendix I).

OTHER EXPENSES:

Itemize by category and unit cost:
- Publication costs
  - Drafting
  - Photographs
  - Page charges
  - Reprints
- Books
- Computer charges
- Service contracts
- Repairs
- Office supplies
- Postage

- Rental and leases
- Fees for services
- Reimbursement for tuition remission for students who work on the project
- Reimbursement for expenses incurred by human subjects who participate in the project

Budget for Entire Project Period (Form, Page 5, Top)   ►

- Account for annual raises for personnel (Cost-of-Living, Merit, Promotion) and predictable changes in fringe benefit rate.
- Check guidelines at your institution and/or NIH to determine appropriate percentages to use to calculate these increases.
- Think about new expenses that may arise in later years of the project—repairs, replacements, beginning new experiments that require new supplies, additional personnel, etc.

Budget Justification (Form, Page 5, Bottom)

Justify everything in the budget that is not obvious. And consider that what is obvious to you may not be obvious to the reviewers. The reviewers will be in a better mood if they do not have to puzzle over things such as unexplained changes in budget for subsequent years. Any changes should be specifically pointed out; it is to your disadvantage if the reviewers think that you are trying to "pull a fast one" by "slipping" extra items into future-year budgets.

There is NO page limit for the budget justification. If this section is written CONCISELY, in clear outline form, using upper-case letters and underlining to make key words stand out and indentation to include secondary information (for example, arithmetic showing how you arrived at the final figures), then each reviewer can choose what to read and what to ignore. The budget discussion at the Study Section meeting generally occurs after the committee has voted on approval of the proposal, but before the members have assigned priority scores. During the budget discussion, reviewers, for the most part, should not have to refer to sections of the proposal other than the budget and budget justification; nor should they have to waste time doing arithmetic—do it for them: Show your work, not just the answer, and be sure it is correct. There is apt to be one reviewer in the crowd who pulls out a pocket calculator and checks the math; incorrect calculations detract from your credibility!

BUDGET FOR ENTIRE PROPOSED PROJECT PERIOD
DIRECT COSTS ONLY

BUDGET CATEGORY TOTALS		1st BUDGET PERIOD (from page 4)	ADDITIONAL YEARS OF SUPPORT REQUESTED			
			2nd	3rd	4th	5th
PERSONNEL *(Salary and fringe benefits)* *(Applicant organization only)*						
CONSULTANT COSTS						
EQUIPMENT						
SUPPLIES						
TRAVEL	DOMESTIC					
	FOREIGN					
PATIENT CARE COSTS	INPATIENT					
	OUTPATIENT					
ALTERATIONS AND RENOVATIONS						
CONSORTIUM/ CONTRACTUAL COSTS						
OTHER EXPENSES						
TOTAL DIRECT COSTS						

TOTAL DIRECT COSTS FOR ENTIRE PROPOSED PROJECT PERIOD *(Item 8a)* ⟶ | $

JUSTIFICATION (Use continuation pages if necessary): Describe the specific functions of the personnel, consultants, and collaborators. For all years, explain and justify any unusual items such as major equipment, foreign travel, alterations and renovations, patient care costs, and tuition remission. For additional years of support requested, justify any significant increases in any category over the first 12-month budget period. Identify such significant increases with asterisks against the appropriate amounts. If a recurring annual increase in personnel or other costs is anticipated, give the percentage. In addition, for COMPETING CONTINUATION applications, justify any significant increases in any category over the current level of support.

Use continuation sheets provided in the PHS-398 kit. (Type your name and social security number onto the sample continuation page provided in the application packet *before* you photocopy the page!)

An indented format makes it easy for reviewers to find increasing levels of detail in the budget justification:

— — — — — — — — — — — — — — — —
— — — — — — — — — —
— — — — —

For example,

SUPPLIES: *$9856*
Animals *$7950*
z Rats . . . .*$xxx*
  x/wk for *y* weeks for the . . . experiments
*x*Rabbits . . . .*$xxx*
  y/wk for *x* weeks for the . . . experiments
Chemicals *$1006*
  . . . , 3 gm/month for *x* months at $*x*/gm . . . *$yyy*
  . . . , 7 gm/month for *x* months at $*x*/gm . . . *$zzz*
Glassware . . . .$ 900

- Footnote budget items on budget pages 4 and 5 and use corresponding numbers for explanations in the budget justification section.
- Justify all personnel.
  - Personnel is likely to be the largest item in your budget. Justify it accordingly!
  - Specify what **unique** role each person will play in the execution of the research. Describe their specific functions in the project.
  - Try to avoid using "To be named;" if you must use it, explain what sort of individual will be recruited (i.e., qualifications: field, specialty within the field, years past B.A. or Ph.D., etc.).
- Explain and justify annual increases in budget items/categories.
- If you request a piece of equipment in the budget, explain why this equipment is necessary for this project.

For example, why is it critical for the experiments? Do not just say that it will let you do an experiment better or faster.

- If a piece of equipment is to be shared—or made available to other investigators for their work—it is sometimes helpful to mention this.

  However, you should give good reasons why *you* are requesting the total cost (rather than sharing it.)

- Check "Equipment" requests against the Resources and Environment page to be sure they are not contradictory.

  Justify *particularly well* equipment also listed under "Major Equipment" on the Resources and Environment page; for example, if you say that your institution has five balances (to convince the reviewer what a super facility it is), you must present a very strong argument for purchasing a sixth one with the requested grant funds.

- Justify and explain new equipment requests in later budget years.
  - If you are requesting a Model XYZ Microscope in the Third year budget and on the Resources and Environment page you write that you have a Model XYZ microscope, explain, for example, that the microscope you now use belongs to Dr. X. Dr. X will be moving to another university in the third year of your project period and will be taking the microscope with her. Therefore, you will need a microscope at that time.

  - If you ask for a piece of equipment in year -03 and justify the request by saying that piece of equipment isn't available at your institution, then you should explain why you're not asking for it in the first year.

    For example, the project for which you need the piece of equipment is not scheduled to begin until year -03.

- For expensive equipment, you may wish to provide a written quote from the company.

  If not included in the quote, calculate an inflation factor and estimate what the price might be at the time the item is to be purchased. Remember: at least a year is likely to elapse between the time you obtain the quote and the time the grant is funded!

- For supplies not in readily available catalogs, if there has been a drastic price increase or if you are requesting money for a large quantity of a particular item, it may help to include receipts of previous purchases or other proof of price and/or actual usage. Reviewers sometimes forget about inflation. It pays to face them with proof of the facts. A little telephone and library research toward creating a realistic budget is time well spent.

- Justify all Travel
  - Specify who will travel and whether or not that person will present a paper.
  - Estimate expenses based on actual meeting places.
      Find out where meetings will be and how much it costs to get there.
  - Specify that costs are based on shared room, tourist class travel, etc.

In these times of "tight" funding, travel sometimes is not considered a very high-priority item. Many reviewers consider one meeting per year per senior investigator reasonable. If you are requesting money for more than one meeting per senior person, it is imperative to justify why it is important for that individual to go to two meetings and how you think she/he will benefit from attendance.

- Justify *all* other expenditures
- **Justify the budget for the total project period**
  - Justify any significant increases in any category over the first 12-month budget period. *Identify such significant increases* with ASTERISKS against the appropriate amounts.
  - Specify: " 'Other Expenses' is increased by an *extra* $1000 (above the annual 4% increase) in year 03 to pay for sharpening our diamond knife (purchased in 19xx)."
  - Or state, for example, "No additional equipment is requested in subsequent years."
  - Don't give the reviewers the opportunity to think you are trying to "put one over" on them.

Sample budget justifications are given in Appendix IV

Biographical Sketches (Biosketches)   ►

(Maximum of 2 pages/person)

- Photocopy the Biosketch form BEFORE filling it out (except for name and Social Security number at top of the page).

BIOGRAPHICAL SKETCH

Give the following information for the key personnel and consultants listed on page 2. Begin with the Principal
Investigator/Program Director. Photocopy this page for each person.

NAME	POSITION TITLE	BIRTHDATE (Mo., Day, Yr.)

EDUCATION (Begin with baccalaureate or other initial professional education, such as nursing, and include postdoctoral training.)

INSTITUTION AND LOCATION	DEGREE	YEAR CONFERRED	FIELD OF STUDY

RESEARCH AND PROFESSIONAL EXPERIENCE: Concluding with present position, list, in chronological order, previous employment, experience, and honors. Include present membership on any Federal Government public advisory committee. List, in chronological order, the titles and complete references to all publications during the past three years and to representative earlier publications pertinent to this application. DO NOT EXCEED TWO PAGES.

*Number pages consecutively at the bottom throughout the application. Do not use suffixes such as 5a, 5b.

- Provide a Biosketch for the Principal Investigator and all other key professional personnel listed on Form page 2.
  - Previous employment—in chronological order (**present position LAST)**
  - Experience (Postdoctoral Training—"Education" box.)
  - Honors and present membership in any federal government Public Advisory Committee
  - Complete references (including titles) to ALL publications *of the past 3 years* and *representative* earlier publications *pertinent* to this application. There is a 2-page limit for each complete Biosketch, so choose publications wisely.

  Note that your own publications may appear in 3 places: Biosketch, Progress Report (section 2, item c), and Literature Cited (section 2, item I).

  Do not provide a standard resume or CV (curriculum vitae) in place of the Biosketch! Use the NIH form and follow the instructions.

Other Support   ►

- Read carefully the instructions given on the Other Support form provided in the application kit.
- Incomplete, inaccurate, or ambiguous information "could lead to delays in the review of the application."
- Notify the Executive Secretary of the Study Section if there are changes in support after you submit the proposal.
- Provide information for all key personnel named on page 2 of the application form.
- List separately
  1. Current active support
  2. Applications pending review or funding
  3. Proposals in preparation or planned
- Include
  - Federal and non-federal support
  - All types of
    - Grants (institutional research, training, etc.)
    - Contracts
    - Fellowships
  - Support administered through another institution
- If your application is part of a larger project,
    give the Principal Investigator/Program Director and other data for the parent project and subproject.

OTHER SUPPORT

(Use continuation pages if necessary)

FOLLOW INSTRUCTIONS CAREFULLY. Incomplete, inaccurate, or ambiguous information about OTHER SUPPORT could lead to delays in the review of the application. If there are changes subsequent to submission, notify the executive secretary of the initial review group.

For each of the key personnel named on page 2, list, in three separate groups: (1) *all* currently active support; (2) *all* applications and proposals pending review or funding; and (3) applications and proposals planned or being prepared for submission. Include *all* Federal, non-Federal, and institutional research, training, and other grant, contract, and fellowship support at the applicant organization and elsewhere. If part of a larger project, identify the principal investigator/program director and provide the data for both the parent project and the subproject. If none, state "none."

For each item give: (a) the source of support, identifying number and title; (b) percentage of appointment on the project; (c) dates of entire project period; (d) annual direct costs; (e) a brief description of the project; (f) whether the item overlaps, duplicates, or is being replaced or supplemented by the present application; delineate and justify the nature and extent of any scientific and/or budgetary overlaps or boundaries; and (g) any modifications that will be made should the present application be funded.

PRINCIPAL INVESTIGATOR/PROGRAM DIRECTOR:
  (1) CURRENTLY ACTIVE SUPPORT: (a)

- For each item
  - Give
    - Source of support
    - ID number
    - Title
    - Percentage of appointment on project
    - Dates of entire project period
    - Annual direct costs
    - Brief description of project
  - Delineate any overlap, duplication, or replacement with/by present application.
    - Justify overlaps, scientific and budgetary.
  - State modifications that will be made if present application is funded.
- **If no other support, write "None."**

Resources and Environment   ➤

- Read carefully the instructions given on the Resources and Environment form provided in the application kit.
- Check in the appropriate boxes on the form, the facilities available at the applicant organization.
  - Check "Other" to describe facilities available at other performance sites and/or field study sites.
- Define the capacity of the facilities.
- Explain pertinent capabilities of the facilities.
- Denote relative proximity of the facilities.
- Detail the extent of availability to the project.
- List major equipment items in the space provided (compare to budget requests!).
  - Specify availability for this project.
  - Note location and pertinent capabilities of each item.
- Provide additional relevant information in the space at bottom of the page.
  - Describe the work environment
    - Colleagues
    - Collaborators
    - Potential for interaction
    - Seminars and Journal Clubs
    - Outside speakers
  - Identify support services and specify availability of each for this project.
    - Consultants
    - Secretaries
    - Machine shop
    - Electronics shop

RESOURCES AND ENVIRONMENT

FACILITIES: Mark the facilities to be used at the applicant organization and briefly indicate their capacities, pertinent capabilities, relative proximity and extent of availability to the project. Use "other" to describe the facilities at any other performance sites listed in Item 9, page 1, and at sites for field studies. Using continuation pages if necessary, include an explanation of any consortium/contractual arrangements with other organizations.

☐ Laboratory:

☐ Clinical:

☐ Animal:

☐ Computer:

☐ Office:

☐ Other (_____):

MAJOR EQUIPMENT: List the most important equipment items already available for this project, noting the location and pertinent capabilities of each.

ADDITIONAL INFORMATION: Provide any other information describing the environment for the project. Identify support services such as consultants, secretaries, machine shop, and electronics shop, and the extent to which they will be available to the project.

SECTION 2: RESEARCH PLAN

The Research Plan is the main (science) part of the grant application and the most important for the review process.

Writing the Research Plan requires much planning and care. It pays to allow yourself plenty of time. It is also a good idea—especially for first-time applicants—to contact Institute Program Personnel and discuss with them matters related to the application process and the relevance of the subject matter of the application you intend to submit in relation to the mandates of that Institute.

The NIH instructions state: "Reviewers often consider brevity and clarity in the presentation to be indicative of a principal investigator/program director's focused approach to a research objective and ability to achieve the specific aims of the project."

You are expected to include sufficient information in the Research Plan to permit an effective review without reference to any previous application.

Renewals

Although Study Section review criteria remain the same, there may be subtle differences in the expectations of the Study Section members for first renewals (the second application to the same agency) compared to second renewals (the third application to the same agency). A first renewal that shows somewhat expanded horizons and new specific aims related to those of the initial proposal may be acceptable if the Principal Investigator has made sufficient progress in the form of substantive original research publications. By the time of the second renewal, reviewers may look for somewhat more than just "linear" progress. The Principal Investigator would do well, at this stage, to demonstrate some maturity of outlook: a realistic assessment of whether the project is worthy of a long-term study or is perhaps in need of a more effective new direction; awareness of and incorporation of appropriate new technology—perhaps from other fields of science; new approaches to the problem; a broader conceptual base; or a more encompassing hypothesis.

General Instructions

Type (print) the Research Plan on the continuation pages provided in the application packet:

- Type your name and social security number onto the sample continuation page provided in the application packet *before* you photocopy the page!
- Photocopy as many of these continuation pages as you think you will need for your application. Save the original in case you need extra copies.
- Stay within the margins indicated on the sample page. Your application is reproduced at NIH in a somewhat smaller format!

Page Limits

There is a 20-page limit for the **Research Plan, items A through D.**

- **Your application may be returned if you exceed the page limitations.**
- You may use any page distribution within this overall limit; but the PHS recommends.

A. *Specific Aims,* **1 page.**

B. *Background & Significance,* **2–3 pages.**

C. *Progress Report,* **6–8 pages** for the narrative portion
    [Or, in a NEW APPLICATION, **C.** *Preliminary Studies* ("Useful but optional" according to NIH instructions)] Submit *maximum of 10* relevant manuscripts (6 copies each) in the Appendix.

D. *Experimental Design and Methods,*
    20 minus the number of pages used for items A-C (i.e., 8–11 pages)

Parts of the Research Plan

Optional, additional Table of Contents for the Research Plan

In addition to the Table of Contents in the NIH form (form page 3) it is sometimes desirable to provide an additional table of contents specifically for the Research Plan, including all subheadings. The reviewers can use this detailed contents to locate specific items readily when they are working on your grant proposal—and during the discussion at the Study Section meeting. The extra table of contents

- Is not useful for proposals with severe page limitations (if you are short of space);

- If included with an NIH proposal, it should be put *before* Research Plan—or into Appendix—and marked "For convenience of reviewers."

The information required in the Research Plan

> *Introduction* [Only required in some cases (see below)].
> *Specific Aims* = What you intend to do.
> *Background and Significance* = What has been done already been done in the field. Why the work is important.
> *Preliminary Studies or Progress Report* = What *you* have done already on this project.
> *Experimental Design and Methods* = How you will fulfill the aims. How you will do the work.

Introduction—Do not exceed 1 page.

INCLUDE ONLY FOR

- Revised application,
  - Delineate all significant changes made.
  - Respond to criticism in the Summary Statement for the previous application.
  - Highlight changes made in the text of the Research Plan by
    - Brackets
    - Indents
    - Different typography
  - Incorporate into the Progress Report/Preliminary Studies any work done since the prior version was submitted.
- Supplemental application,
  - Explain the significance with respect to the original proposal.

A. Specific Aims

In 1 page (recommended maximum),

1. State the broad long-term objectives of the proposal.
2. Describe concisely and realistically
   a. What the specific research described in the application is intended to accomplish
   b. Any hypotheses to be tested
      - Avoid grandiose designs.
      - Ask clear specific questions.
      - Have clear hypotheses.

- State hypotheses in form of short bulleted list.
- Avoid narrative paragraphs.

- "To study the effect of substance X on system Y" is *not* a good specific aim!
- Understand the difference between
  - *broad, long-term objectives* e.g., "Eradicate diabetes" (hard to quantify progress) and
  - *specific aims*, e.g., "Develop a method to continuously measure blood sugar levels" (something that could be crossed off a list of *n* items needed to further the broad, long-term objectives).

B. Background and Significance

In 2–3 pages (recommended maximum),

1. BRIEFLY sketch the BACKGROUND for the proposal.
2. Critically EVALUATE the existing knowledge.
3. Specifically identify the GAPS the project is intended to fill.
4. State CONCISELY the importance of the research by RELATING the Specific Aims to the Broad, Long-term Objectives.
5. Reference this section (especially Background).
   The references go into Literature Cited, item I (which has a limit of 4 pages).

Use this section of the grant application to demonstrate your understanding of the subject and justify the need for the proposed research. State clearly why the information to be obtained is useful; that is, what you can do with the information after you get it. If appropriate, explain the clinical relevance of your proposed research. Make it clear in the Background section which previous work was done by others and which by you, the applicant.

Background discussions should avoid fanning the flames of scientific controversies. Be strictly scientific and unbiased and let the data speak for you. Someone on the Study Section may have a strong bias in the debate that may not coincide with yours!

References cited by author and year in the text and listed in alphabetical order (and numbered) in the bibliography are more meaningful to the reviewer than references cited by number. References cited only by number cause the reviewer to have to flip back to the bibliography pages frequently to determine what the reference is. In contrast, references cited by author and year in the text, are likely to mean something to the reviewer at once. However, with current page limitations, this method of citation may take up too much valuable space. In addition, this method of citation can interrupt the flow of text for the reader when there are multiple citations at a given place. You will have to make a judicious decision about the best method for citing references in your proposal considering the positive and negative aspects of each method.

If you refer to a long article (for example, a review article), put a note in the text to the effect that "discussion pertinent to the subject may be found on p. 15–18, 29–32, and 56 in Wade and Jade, 1959 (reference 43)." The reviewer may want to check a statement without wading through a 63-page article to find it. If the article is not readily attainable, provide photocopies of the pertinent pages for the reviewers (see section on bibliography, below).

C. Preliminary Studies

In 6–8 pages* (recommended maximum)

Optional for NEW Applications
New applicants may use this section to provide information that will help to establish their experience and competence to pursue the proposed project.

Although this section is "optional" according to the NIH instructions, it is very important that you provide preliminary data that show that your project is feasible—and do-able by you.

1. Discuss preliminary studies, *by the Principal Investigator* (PI), pertinent to the application.
2. Provide any other information that will help to establish the experience and competence of the Principal Investigator to pursue the proposed project.
3. Give titles and complete references to appropriate publications and manuscripts **accepted** for publication.

   Submit 6 copies each of *NO MORE THAN 10* such items as an Appendix (Submit them as collated sets).

---

* For the narrative portion. Does not include list of professional personnel, list of publications, or appendix items.

Any evidence that the project is realistic, and/or that you can handle it, is valuable. Data that indicate that your basic premises—your hypotheses—are correct, are especially helpful for bridging the credibility gap for new applicants. A photocopy of a curve from even a single good, relevant experiment that you have done is better than no preliminary data, but make it neat and understandable to the reviewers. Explain what is in the figure and label the coordinates properly. A curve derived from an in-house experiment, labeled with lab jargon that you know, may not be comprehensible by someone else! Do not include any preliminary data in this section that resulted from experiments that you say in the application you propose to carry out in the forthcoming project!

In renewal applications, PRELIMINARY STUDIES is replaced by the PROGRESS REPORT.

C. Progress Report

In 6–8 pages* (recommended maximum)

Required for competitive renewal and supplemental applications—in place of "PRELIMINARY STUDIES"

1. Give dates of period covered since last competitive review. (Note that this does not coincide with project period dates.)
2. List key personnel who have worked on the project in this period.
   • Name
   • Title
   • Dates of service
   • % appointment devoted to project
3. Summarize Specific Aims (item A) of preceding application and give succinct account of progress (published and unpublished) toward their achievement.
   • Number items in the progress report to correspond to numbers of Specific Aims of the **preceding** proposal.
   • Reviewers are often provided with a copy of your previous proposal. **But,** the instructions specify that you "include

---

* For the narrative portion. Does not include list of professional personnel, list of publications, or appendix items.

sufficient information in Section 2 to facilitate an effective review *without* reference to any previous application."

4. Summarize importance of the findings. (Don't just list the findings!)
5. Discuss any changes in original Specific Aims.
6. Give titles and complete references to all publications, manuscripts **accepted** for publication, patents, invention reports, and other printed materials that have resulted since the last competitive review. Clearly distinguish between original papers (research reports), reviews, books, and abstracts: **Group them using sub-headings.**

Submit 6 copies each of NO MORE THAN 10 such items as an appendix. (Submit them as collated sets.)

The Progress Report is very important. For renewal applications clearly note which of the original aims of the previous proposals have been accomplished, which have not, and why. Write the Progress Report so that the reviewer can easily follow along in the preceding application (the reviewer is usually provided with a copy), and refer to it using the same numbering system. For example:

In the preceding proposal (give date) I (we) outlined *x* specific aims. (Summarize the specific aims of the previous proposal.)

No. 1 has been accomplished in that . . . and a publication describing the results appeared in . . . " (give reference).

No. 2 was not pursued after some initial experiments because we ran into an unexpected, severe experimental difficulty." (State briefly what the difficulty was).

No. 3 was started in the last year. One publication has resulted (give reference) but the project has evolved into a more extensive one than originally anticipated; new methodology, described in the current proposal, will have to be employed to further evaluate . . . . " (Then, in the Specific Aims of the renewal application, one specific aim would be related to the continuation of this work.)

No. 4 Work relating to Specific Aim 4 has just begun. The figure below shows the results of the first three experiments and indicates . . . . We expect this aspect of the project to be complete by the end of the current grant period.

Remember that you are re-applying about a year before the present grant period is up.

In listing your publications in the progress report, you may want to list first the papers on which you are the only author. (If you are the sole author and/or first author on only a few papers, explain why. Study Sections do not like applicants to suffer from "apublishanemia." Obviously, you must think about your publication record long before it is time to write the renewal application.) DO include papers "In Press." The official instructions (9/86 revision) state that only published or "In Press" papers should be listed. However, if you have only a small number of publications, but have a paper that has been submitted for publication or is in preparation but fairly complete, call NIH and ask for permission to submit copies. For each unpublished paper listed, you should submit preprints in the Appendix, and indicate in the list of publications that the preprint is provided.

D. Experimental Design and Methods

(Limit of 20 pages minus the number of pages used for items A–C = 8–11 pages)

- Outline the *experimental design* and *procedures* to be used to accomplish the Specific Aims of the project.
- Distinguish between the overall experimental design and the specific methods:
  - Experimental design
    - To label Q-protein with fluorescent probes at specific amino acid sites and use the probes as indicators of changing intermolecular interactions associated with the functions of Q-protein in the presence of X-protein.
  - Specific methods
    - Techniques for labeling with probe reagents
      1.) . . .
      2.) . . .
    - Determination of specificity of labeling
      - Separation and identification of fluorescent peptides by HPLC and gel electrophoresis after enzymatic digestion of protein
      - Analysis of labeled peptides on amino acid analyzer/sequencer
- Number the experimental designs and methods in this section to *correspond* to the numbers in Specific Aims, item A.
- Use sub-numbering within this section when describing several methods applicable to the same Specific Aim.

- *Do not repeat* identical procedures that apply to more than one Specific Aim. Describe them once and then refer the reader back to that section—or group such procedures in a section of "General Procedures" and refer to them as appropriate.
- Describe and/or reference protocols.
  - Describe and reference protocols that are new or unlikely to be known to reviewers. If in doubt, give a reference to the methodology and then provide 2 copies of the actual reference (a reprint or a photocopy of the article) in the Appendix for use by the primary reviewers.
  - Reference, but do not describe, well-known procedures.
- For new methods, explain *why* they are *better* than existing methods.
- Discuss CONTROL EXPERIMENTS.
- Explain how the data are to be *collected, analyzed,* and *interpreted*.
- Discuss potential *difficulties* and *limitations* of the proposed procedures and *alternative approaches* to achieve the aims.
- Point out procedures, situations, or materials that may be *hazardous* to personnel and describe *precautions* to be exercised.
- Provide a tentative SEQUENCE or *timetable* for the project (be realistic, not exact.).
- Document proposed collaborative arrangements with letters from the individuals with whom you propose to work, and define what role each will play in the project.

The Experimental Design and Methods section is an important part of the Research Plan. You have said in the Specific Aims what you propose to do; now you are telling the reviewers how you propose to do it. Explain why the particular approach that you describe was chosen to attack the problem that you plan to research. Convince the reviewers that you can do what you propose, and that the necessary facilities and equipment are available to you.

"Cookbook" repetitions of techniques copied from published papers do not convince reviewers of your expertise. If you find it necessary to detail such a technique, describe it in the context of your specific research problem and experiments.

Describe *briefly* what might be expected in a given set of experiments. For example: "If the data come out thus and so, then it means . . . and we will do . . . ; on the other hand, if the data turn out to be . . . , it might mean . . . and we will proceed as follows. . . ." Don't speculate on experimental outcomes for which you can propose no further experimental progress.

TRY TO CONVINCE THE REVIEWER THAT YOU HAVE NOT MERELY GONE TO THE LIBRARY BUT THAT YOU REALLY UNDERSTAND AND KNOW HOW TO CARRY OUT THE RESEARCH AND ARE FAMILIAR WITH THE TECHNIQUES AND THEIR SHORTCOMINGS.

E. Human Subjects

- See regulations about use of Human Subjects in NIH Instructions.
- Need approval from Institutional Review Board (IRB).

  If your studies involve HUMAN SUBJECTS, you must address these 6 points in *item E*.
  No page limit; be brief.

1. Detailed description of the proposed involvement of human subjects as PREVIOUSLY outlined in item D
   - Characteristics of subject population
     - Anticipated number of subjects
     - Ages (age ranges)
     - Sex
     - Ethnic background
     - Health status
   - Criteria for inclusion or exclusion
   - Rationale for involvement of
     - Fetuses
     - Pregnant women
     - Children
     - Human *in vitro* fertilization
     - Prisoners or other institutionalized or "vulnerable" individuals
2. Identify sources of research material.
   - Specimens
   - Records
   - Data
   (Will you use existing material or gather material especially for the research?)
3. Describe plans for recruitment and for consent procedures.
   - How subjects will be recruited
   - Circumstances under which consent will be sought and obtained

- Who will seek consent
- Nature of information to be provided to prospective subjects
- Method of documenting consent
- State if the IRB has authorized a modification or waiver of the elements of consent or the requirement of documentation of consent.

(The consent form must have IRB approval.)

(DO NOT SUBMIT THE CONSENT FORM unless it is requested.)

4. Describe potential risks.
   - Physical
   - Psychological
   - Social
   - Legal
   - Other

   (Assess likelihood and seriousness.)

   (Where appropriate, describe alternative treatments and procedures that might be advantageous to the subjects.)

5. Describe procedures to minimize potential risks and assess their likely effectiveness.
   - Include risks to confidentiality.
   - Discuss provisions for intervention in case of adverse effects to subjects.
   - Describe provisions for monitoring the data collected to ensure safety of subjects.

6. Discuss RISK/BENEFIT RATIO.
   - Anticipated benefits to subjects
   - Importance of knowledge that may be expected to result (Benefit to society)

- Name any test items involved and state whether
  - 30-day interval has elapsed or been waived
  - Use of test item has been withheld or restricted by FDA (Consider investigational new drug, device, or biologic)
- If you have designated exemptions from the human subjects regulations on the face page, provide information to show propriety of exemption.
- If in doubt (exempt category or not, etc.), consult with NIH Office for Protection from Research Risks *before* you plan/write the proposal.

- IRB review is best completed before submission of the application—but, at latest, within 60 days after submission.
- It is YOUR responsibility to send certification of approval.
- **If certification is not received by time of Study Section Meeting, application will be deferred to next review cycle.**

F. Vertebrate Animals

- See regulations for use and care of vertebrate animals in NIH Instructions.
- Need approval from Institutional Animal Care and Use Committee (IACUC)

If you plan to use vertebrate animals, you must address these 5 points in *item F*.
No page limit; be brief.

1. Describe in detail the proposed use of animals.
   Identify
   - Species
   - Strains
   - Ages
   - Sex
   - Numbers of animals to be used

2. Justify
   a. Use of animals
   b. Choice of species
   c. Number to be used
      (Give additional rationale if animals are scarce, costly, or to be used in large numbers.)

3. Describe veterinary care of animals.

4. Describe procedures to minimize the animals' discomfort, distress, pain, and injury.
   Discuss use of

   - Analgesics
   - Anesthetics
   - Tranquilizers
   - Restraining devices

5. Describe euthanasia methods and reasons for selection.
   - State whether methods to be used are recommended by

Panel on Euthanasia of American Veterinary Medical Association.
If not, justify.

G. Consultants/Collaborators

- Provide "Letter of Confirmation" from each such person (include role in project).
- Provide Biosketch for each such person.

H. Consortium/Contractual Arrangements

- Provide a detailed explanation of the arrangements
- Programmatic
- Fiscal
- Administrative
- Provide a statement about interorganizational agreements regarding compliance with pertinent Federal regulations and policies.
- Provide letters confirming interorganizational agreements.
- If the majority of the work is not being done by you, explain why you are the grantee.

See NIH instructions (Page 14, Item 9; Page 19, top paragraph; Page 22, Item H) in Appendix I.

I. Literature Cited (Bibliography)

4 pages maximum

- Acknowledge the work of others, including your competitors.
  Do not let the reviewers think that you are biased or arrogant.
- Be thorough, relevant, and current.
- Reviewers are interested in how up to date you are. A grant application submitted in Nov. 1988, in which the latest reference cited is from March, 1987, does not "sit well" with the Study Section, unless you specifically point out that no publications in the field have appeared since then.
- Article titles are optional but bibliographies without titles make more work for reviewers. On the other hand, titles take up precious space!
- Use a consistent format. For example, all authors, article title (optional), journal title, vol. no., page nos., year.
- Be sure every citation in the text is listed in the bibliography.

• Be sure every citation in the bibliography is referred to in the text.

Choose wisely what you will include. Your choice of citations will tell the reviewer about your quality as a scientist—your ability to evaluate the work of others and to distinguish the important from the mundane.

The use of the author-year (in the text) citation system is much more meaningful to reviewers than numbers; it saves them the time of flipping back to the bibliography whenever they come to a numbered citation. If you use this system, you should number the articles in the bibliography as well as present them in alphabetical order. The numbers make it easier for reviewers to refer to them during the discussion (e.g., "Doesn't Homenflof have more recent references on . . . than those cited at numbers 37 to 41 on p. 80!"). The disadvantages of the author-year system are (1) it takes up more space, and (2) multiple citations cause a long break in the text which can be confusing to the reader.

If the bibliography contains obscure references that *you* went to a lot of trouble to obtain, and that, therefore, are likely not to be readily available to the reviewer—and if the reference is important in the context of the proposal—provide several copies for use by the primary reviewers. If an obscure reference is *not* very important , provide 2 photocopies of the summary or omit the citation. For foreign language references not available in many libraries, provide the English summary. Provide copies of abstracts not published in major journals. For each such item provided (in duplicate), attach a note specifying that it is for the 2 primary reviewers. If the topic of your proposal is unique, provide 3 or 4 copies of the materials, because there are likely to be one or more outside reviewers.

Other Parts of the Application

Checklist   ➤

(Form in application kit)

- Required as the **LAST PAGE** of the signed original of the application
- Number the checklist page appropriately.
- Do not duplicate this page for the other 6 copies of the application.
- This form is NOT part of the review process.

Note added in second printing: The Checklist page has been changed in the PHS-398 (Revised 10/88).

CHECKLIST

Check the appropriate boxes and provide the information requested. Make this page the last page of the signed original of the application. *Do not attach copies of this page to the duplicated copies of the application.* Upon receipt and assignment of the application by the PHS, this page will be separated from the application. The page will *not* be duplicated, and it will *not* be a part of the review process. It will be reserved for PHS staff use only.

TYPE OF APPLICATION

☐ NEW application *(This application is being submitted to the PHS for the first time.)*

☐ REVISION of application number: _____
(This application replaces a prior unfunded version of a new, competing continuation or supplemental application.)

☐ COMPETING CONTINUATION of grant number: _____
(This application is to extend a funded grant beyond its current project period.)

☐ SUPPLEMENT to grant number: _____
(This application is for additional funds to supplement a currently funded grant.)

☐ CHANGE of principal investigator/program director.
Name of former principal investigator/program director: _____

☐ FOREIGN application. *(This information is required by the U.S. Department of State.)* City and country of
birth and present citizenship of principal investigator/program director: _____

ASSURANCES *(See GENERAL INFORMATION section of instructions.)*

a. Civil Rights Form HHS 441	b. Handicapped Individuals Form HHS 641	c. Sex Discrimination Form 639-A	d. Scientific Fraud (Misconduct) Assurance
☐ Filed ☐ Not filed	☐ Filed ☐ Not filed	☐ Filed ☐ Not filed	☐ Administrative review process has been established. Reporting requirements of the published scientific misconduct regulations will be followed.

INDIRECT COSTS

Indicate the applicant organization's most recent indirect cost rate established with the appropriate DHHS Regional Office, or, in the case of for-profit organizations, the rate established with the appropriate PHS Agency Cost Advisory Office. If the applicant organization is in the process of initially developing or renegotiating a rate, or has established a rate with another Federal agency, it should, immediately upon notification that an award will be made, develop a tentative indirect cost rate proposal based on its most recently completed fiscal year in accordance with the principles set forth in the pertinent *DHHS Guide for Establishing Indirect Cost Rates,* and submit it to the appropriate DHHS Regional Office or PHS Agency Cost Advisory Office. Indirect costs will *not* be paid on foreign grants, construction grants, grants to Federal organizations, and grants to individuals, and usually not on conference grants. Follow any additional instructions provided for Research Career Development Awards, Institutional National Research Service Awards, and the specialized grant applications listed in the GENERAL INSTRUCTIONS section.

☐ DHHS Agreement Dated: _____   ☐ No Indirect Costs Requested.

☐ DHHS Agreement being negotiated with _____ Regional Office.

☐ No DHHS Agreement, but rate established with _____ Date _____

CALCULATION*

a. First 12-month budget period:
Amount of base $_____ × Rate applied _____% = Indirect costs (a) $_____

b. Entire proposed project period:
Amount of base $_____ × Rate applied _____% = Indirect costs (b) $_____

(a) Add to total direct costs from page 4 and enter new total on FACE PAGE, Item 7b
(b) Add to total direct costs from page 5 and enter new total on FACE PAGE, Item 8b

*Check appropriate box(es):

☐ Salary and wages base   ☐ Modified total direct costs base   ☐ Other base (Explain below)

☐ Off-site, other special rate, or more than one rate involved (Explain below)

Explanation *(Attach separate sheet, if necessary.):*

*This is the required last page of the application. Number it appropriately.

Personal Data on Principal Investigator　　➤

(Form in application kit)

(OPTIONAL)

- Data provided by you are confidential.
- If you do not wish to provide the requested information, attach the form without filling out the information.
- DO NOT give this form a PAGE NUMBER.
- Attach this form to the signed original of the application—following the **CHECKLIST.**
- Do NOT duplicate this form.
- This form gets separated from the rest of the application before duplication.
- This form is NOT part of the review process.

Assurances

See NIH instructions, pages 4 to 8 (Appendix I)

- **Human subjects**
  Enter appropriate information in item 4 on Face page

- **Vertebrate animals**
  Enter appropriate information in item 5 on Face page

- **Recombinant DNA**
  - Guidelines are available from the Office of Recombinant DNA Activities, NIH, Bethesda, MD, 20892.
  - All research involving recombinant DNA techniques that is supported by the DHHS must meet the requirements of these guidelines.
  - Recombinant DNA molecules are defined as
    1. Molecules which are constructed outside living cells by joining natural or synthetic DNA segments to DNA molecules that can replicate in a living cell, or
    2. DNA molecules that result from replication of the DNA molecules described in (1) above

- **Protection Against Scientific Fraud**
  - Your Institution must have submitted assurance that it
    1. Has established an administrative process to review reports of scientific fraud related to biomedical and behavioral research conducted at or sponsored by your institution

Attach this form to the signed original of the
application after the CHECKLIST. Do not duplicate.

PERSONAL DATA ON
PRINCIPAL INVESTIGATOR/PROGRAM DIRECTOR

The Public Health Service has a continuing commitment to monitoring the operation of its review and award processes to detect—and deal appropriately with—any instances of real or apparent inequities with respect to age, sex, race, or ethnicity of the proposed principal investigator/program director.

To provide the PHS with the information it needs for this important task, complete the form below and attach it to the signed original of the application after the CHECKLIST. *Do not attach copies of this form to the duplicated copies of the application.*

Upon receipt and assignment of the application by the PHS, this form will be separated from the application. This form will *not* be duplicated, and it will *not* be a part of the review process. Data will be confidential, and will be maintained in Privacy Act record system 09-25-0036, "Grants: IMPAC (Grant/Contract Information)." All analyses conducted on the data will report aggregate statistical findings only and will not identify individuals.

If you decline to provide this information, it will in no way affect consideration of your application.

Your cooperation will be appreciated.

DATE OF BIRTH *(month/day/year)*	SEX
	☐ Female ☐ Male

RACE AND/OR ETHNIC ORIGIN *(check one)*

☐ American Indian or Alaskan Native

☐ Asian or Pacific Islander

☐ Black, not of Hispanic origin

☐ Hispanic

☐ White, not of Hispanic origin

NOTE: The category that most closely reflects the individual's recognition in the community should be used for purposes of reporting mixed racial and/or ethnic origins. Definitions are as follows:

American Indian or Alaskan Native: A person having origins in any of the original peoples of North America, and who maintains cultural identification through tribal affiliation or community recognition.

Asian or Pacific Islander: A person having origins in any of the original peoples of the Far East, Southeast Asia, the Indian subcontinent, or the Pacific Islands. This area includes, for example, China, India, Japan, Korea, the Philippine Islands and Samoa.

Black, not of Hispanic origin: A person having origins in any of the black racial groups of Africa.

Hispanic: A person of Mexican, Puerto Rican, Cuban, Central or South American or other Spanish culture or origin, regardless of race.

White, not of Hispanic origin: A person having origins in any of the original peoples of Europe, North Africa, or the Middle East

2. Will report to the Secretary of DHHS any investigation of alleged scientific fraud that appears substantial
- Scientific fraud is defined as
  1. Serious deviation (such as fabrication, falsification, or plagiarism) from accepted practices in carrying out research or in reporting the results of research, or
  2. Material failure to comply with Federal requirements affecting specific aspects of the conduct of research, e.g., the protection of human subjects and the welfare of laboratory animals.
  (See NIH Guide for Grants and Contracts, Vol. 15, #11, July 18, 1986.)

- **Civil Rights**
  - Check the appropriate box on the Checklist page.
  - Verify by the signatures on the FACE PAGE.
  - Does not apply to foreign applicant organizations
  - The Assurance of Compliance Form HHS **441** is available from the Office of Grants Inquiries, Division of Research Grants, NIH, Bethesda, MD 20892.

- **Handicapped Individuals**
  - Check the appropriate box on the checklist page.
  - Verify by the signatures on the FACE PAGE.
  - Does not apply to foreign applicant organizations
  - The Assurance of Compliance Form HHS **641** is available from the Office of Grants Inquiries, Division of Research Grants, NIH, Bethesda, MD 20892.

- **Protection Against Sex Discrimination**
  - Check the appropriate box on the checklist page.
  - Verify by the signatures on the FACE PAGE.
  - Does not apply to foreign applicant organizations
  - The Assurance of Compliance Form HHS **639-A** is available from the Office of Grants Inquiries, Division of Research Grants, NIH, Bethesda, MD 20892.

Note added in second printing: See *NIH Guide*, Vol. 18, No. 20, June 9, 1989 about "Other Support," p. 2 and about "Misconduct in Science Assurance," p. 3.

SECTION 3: APPENDIX

(Submit 6 collated sets.)
Note: Original + 5 sets—in contrast to body of proposal, for which you must submit the Original + 6 sets

What to Put Into the Appendix

1. SUPPLEMENTARY MATERIAL (RELEVANT TO PRE-LIMINARY STUDIES OR PROGRESS REPORT, section 2, item C)
   Graphs, diagrams, tables, charts that are not essential, but helpful and relevant to documenting progress
      [If essential to the evaluation of the Research Plan, in-corporate these items in body of application. (Reduce to save space, using photocopy machine, and wrap text around graphic.)]

2. Photographs, oversized documents, materials that do not reproduce well
   (Keep materials in item (1) and (2) above to a minimum.)

3. **Maximum of 10 documents such as**
   • Publications or Manuscripts ACCEPTED for publication
   • Patents or Invention reports
   • Other printed materials that have resulted since the last competitive review
      • NEW applicants may provide similar background materials to document preliminary studies.

4. Materials intended to help the primary reviewers by saving them a trip to the library (See Experimental Design and Methods, section 2, item D. These reprints/abstracts need only be submitted in duplicate or triplicate.)

How to Prepare the Appendix for the Final Draft

• Identify each appendix set with the name of the Principal Investigator/Program Director and the Project Title.
• Provide list of appendix items in 2 places:
   • At bottom of page 3 (Table of Contents)
   • On a separate sheet at the front of each collated Appendix set
• Label each appendix item (Name, Social Security number, Project title, Title of item).

- Be sure each appendix item is referred to in the text of the application.
- Be sure each appendix item referred to in the text of the application is provided and entered in the list of appendix items.
- Do not number appendix pages.
- Do NOT mail the Appendix separately.

NOTE: NIH does not duplicate the Appendix with the rest of the application.

The Appendix is given, in original form, to the 2 or 3 primary reviewers. The remaining copies are available at (or before) the Study Section meeting for other members who request to see the Appendix.

The Appendix is **NOT** to be used to circumvent the page limitations in the Research Plan.

NOTE: "AN APPLICATION MAY BE RETURNED IF THE APPENDIX FAILS TO OBSERVE THE SIZE LIMITATIONS."

INCOMPLETE APPLICATIONS

An application will be considered incomplete and RETURNED TO THE PRINCIPAL INVESTIGATOR if

- It is illegible

- It does not conform to the instructions

- The material presented is insufficient to permit adequate review

SENDING ADDITIONAL INFORMATION (AFTER THE PROPOSAL HAS BEEN SUBMITTED)

- Send additional or corrective material, pertinent to an application, after the receipt date, ONLY if it is specifically solicited OR agreed to by prior discussion with an appropriate Public Health Service staff member, usually the Executive Secretary of the Study Section.

- Send 6 copies (if it is months before the Study Section Meeting) to 20 copies (if it is only a few weeks before the Study Section Meeting) of the item, along with a cover letter to the Executive Secretary of the assigned Study Section—even as late as 4 weeks *before* the Study Section Meeting.

- Mail the materials to the Executive Secretary of the Study Section to which your application has been assigned. Your materials are likely to get lost if you address them simply to "Division of Research Grants."

  Enclose a self-addressed, stamped postcard—to receive acknowledgement that the materials you sent were received by the Executive Secretary. Call the Executive Secretary if your postcard is not returned within 2 weeks.

- *At the same time,* send a copy of the letter and the item(s) to your Health Scientist Administrator asking her/him to be sure that the new material has been distributed to the Study Section Members.

PART

III

Planning
Your
Grant Proposal

PLANNING THE GRANT PROPOSAL

The most important part of a grant proposal is the idea: the major subject and content of the proposed research (the Research Plan, section 2 of the grant application). The Research Plan should be innovative, have a clear rationale, and obvious significance; it should be focused, well thought out, and timely. It should address a specific problem or set of related problems that can be solved by a logical sequence of experiments.

For NIH proposals, clinical relevance is also helpful but an artificial or overly tenuous, circuitous relevance should not be invented for the proposal. You should consult the funding agency to determine whether your ideas are considered to have a high priority in the view of that agency. If so, indicate that in the proposal. For example, the National Eye Institute has a 5-year plan. The *NIH Guide for Grants and Contracts* is also a good place to get ideas of current interests at NIH. (There is no charge for being on the mailing list for the NIH Guide. See Appendix XI, Resources.) See also *NIH Guide*, Vol. 18, No. 20, June 9, 1989, p. 4.

Don't try to incorporate every idea you have about all interesting topics into one grant proposal. Although it is important that you have expertise ("a track record") in the proposed field of research, do not be discouraged if you are a new entrant into the field. If your training was good, and your idea is good, well thought out, and well presented (written), you stand a good chance of getting funded. At present, the percentage of new applicants who are funded is about the same as that of previous grantees who get funded. However, pilot experiments and presentation of preliminary experimental results are imperative. (Some Institutes provide small grants for pilot projects.)

A clear, concise, but adequately detailed description of the Experimental Design and Methods to be used to achieve the proposed research goals is essential in section 2, item D of the application. Don't present a global set of experiments. Experiments should be feasible and designed in such a way that they answer specific questions and that one experiment leads logically to the next.

A realistic grasp of what personnel, equipment, supplies, and so forth will be required to do the project and how much can be accomplished in the requested time is absolutely necessary. A reasonable budget reflects your thoughtfulness and knowledge about the costs associated with your research. Reviewers may consider you naive if you underbudget or greedy if you overbudget. Likewise, reviewers become wary if you propose 10 years of work in a 3-year grant request or attempt to draw a 1-year project out to 3 years. A concise schedule indicating the aspects of the project planned for each of the proposed years (at the end of Experimental Design and Methods section) is a help to the reviewer, but a detailed analysis of what you will do week by week or month by month is unnecessary. Exaggerated detail often provides comic relief for the reviewers and detracts from your credibility as a professional, experienced scientist.

Discussion of your ideas with more established and experienced colleagues, before writing the proposal, can save you hours of valuable time. Having them critique the application can help you avoid pitfalls and gain clarity in your presentation: You know what you want to say; do others perceive what you intend them to?

BEFORE YOU WRITE YOUR GRANT PROPOSAL

Before you plan your project—and again, before you begin to write your grant proposal—carefully read the instructions for completing the application, in the case of NIH, the NIH Instruction Booklet. Some aspects of the instructions are changed occasionally by NIH *without printing new editions of the instruction booklet*. These changes are generally explained on loose sheets added into the application kits and are also announced in the NIH Guide. The changes may be important. So, always read the additional instruction sheets that you may find in the grant application kit and keep up to date with the NIH Guide. Do not assume you know the instructions by remembering them from the last time you submitted an application.

After you have read the instruction booklet but before you begin writing your own proposal, read one or more well-written, successful applications that have received high priority scores and have been funded for 3 or 5 years. You will be able to find such proposals at many research institutions. Perhaps the grantees will allow you to read not only the proposals, but also the corresponding "pink sheets." Reading these documents will give you a better idea of what the instructions mean and what meets with Study Section approval.

PLANNING THE RESEARCH PLAN

Aspects of proposal preparation
- Deciding what you are going to do (propose)
- Planning the project
- Doing preliminary (feasibility) studies
- Describing what you are going to do (writing the proposal)
- Developing a realistic budget

Getting Started

Write down the answers to the following questions:
- What is to be done? What is the hypothesis to be tested or question(s) to be answered?
- Is the work original?
- Are you and your team aware of what's been done in this and related fields? (Background)
- Why is the work worth doing? (Significance)
- What is the long-range goal?
- What are the specific objectives?
- Do the specific objectives lead toward accomplishment of the long-range goal?
- Is the methodology "state of the art?"
- Who will do the work? (The reputation of the grantee and her/his team)
- Why should the granting agency let **YOU** do the project? (What are your unique qualifications?)
- How long will the work take?
- How much will the project cost (budget) and why (budget justification)?
- What facilities will the work require?
- Do you have access to such facilities?
- What are the expected results?
- What are your contingency plans in case you hit a "snag?"

- Where will the work be carried out (project site)?
- What is the cost/benefit ratio for the project?
  - How will the project benefit your institution?
  - How will the project benefit the granting institution?
  - How will the project benefit society? (Health relatedness)
  - For corporation grants: How will the project make money for, or add to the stature of, the corporation?
- What other funds are available to support your project?
- If not applying to NIH, does the agency require a pre-application?

Writing
Your
Grant Proposal

✳ **CONSIDER THAT THE WAY YOU WRITE YOUR GRANT APPLICATION TELLS THE REVIEWER A LOT ABOUT YOU—as a scientist and as a person.**

- Do you show originality of thought?
- Do you plan ahead—and do so with ingenuity?
- Do you think logically and clearly?
- Are you up to date in all matters relevant to your project?
- Do you have good analytical skills?
- Do you recognize limitations, pitfalls?
- Do you have good managerial skills? How do you handle a budget?
- How meticulous are you? How much care do you give to detail?

BEGIN TO WRITE YOUR GRANT PROPOSAL EARLY.

- It may take anywhere from several weeks to several months to prepare a good grant application.
- Set deadlines for yourself for finishing the outline, first draft, second draft, etc.
- A hastily prepared application is often a poorly prepared application.
- Have a good second draft of the proposal ready —to send to colleagues for appraisal—at least 4–5 weeks before the grant application is due at your Institution's Grants Administration Office (often 2 - 4 weeks before the grant proposal is due at NIH).

     NEW grant applications are due Feb. 1, June 1, Oct. 1.
     RENEWAL applications are due Mar. 1, July 1, Nov. 1.
     REVISED applications are due Mar. 1, July 1, Nov. 1. (See NIH Guide, Vol. 17, #14, April 15, 1988, page 1.)

- A missed deadline—even one day late—may cost you 4 months of time!

Leave yourself ample time to

- THINK
- PLAN
- PREPARE
- OUTLINE
- WRITE
- REVISE
- GET HELP
- REVISE
- POLISH
- GET ADMINISTRATIVE APPROVAL
- PHOTOCOPY
- MAIL (In time to be *received* by the deadline)

Read and Follow Instructions Meticulously

- KEEP TO THE **PAGE LIMITS.**
- Stay within the recommended margins (the proposal gets copied and reduced).
- PUT INFORMATION ONLY WHERE IT BELONGS. (Don't put background information into Specific Aims or Specific Aims into Experimental Design and Methods, etc.)

Use a Checklist

Use the printed checklist that NIH requires as the last page of the application and the one provided in *Appendix III* of this book:

- When you plan the proposal (before you begin writing)
- Before you finish the second draft
- Before you finish the last draft

WRITING THE RESEARCH PLAN

MAKE AN OUTLINE for each section of the proposal. The time you spend making an outline will probably be regained many times over in the time you save at the writing and editing stages.

- Use index cards, 3M Post-it Notes, Word processors, OUTLINE PROCESSORS.
  (Word processors are very useful but are not a substitute for making an outline. Make an outline on your word processor and then write from the outline.)

- Your outline should fit **logically** into the obligatory outline given in the NIH instructions.
- **OUTLINES ARE MUCH EASIER TO REVISE THAN TEXT.**
- Check the outline for logical progression of ideas, parallel construction, and adequacy of detail.
- **Don't** begin to **write until you are 99.99% happy with your outline.**

WHEN YOU BEGIN TO WRITE:

- PLAN TO INCLUDE WELL-DESIGNED AND CAREFULLY LABELED TABLES AND FIGURES.
- Prepare **FIGURES, TABLES, AND PHOTOGRAPHS (PLATES) BEFORE** you write the proposal.
  - Use them as a guide to organize your material (sequence).
  - Be sure they are referred to in the text.
  - Be sure they are interpreted in the text.
  - Be sure the legends, units, and findings agree with statements in the text.
- PLAN TO REFER TO THE LITERATURE THOUGHTFULLY, THOROUGHLY, AND SELECTIVELY.

Writing the First Draft

- FOLLOW THE OUTLINE.
- Try to write each section at one sitting; if the section is too long, try to write each sub-section at one sitting.
- It is acceptable to use the first person in writing the research plan. (Note, however, that the first person is not to be used in the DESCRIPTION (ABSTRACT) of the proposal.)
- Don't worry about "niceties" in the first draft; just "let it flow!"

WRITE TO EXPRESS, NOT TO IMPRESS!

Never assume that the reviewers will "know what you mean."

Revising the First Draft

When You Revise the First Draft, Think About

- **ACCURACY**
- **CLARITY**
- **CONSISTENCY**

- **BREVITY** Concise
- **EMPHASIS**
- **STYLE AND TONE**

Be Accurate

- Provide correct information to maintain your credibility.
- Convey correctly the information you provide.
  - Use words correctly.
  - Don't call something a fact unless it *is* a fact.

Be Clear

- The reviewer should be able to
  - Understand easily what you wrote
  - Perceive easily how you got from point A to point B
    - Use a logical sequence of presentation.
    - If you discuss 3 topics, give similar information—in the same sequence—about each topic.
    - "Method" 1 should go with Specific Aim 1, etc.
    - Don't use "BIG" words (never send your reader to the dictionary).
    - Don't use JARGON! Terminology limited to a given field may be unfamiliar—and irritating—to a reviewer who is not in that field.
    - Don't use the words *former* and *latter*—it slows the reader down.
- Start each paragraph with a good, informative **TOPIC SENTENCE.** What are you going to tell the reader in that paragraph?

- **Avoid Ambiguity**
  - Misplaced Modifiers
  - Uncommitted pronouns
  - Words that can be interpreted in more than one way
  - Complex sentences

SEE APPENDIX X

Think about possible gaps between what you *intend* to convey and what the reader may *perceive*.

- **AVOID IRRELEVANT INFORMATION**

i.e., INFORMATION THAT IS IRRELEVANT IN A GIVEN CONTEXT

- Don't "pour out" all you know just to impress the reader.
- Think about what the reader needs (wants) to know in relation to *this* section of *this* proposal about *this* subject (project).
- Irrelevant information may confuse the reader.

Be Consistent

- In the outline form, are your headings I, II, III; A, B, C; and 1, 2, 3 at the same levels of importance?
- It is difficult but essential to maintain a good outline within the confines of the one imposed by the NIH instructions.
- **AN OUTLINE PROCESSOR CAN HELP IMMENSELY.**

Be Consistent

- Text should agree with the information in figures and figure legends (including the units you use).
- Terminology and abbreviations should be the same throughout. Do not use different words for the same thing just for literary reasons. Use of different terms for the same thing may create ambiguities. Ambiguities slow the reader down.
- Tenses should be uniform throughout the document or at least throughout a section of the document.
- Subjects and verbs should agree (singular or plural):
  The GROUP of scholars IS getting an award.
  The SCHOLARS ARE getting an award.

Be Consistent

Appropriate sections of the proposal should agree with each other:

- Body of proposal with description (abstract)
- Specific Aims with Methods
- Methods with Budget
- Budget requests with Facilities Available

Separate clearly what you say you

- Have done (Progress Report)
- Are doing now (time between writing proposal and, you hope, funding)
- Propose to do in next project period
- Want to do in the future (or should do) but are *not* planning to do in the next project period. That is, be very explicit about

designating what might be a direction for a subsequent renewal project period but is not a current aim.

Be Brief (Concise But Complete)

In the case of a competitive renewal application, the reviewers usually are provided with a copy of your previous research proposal. Nevertheless, the instructions specify that the present application must be complete by itself.

In expository writing, the reader wants the *maximum* information in the *minimum* number of words.

AVOID INFORMATION IRRELEVANT **IN THE CONTEXT** OF THE PROPOSAL.

AVOID REDUNDANCY AND UNNECESSARY WORDS.

They waste your space (page limitations).
They waste the reviewer's precious time.
They may irritate the reviewer.
They may confuse the reviewer. (Why is the writer telling me this again?)

See Appendix X

Think About Emphasis

• Don't begin a paragraph with unimportant words. (Consider IMPACT)
• In a compound sentence, put the important phrase first.

See Appendix X

Think About Style and Tone

• Use simple words, short direct sentences, and short paragraphs that begin with **informative topic sentences.**
• Avoid modifiers that do not add to the critical essence of what you want to say:
    This *cleverly conceived* experiment . . .
• Replace "opinion" modifiers with quantitative modifiers.
    Not: *most* or *many*   But: 68–70%
• Don't overstate your case.
    Avoid superlatives unless you are very sure "it" really is *best, most*, etc.
• Try not to split infinitives.

- Try to be positive (mood and tone are "contagious").
- **Avoid "Pompous" Language**
  - Don't write: "Nosocomial infection;" Write: "Hospital-acquired infection"
  - Don't write: "Iatrogenic condition;" Write: "Physician-induced condition"

  (Your reviewer may not be an MD)

  Avoidance of unnecessary, "heavy," medical jargon is especially important if you are an M.D. researcher proposing a project that involves a lot of basic science. Such a proposal is likely to have at least one Ph.D. reviewer. Sending this reviewer on frequent trips to a medical dictionary wastes her/his time!

Make the grant proposal short but thorough; do not repeat, but rather refer to, material in other sections. For example, say "As discussed in section Y on page X" or "See section Y, page X."

Strictly adhere to the page limitations. If you are strapped for space, consider that 12-letters-per-inch type allows more text on a page than 10-letters-per-inch, but remember that choice of the type size is sometimes important to keep things looking neat. Legibility is very important. Don't antagonize your reviewer by using smaller than 10 or 12 pitch type (to circumvent the page limitations!) or fancy fonts that are hard to read. Good "letter quality" print should be used in all drafts that will be read by others; some people find dot-matrix print difficult to read.

When you have edited your first draft in accordance with each of the above criteria, print out a second draft and check it again.

Revising the Second Draft

SELF-EDITING THE SECOND DRAFT

In the Second Draft, Watch Out For

- Lack of logical flow
- Bad grammar (especially the kind that causes ambiguity)
- Jargon
- Insufficient references
- A messy presentation (e.g., too many typos or spelling errors)
  Reviewer may extrapolate: Carelessness in writing indicates carelessness in experimentation!
- Circular sentences
  "The important conclusion from these findings is . . . " But instead of giving a conclusion, you repeat the findings!
- Sentences and paragraphs that are too long

HAVING OTHERS EDIT THE SECOND DRAFT

When You Have a Good Second Draft, Get Help From Computers, Colleagues and/or Consultants.

COMPUTER AIDS

- Outline processors
- "Search mode" in word processors to find over-used words
- Spelling checkers
- Stylistics and grammar checkers (Some computer programs can check for passive versus active verb constructions, sentence length, vague phrases, incorrect punctuation, missing spaces, overused words, etc.)

COLLEAGUES

Edit your own first and second draft. Send colleagues the **GOOD** second draft to read.

- I'll read your grant/you read mine
  - Ask ahead of time
  - Give them **at least** 2 weeks to read your proposal
- In-house "study section" (if your institution has one)

Have at least 3 people review your grant before you write your final draft:

1. Someone who understands your specific research—to check for accuracy.
2. Someone who understands science and research but does **NOT** know about your specific research—to check for clarity.
3. Someone who is a good editor—to help you polish the proposal.

People who know your field can make valuable scientific suggestions, but someone not totally familiar with your specific area of research may be a better judge of clarity (and may, in some cases, better simulate the reviewer). Likewise, someone who is a successful proposal-writer (preferably multiple successes) and has had experience as a reviewer can have valuable comments even if he/she knows little about the field. Lastly, someone with good editorial skills can help with the final polishing of the proposal. It is optimal for the success of your grant proposal to have it read by each of these types of critics.

The best stage at which to have a candid and "savvy" colleague read the application is at the stage when you have a clean, comprehensible draft. This draft should be easy for a colleague to understand but should not be at the stage where you will feel resentful about making suggested changes. Check a single-spaced draft for page limits. But, if possible, send readers a double-spaced copy with wide margins to make it easy for them to insert suggested changes.

It is at this stage, if you get there early enough, that it is sometimes possible and advisable also to send a copy to your health scientist administrator at NIH and ask him/her for comments on the adequacy of the presentation. It is within the jurisdiction of the health scientist administrator to prereview drafts of a grant application, if she/he is requested to do so by the Principal Investigator—but such prereview will be only with respect to form (i.e., for grantsmanship, not for scientific merit). Your health scientist administrator should be able to discuss with you the appropriateness of various components of your application but if you wish to use this "service," the grant application must be sent to the health scientist administrator several months before the required submission date! Do not count on the health scientist administrator to make suggestions about material (scientific) content, give "estimates" on fundability, or do editing.

Don't change the draft you gave to the readers while the readers have that draft.

> You will have a lot of trouble locating changes suggested by the readers if you have generated a new draft!

REVISE the second draft after you get **all** the copies back.

> INCORPORATE THE READERS' SUGGESTIONS (only those that are appropriate) during this revision. You will then have a pre-final draft.

REVISING THE PRE-FINAL DRAFT

> This is your last opportunity to make substantive changes. Be sure you are satisfied with your proposal before you do the final polishing and checking.

POLISHING AND CHECKING THE PRE-FINAL DRAFT of the Research Plan and the rest of the application.

See Appendices I, III and X.

- Have you rechecked the budget calculations?
- Have you checked that budget totals are entered in items 7 and 8 of the face page?
- Have you signed the application? (Before photocopying!)
- Has the responsible institutional official signed the application? (Before photocopying!)
- Do you have a table of contents?
  ARE THE PAGE NUMBERS FILLED IN—on the text pages?—in the table of contents?—and IN ACCORDANCE WITH THE PAGE NUMBERS OF THE FINAL DRAFT?
- Have you compared the project desription (ABSTRACT; form page 2) with the final version of the application to be sure it is appropriate and parallel?
- Do you have a tentative timetable for your project (at the end of the Experimental Design and Methods section?)
- Do you have a biographical sketch for each professional person listed under "Personnel" and "Consultants?"
- Do you have a letter of collaboration for each Consultant and "outside" collaborator?
- Do you have the necessary documentation for consortium/contractual arrangements?
- Have you completed the necessary forms concerning
  - Other Support
  - Resources and Environment
    (Be sure "Facilities" and "Equipment" are not at odds with equipment asked for in the budget)
  - Personal Data on Principal Investigator
  Are the forms in the correct places in the application?
- Have the dates of the various institutional agreements been filled in on the Face Page and Checklist Page?
- Have the indirect costs been calculated on the Checklist Page and filled in on the Face Page?
- Is the Appendix complete and in order (collated)? Is each appendix item labeled correctly?
- Have you included a list of appendix items as a cover sheet for the Appendix?
- Have you made a final check of all items against the checklist provided by NIH?
- Is the NIH checklist filled in and included? Have you numbered it as the last page of the application?
- Have you checked the formatting of each page? (Including margins)

- Have you checked that no page limits have been exceeded in the final format?
- Is your name and social security number typed at the top of every page?
- Are the pages all numbered consecutively and correctly? (No pages 5, 5A, 5B, 6, . . . !).

The final copy of the grant proposal should look neat. Spelling and grammar should be correct. Poor grammar makes extra work for the reviewers and, if they are of the "old school," may "sour" them about the applicant. Certain spelling and grammatical errors, or a large number of such mistakes, may provide "comic relief" during the long and tedious Study Section meetings. Be sure your proposal is not used for this purpose. An occasional minor error is no calamity—and a neatly "whited-out" correction is perfectly acceptable. But, a sloppy-looking grant application may give the reviewers the idea that this is a reflection of how you do your science. If a reviewer feels an applicant could not be bothered putting out a decent final product, the reviewer is likely to start her/his review of your grant proposal with a negative view.

If all of the above are in order, you can prepare your application for submission.

Preparing the Application for Submission

- Print out (or type) a final draft.
- Make the appropriate number of photocopies of the application and the Appendix.
  Aside from the 6 photocopies of the application and 5 photocopies of the appendix required by NIH, you will need extra copies of the application for yourself and for the grants management office, and perhaps other administrative offices, of your own institution.
  - Use paper clips or rubber bands to fasten pages together. (Do not staple or bind!)
  - Use folders or lower halves of manila envelopes to keep copies neat.
  - Label items: "Original Application," "Original Appendix," etc.
- If you want to, provide a cover letter requesting (suggesting) a particular Study Section—and the reason you are making the request—and attach it (paper clip) to the front of the original copy of the application.

• Self-address, STAMP and include a postcard that someone at NIH can drop in the mail to confirm receipt of your proposal. The postcard can simply say:

> "Grant Application: (Fill in your grant proposal title) by (Fill in your name) was received at DRG
>
> by _____
>
> on (date) _____
>
> Thank you."

Mailing the Application

MAIL **ORIGINAL** + **6** COPIES OF THE APPLICATION = **7** COMPLETE SETS*

MAIL 6 COMPLETE SETS OF THE *APPENDIX*

• Use boxes from bond paper , etc., to pack application so that it arrives at NIH in good condition.
• Use the mailing label provided in the middle of the application kit (just after the sample continuation sheet and before the first blue page).
• Use the proper amount of postage. (Weigh it; don't guess.)
• Mail the application in *ample* time. (The deadlines at NIH refer to receipt dates, not postmarks.)
• Get a legible proof-of-mailing receipt from the mail carrier dated at least 1 week prior to due date (see next to last paragraph on page 11 of NIH instructions in Appendix I). Such a receipt costs only $0.45.

On arrival at NIH, each application is stamped with the arrival date in large letters! It is important that your application arrive on time. If you cannot mail the application early enough to use regular mail, use U.S. Postal Service Express Mail or a private express mail service such as Federal Express.

---

* NIH has announced a new expedited review of grant applications related to AIDS research. Beginning April, 1989, such proposals require submission of the original + 24 legible copies. (See NIH Guide, Vol. 18, #15, April 28, 1989, page 1.)

IMPENDING CHANGES IN PROCEDURE FOR SUBMISSION OF GRANT APPLICATIONS

National Institutes of Health (NIH)

NIH GRANT RO1 APPLICATION PROTOTYPE SOFTWARE PROGRAM

The National Institutes of Health, Division of Computer Research and Technology, in conjunction with the Division of Research Grants, is developing a computer software program for the Apple Macintosh Computer and for the IBM PC (and compatibles) for the purpose of facilitating the processing of RO1 grant applications to the National Institutes of Health.

The program is expected to be implemented in 1990 and will allow investigators to submit grant proposals (administrative information and the Research Plan) to NIH directly on a Macintosh or IBM PC floppy disk or, ultimately, via a telecommunications network. Initially, certain materials, such as electron micrographs, will continue to be submitted by mail.

The computerization will expedite the processing of proposals, eliminate paperwork and save time and money now expended in retyping information from grant applications. Information necessary for NIH purposes will be transferred at NIH directly from the disks to avoid retyping and the resultant errors. The program is also intended to expedite grant application assignment to Study Sections for initial scientific review, and to Institutes for potential funding. Computer matching of elements of a grant application with the expertise of particular Study Sections would provide more accurate assignments than are now possible by referral officers. Revised applications, now often assigned to the same Study Section that reviewed the original proposal, will be assigned to Study Sections based on more rigorous scientific criteria.

Reviewers will receive grant proposals on floppy disks and will write their reviewers' reports directly on these disks. After the Study Section meeting, the executive secretary will develop the summary statements from the reviewers' reports directly on the computer disks. Reviewers' reports will be in locked files to insure the confidentiality of the review process. Methods involving passwords and/or encryption will insure that certain documents are not accidentally changed or tampered with during the process.

From the point of view of the investigator, there should be a significant reduction of the application cycle time, as well as better matching of applications with Study Sections and Institutes for purposes of grant review and funding. The new system will also avoid large amounts of paperwork and the mailing of large packets, and will save on postage, especially the express postage used by so many investigators.

National Science Foundation (NSF)

The National Science Foundation is taking a more general approach to the problem of electronic information transfer. The aim of NSF is to permit transfer of all types of graphics, as well as text, within grant proposals. The first phase of the project now underway at NSF will be limited to transmission of the administrative data in the application.

TRACKING THE APPLICATION

Follow the travels of your application after it is sent to the granting agency—in this case, NIH:

- Did you get the self-addressed postcard back?
- Did you receive your proposal ID # and Study Section assignment from NIH?
- What are your Study Section and Institute assignments?
- When does your Study Section meet?
- Who are the members of the Study Section?

As soon as you get your assignment, call your Executive Secretary to find out if there is anyone on the Study Section who is not listed in the NIH list of Initial Review Group (IRG) members.

It is **your responsibility** to contact the Division of Research Grants (DRG) Referral Office if you do not get, within 6 weeks of submitting the application, the Study Section assignment (including the name, address, and phone number of the Executive Secretary—and the number assigned to your application).

In the months between submission of your application and the Study Section meeting, things may happen that might help your proposal get a better review. You may get some new exciting data, an additional paper may be accepted for publication, you may get a promotion—or something else may occur that would strengthen your application. It is to your advantage to inform the Study Section about such matters.

If you have something to send, contact the Executive Secretary of your assigned Study Section and ask for permission to send supplementary materials. If permission is granted, write a letter (enclose new data, reprints, preprints, etc., original + 6 copies) to the Executive Secretary of the Study Section asking him/her to release this additional information to the reviewers. However, do not send data just to impress the reviewers that you are working hard. Do not send data that you would not have put into the original grant application.

In fairness to the Executive Secretary, staff, and the Study Section, the optimal time to send such additional data is more than 6 weeks before the Study Section meeting. However, if an experiment that will help the status of your grant proposal comes out a week before the meeting, call NIH. If you get permission, send the materials by express mail; there is no harm in trying.

If you do send material close to the time of the Study Section meeting, send 16 to 20 copies to save NIH the task of making photocopies.

Enclose a self-addressed, stamped postcard with the materials you send so that you can get acknowledgement of receipt of the materials.

Also, if you get permission and send additional materials to the Executive Secretary, send a copy of the materials and the cover letter to the Health Scientist Administrator or Program Director at the potential funding Institute and ask her/him to check that the materials have reached the Study Section members.

Be sure you have received your "pink sheets" 4 to 6 weeks after the Study Section meeting. (The Executive Secretary needs time to write about 60 to 100 or more of these after the meeting. She/he must synthesize these Summary Statements from 2 or 3 written reports of the primary reviewers and the discussion during the meeting that follows the oral reading of these reports. It is no easy task! Don't call about your "pink sheets" immediately after the Study Section meeting.)

What To Do If Your Application is Not Funded

1. SUBMIT A REVISED APPLICATION.

If your priority score warrants it and if you have funds to tide you over for another grant processing cycle, revise the proposal and try again. As funding decreases, it is becoming almost more the rule, than the exception, to have to revise at least once.

IF YOU PREPARE A **REVISED APPLICATION:**

- Be sure it has substantive improvements.
  "A revised application will be returned if substantial revisions are not clearly apparent."
- Be sure it is responsive to all questions and criticisms raised in the summary statement.
- Get help from your Health Scientist Administrator.
- Indicate all substantive changes you have made in the application.
  - "Highlight these changes within the text of the Research Plan by appropriate bracketing, indenting or changing of typography."
  - Discuss these changes in Section 2: INTRODUCTION to the RESEARCH PLAN (1-page limit).
- "Incorporate into the Progress Report/Preliminary Studies any **pertinent** work you have done since the prior version of the proposal was submitted."
- Note that the deadline for submission of revised applications is the same as for competitive renewals (March 1, July 1, November 1) whether the revised application is for a new or a competing continuation grant.

SOME HINTS ABOUT THE SUMMARY STATEMENT (*"PINK SHEETS"*)

The Summary Statement is largely a combination of the reports of the 2 primary reviewers. Sometimes one can detect the "cut-and-paste" nature of the "pink sheets" and even can distinguish between the comments of the 2 reviewers. Did they agree or disagree? What were their individual "gripes with your proposal? There is an "art" to reading between the lines of the Summary Statement. Learn to interpret the "pink sheets" and to use them to write a better revision.

- Comments that represent the proposal inaccurately often result from unclear writing by the Principal Investigator.
- Criticisms about protocols, techniques, or data analysis often indicate the Principal Investigator didn't do enough homework.
- If the critique questions the ability of the Principal Investigator to carry out the proposed work, an appropriate collaborator may be in order.
- If the critique questions the choice of problem, ask yourself if the

significance was poorly explained (rewrite)—OR—if the problem per se lacks merit (pick a new problem)

If the **Summary Statement ("Pink Sheet")** is not sufficiently explicit about what the Study Section did, and did not, like about your proposal, you can sometimes get additional information by contacting your HEALTH SCIENTIST ADMINISTRATOR or the Executive Secretary of your Study Section.

Your Health Scientist Administrator is likely to have been present during the review of your application and may be able to provide some insight into what the reviewers did and did not like about your the project. Your Health Scientist Administrator can also help you respond to the Study Section critique if you plan to revise your application.

If you submit a revised application, remember that the composition of the Study Section changes with time. Although a re-submitted application is frequently given back to the same reviewers, this is not always the case.

2. WRITE A REBUTTAL.

You may request corrective action by the Public Health Service if you think there has been serious error in

1. The assignment of your application (*prior to* the Study Section meeting)
   Write to the Executive Secretary.
2. The process or substance of the review of your application (*after* the Study Section meeting)

If you do not agree with something in the Summary Statement or think the reviewers have misunderstood your intent, call your Health Scientist Administrator. She/he may be able to intervene prior to the Council meeting in some cases. You also may discuss with your Health Scientist Administrator the advisability of submitting written information on behalf of your application for consideration by the Council.

Contact your Health Scientist Administrator at the Institute.

• The Institute Program Staff decide on a response.
• The Institute Program Staff sends a reply.

Detailed information about communicating concerns as to the review of an application—and as to the options open to the Institute Program Staff—is available from the Office of Grants Inquiries, Division of Research Grants, NIH, Bethesda, MD 20892 (See page 3 of the NIH instructions, Appendix I).

If you decide to write a letter of rebuttal, be sure it is constructive and written in a positive tone.

No "Sour Grapes"

- Do not *COMPLAIN* to the granting agency.
- Do not berate the Institute staff about what is in the "pink sheets"—no matter how "right" you are.
  - The Institute staff does not initiate the critique.
  - The Institute staff is only the intermediary between the reviewers and the Principal Investigator.
  - The Institute staff generally does not communicate with the Study Section about an application once the Study Section meeting is over.
  - The Institute staff consists of professionals. They are also human beings; treat them with courtesy and respect.

Intrusion of sarcasm, righteous indignation, and/or "sour grapes" statements in a letter of rebuttal helps no one, least of all you!

Under no circumstances should you attempt to contact individual Study Section members. Never put a Study Section member in a compromising position by either trying to influence him/her personally before the Study Section meeting, or by asking for the results of the deliberations of the Study Section after the meeting.

A FINAL WORD

If you get a chance to be an ad hoc reviewer on a Study Section (i.e., on a one-time basis), take it! Watching the peer review system work, from the inside, and observing and experiencing the enormous task of the reviewers, will not only be enlightening but is almost guaranteed to improve the writing of your own grant applications.

GOOD LUCK!

Appendix I

Instructions (Form PHS–398; Revised 9/86)
For NIH-R01 Application

On the following pages is a copy of the NIH instructions as revised September, 1986. The bold print and italics are as found in the NIH instructions. I have added additional italics to emphasize items in the instructions that I deem particularly noteworthy. I have also indicated, to the nearest full line of text (for reasons of style), where each pagebreak of the original NIH instructions occurs.

Instruction Sheet for PHS 398   Form Approved through 9/30/89
Rev. 9/86   OMB No. 0925–0001

U.S. DEPARTMENT OF HEALTH
AND HUMAN SERVICES
Public Health Service

GRANT APPLICATION FORM PHS 398

GENERAL INFORMATION

Introduction

The Public Health Service (PHS) requests the information described in these instructions pursuant to its statutory authorities for awarding grants, contained in Sections 301(a) and 487 of the PHS Act, as amended (42 USC 241a and 42 USC 288). *Lack of sufficient information may hinder the PHS's ability to review an application and to monitor the grantee's performance.* Therefore, such information must be submitted if an application is to receive due consideration for an award.

The PHS requests the Social Security Number for the purpose of accurate identification, referral, and review of applications and for efficient management of PHS grant programs. *Provision of the Social Security Number is voluntary.* No individual will be denied any right, benefit, or privilege provided by law because of refusal to disclose his or her Social Security Number.

Government Use of Information

In addition to using the information provided for reviewing applications and monitoring grantee performance, the *PHS may use the information to identify candidates who may serve as ad hoc consultants, committee, or national advisory council and board members* and to analyze costs of proposed grants.

The PHS maintains applications and grant records as part of a system of records as defined by the *Privacy Act:* 09–25–0112, "Grants: Research, Research Training, Fellowship, and Construction Applications." The Privacy Act of 1974 (5 USC 552a) *allows disclosures for "routine uses"* and for permissible disclosures.

Some routine uses are:

1. To the cognizant audit agency for auditing;

2. To a congressional office from the record of an individual in response to an inquiry from the congressional office made at the request of the individual;

3. To qualified experts, not within the definition of Department of Health and Human Services (DHHS) employees as prescribed in DHHS regulations (45 CFR 5b.2), for opinions as a part of the application review process;

End of Page 1 of NIH instructions.

---

4. To a Federal agency, in response to its request, in connection with the letting of a contract or the issuance of a license, grant, or other benefit by the requesting agency, to the extent that the record is relevant and necessary to the requesting agency's decision on the matter;

5. To organizations in the private sector with which the PHS has contracted for the purpose of collating, analyzing, aggregating, or otherwise refining records in a system. Relevant records will be disclosed to such a contractor, who will be required to maintain Privacy Act safeguards with respect to such records; and

6. To the applicant organization in connection with performance or administration under the terms and conditions of the award, or in connection with problems that might arise in performance or administration if an award is made.

7. Another routine use is to the Department of Justice, to a court or other tribunal, or to another party before such tribunal, when one of the following is a party to litigation or has any interest in such litigation, and the DHHS determines that the use of such records by the Department of Justice, the tribunal, or the other party is relevant and necessary to the litigation and would help in the effective representation of the governmental party:

a) the DHHS, or any component thereof;

b) any DHHS employee in his or her official capacity;

c) any DHHS employee in his or her individual capacity where the Department of Justice (or the DHHS, where it is authorized to do so) has agreed to represent the employee; or

d) the United States or any agency thereof, where the DHHS determines that the litigation is likely to affect the DHHS or any of its components.

8. *A record may also be disclosed for a research purpose,* when the DHHS:

a) has determined that the use or disclosure does not violate legal or policy limitations under which the record was provided, collected, or obtained;

b) has determined that the research purpose (1) cannot be reasonably accomplished unless the record is provided in individually identifiable form, and (2) warrants the risk to the privacy of the individual that additional exposure of the record might bring;

c) *has secured a written statement* attesting to the recipient's understanding of, and willingness to abide by these provisions; and

d) has required the recipient to:

(1) establish reasonable administrative, technical, and physical safeguards to prevent unauthorized use or disclosure of the record;

(2) remove or destroy the information that identifies the individual at the earliest time at which removal or destruction can be accomplished consistent with the purpose of the research project, unless the recipient has presented adequate justification of a research or health nature for retaining such information; and

---

End of Page 2 of NIH instructions.

---

(3) make no further use or disclosure of the record, except (a) in emergency circumstances affecting the health or safety of an individual, (b) for use in another research project, under these same conditions, and with written authorization of the DHHS, (c) for disclosure to a properly identified person

for the purpose of an audit related to the research project, if information that would enable research subjects to be identified is removed or destroyed at the earliest opportunity consistent with the purpose of the audit, or (d) when required by law.

The Privacy Act also authorizes *discretionary disclosures* where determined appropriate by the PHS, including to law enforcement agencies; to the Congress acting within its legislative authority; to the Bureau of the Census; to the National Archives; to the General Accounting Office; pursuant to a court order; or as required to be disclosed by the Freedom of Information Act of 1974 (5 USC 552) and the associated DHHS regulations (45 CFR 5).

The PHS also maintains management information related to grants as part of another Privacy Act system of records: 09–25–0036, "Grants: IMPAC (Grant/Contract Information)."

Information and Actions Available to the Principal Investigator/Program Director

Under the provisions of the Privacy Act, *principal investigators/program directors may request copies of records pertaining to their grant from the PHS component responsible for funding decisions.* Principal investigators/program directors are given the *opportunity* under established procedures *to request that the records be amended if they believe they are inaccurate, untimely, incomplete or irrelevant.*

Beyond the statutory requirements of the Privacy Act, the *PHS automatically informs the principal investigator/program director about the acceptance of an application and its assignment to an initial review group (IRG) and PHS awarding component.* In addition, *as soon as possible after each IRG meeting, some components of the PHS automatically send the principal investigator/program director a summary statement of the IRG's findings and recommendations ("pink sheet") with the priority score displayed. Within 30 days after each subsequent national advisory council or board meeting, the PHS shall automatically notify the principal investigator/program director and the applicant organization of the council's or board's recommended action.* If the council or board recommends an action other than that recommended by the IRG, the PHS will send a letter indicating the variant action and its rationale.

Subsequent decisions concerning the *funding of applications recommended for approval will also take into account elements such as the relevance of the goals of the proposed research to the missions of the awarding component, program balance, overlapping support from other agencies, and availability of funds.* The PHS will notify the principal investigator/program director and the applicant organization of the final disposition of the application.

A principal investigator/program director may request corrective action by the PHS if he or she believes that the assignment of an application or the process or substance of its review is seriously in error. A request must first be directed to the PHS component which at the time is responsible for the application. *The executive secretary of the IRG is the appropriate addressee for such matters prior to the IRG meeting; the PHS funding component is responsible for such matters after the initial review has been completed. Further information* about communicating concerns regarding the review of an application is available from the *Office of Grants Inquiries, Division of Research Grants, National Institutes of Health, Bethesda, MD 20892.*

End of Page 3 of NIH instructions.

Information Available to the General Public

The *PHS makes information about awarded grants available to the public, including the title of the project, the grantee institution, the principal investigator/program director, and the amount of the award. The Description on page 2 of a funded research grant application is sent to the National Technical Information Service (NTIS), U.S. Department of Commerce, where the information is used for the dissemination of scientific information* and for scientific classification and program analysis purposes. *These Descriptions are available to the public* from the NTIS.

The Freedom of Information Act and the associated DHHS regulations require the release of certain information about grants upon request. Release does not depend upon the intended use of the information. Confidential financial material and material that would affect patent or other valuable rights are deleted. Although the grantee institution and the principal investigator/program director will be consulted about any such release, the final determination will be made by the PHS. The following materials are generally available for release upon request: all funded grant applications as well as their derivative unfunded and pending noncompeting continuation, competing continuation, and supplemental grant applications; progress reports of grantees; and final reports of any review or evaluation of grantee performance conducted or caused to be conducted by the DHHS. *Generally* not *available for release to the public are new grant applications for which awards have* not *been made, evaluative portions of site visit reports, and summary statements ("pink sheets") of findings and recommendations of review groups.*

Human Subjects

The DHHS regulations for the protection of human subjects provide a systematic means, based on established internationally recognized ethical principles, *to safeguard the rights and welfare of individuals who participate as subjects in research activities* supported or conducted by the DHHS. The regulations require that applicant organizations establish and maintain appropriate policies and procedures for the protection of human subjects. *These regulations, 45 CFR 46,* Protection of Human Subjects, *are available from the Office for Protection from Research Risks, National Institutes of Health, Bethesda, MD 20892.*

The regulations stipulate that an applicant organization, whether domestic or foreign, bears responsibility for safeguarding the rights and welfare of human subjects in DHHS-supported research activities. The regulations *define "human subject"* as "a living individual about whom an investigator (whether professional or student) conducting research obtains (1) data through intervention or interaction with the individual or (2) identifiable private information." The *regulations extend to the use of human organs, tissues, and body fluids* from individually identifiable human subjects as well as to *graphic, written, or recorded information* derived from individually identifiable human subjects. The *use of autopsy materials* is governed by applicable state and local law and *is not directly regulated by 45 CFR 46.*

An *applicant organization* proposing to conduct non-exempt research involving human subjects *must file an Assurance of Compliance with the Office for Protection from Research Risks (OPRR).* As part of this Assurance, which commits the applicant organization to comply with the DHHS regulations, the applicant organization *must appoint an institutional review board (IRB),* which is required to review and approve all non-exempt research activities involving human subjects.

Exempt from coverage by the regulations are activities in which the only involvement of human subjects will be in one or more of the following six categories.

1. *Research conducted in established or commonly accepted educational settings, involving normal educational practices,* such as (i) research on regular and special education instructional

---

End of Page 4 of NIH Instructions.

---

strategies, or (ii) research on the effectiveness of or the comparison among instructional techniques, curricula, or classroom management methods.

2. Research involving the use of *educational tests* (cognitive, diagnostic, aptitude, achievement), *if* information taken from these sources is recorded in such a manner that *subjects cannot be identified,* directly or through identifiers linked to the subjects.

3. Research involving *survey or interview procedures, except where* all of the following conditions exist: (i) responses are recorded in such a manner that the *human subjects can be identified,* directly or through identifiers linked to the subjects; (ii) the subject's responses, if they became known outside the research, could reasonably *place the subject at risk of criminal or civil liability* or be *damaging to the subject's financial standing or employability;* and (iii) the research *deals with sensitive aspects of the subject's own behavior,* such as illegal conduct, drug use, sexual behavior, or use of alcohol. All research involving survey or interview procedures is exempt, without exception, when the respondents are elected or appointed public officials or candidates for public office.

4. Research involving the *observation* (including observation by participants) *of public behavior, except* where all of the following conditions exist: (i) observations are recorded in such a manner that the *human subjects can be identified,* directly or through the

identifiers linked to the subjects; (ii) the observations recorded about the individual, if they became known outside the research, could reasonably *place the subject at risk of criminal or civil liability* or be *damaging to the subject's financial standing or employability;* and (iii) the research *deals with sensitive aspects of the subject's own behavior* such as illegal conduct, drug use, sexual behavior, or use of alcohol.

5. Research involving the *collection or study of existing data, documents, records, pathological specimens, or diagnostic specimens,* if these sources are *publicly available* or if the information is recorded by the investigator in such a manner that *subjects cannot be identified,* directly or through identifiers linked to the subjects.

6. Unless specifically required by statute, *research and demonstration projects which are conducted by or subject to the approval of the DHHS, and which are designed to study, evaluate, or otherwise examine: (i) programs under the Social Security Act, or other public benefit or service programs; (ii) procedures for obtaining benefits or services under those programs; (iii)* possible changes in or alternatives to those programs or procedures; or (iv) possible changes in methods or levels of payment for benefits or services under those programs. However, if following review of proposed research activities that are exempt from these regulations under this paragraph, the Secretary of the DHHS determines that a research or demonstration project presents a danger to the physical, mental, or emotional well-being of a participant or subject of the research or demonstration project, then Federal funds may not be expended for such a project without the written informed consent of each participant or subject.

Investigators who conduct *research involving fetuses, pregnant women, children, human* in vitro *fertilization, or prisoners must* follow the provisions of the regulations in Subparts B, C, and D of 45 CFR 46, which describe the *additional protections required for these subjects.*

No DHHS award for non-exempt research involving human subjects will be made to an applicant organization unless that organization is operating in accord with an approved Assurance of Compliance and provides certification that the IRB has reviewed and approved the proposed activity in accordance with the DHHS regulations. Copies of the approved Assurance of Compliance are available to every researcher at the applicant organization. No award to an individual will be made unless that individual is affiliated with an organization that accepts responsibility for compliance with the DHHS regulations and has filed the necessary Assurance with OPRR. Foreign applicant organizations must also comply with the provisions of the regulations.

End of Page 5 of NIH instructions.

Research investigators are entrusted with an essential role in assuring the adequate protection of human subjects. In activities they conduct or which are conducted under their direction, they have a direct and continuing responsibility to safeguard the rights and the welfare of the individuals who are or may become subjects of the research. Investigators must comply with the DHHS regulations, with the applicant organization's Assurance of Compliance, and with the requirements and determinations of the IRB concerning the conduct of the research. *Investigators must ensure the minimum of unnecessary risks to subjects by using procedures which are consistent with sound research design.* Whenever appropriate, investigators should use procedures already being performed on the subjects for diagnostic or treatment purposes. *Risks to subjects must be reasonable in relation to anticipated benefits,* if any, *to subjects, and to the importance of the knowledge that may reasonably be expected to result.* Investigators must *obtain* the legally effective *informed consent* of each subject or of the subject's legally authorized representative *before involving the subject* in the research, to the extent required by and in accordance with 45 CFR 46, or as required by applicable Federal, State, or local law. *The consent form must be approved by the IRB.*

Vertebrate Animals

The *PHS Policy on Humane Care and Use of Laboratory Animals by Awardee Institutions* requires that applicant organizations establish and maintain appropriate policies and procedures to *ensure the humane care and use of live vertebrate animals involved in research activities* supported by the PHS. This policy implements and supplements the *U.S. Government Principles for the Utilization and Care of Vertebrate Animals Used in Testing, Research, and Training* and *requires that institutions use the Guide for the Care and Use of Laboratory Animals* as a basis for developing and implementing an institutional animal care and use program. This policy does not affect applicable State or local laws or regulations which impose more stringent standards for the care and use of laboratory animals. All institutions are required to comply, as applicable, with the Animal Welfare Act as amended (7 USC 2131 et sec.), and other Federal statutes and regulations relating to animals. *These documents are available from the Office for Protection from Research Risks, National Institutes of Health, Bethesda, MD 20892.*

The policy stipulates that an applicant organization, whether domestic or foreign, bears responsibility for the humane care and use of animals is PHS-supported research activities. The PHS policy defines "animal" as "any live, vertebrate animal used or intended for use in research, research training, experimentation or biological testing or for related purposes." *An applicant organization proposing to use vertebrate animals in PHS-supported activities must file an Animal Welfare Assurance with the OPRR.* As part of this Assurance, which commits the applicant organization to comply with the PHS policy, the applicant organization *must appoint an institutional animal care and use committee(IACUC)* which is required to review and approve those sections of applications for PHS support that involve vertebrate animals.

No PHS award for research involving vertebrate animals will be made to an applicant organization unless that organization is operating in accord with an approved Animal Welfare Assurance and provides verification that the IACUC has reviewed and approved the proposed activity in accordance with the PHS policy. Applications may be referred by the PHS back to the IACUC for further review in the case of apparent or potential violations of the PHS policy. Copies of the approved Animal Welfare Assurance are available to every researcher at the applicant organization. *No award* to an individual will be made *unless* that *individual is affiliated with an organization that accepts responsibility for compliance with the PHS policy and has filed the necessary Assurance with OPRR.* Foreign applicant organizations applying for PHS awards for activities involving vertebrate animals are required to comply with PHS policy or provide evidence that acceptable standards for the humane care and use of animals will be met.

Research investigators are entrusted with an essential role in assuring the humane care and use of animals. In activities they conduct or which are conducted under their direction, they *have a direct and continuing*

End of Page 6 of NIH instructions.

----

responsibility to see that animals are adequately cared for and used. Investigators must comply with the PHS policy, with the applicant organization's Animal Welfare Assurance, and with the requirements and determinations of the IACUC concerning the conduct of the research. *Investigators must ensure that discomfort, distress, pain, and injury to the animals are avoided or minimized, consistent with sound research design;* that *no more animals are used than are necessary to reach sound scientific conclusions;* and that, *when appropriate, animals are painlessly sacrificed* in accordance with methods of euthanasia approved by the Panel on Euthanasia of the American Veterinary Medical Association.

Recombinant DNA

The current *NIH Guidelines* for Research Involving Recombinant DNA Molecules and announcements of modifications and changes to the *Guidelines* are *available from the Office of Recombinant DNA Activities, National Institutes of Health, Bethesda, MD 20892.* All *research* involving recombinant DNA techniques that is supported by the DHHS *must meet the requirements of these Guidelines.* As defined by the *Guidelines,* recombinant DNA molecules are either: (1) molecules which are constructed outside living cells by joining natural or synthetic DNA segments to DNA molecules that can replicate in a living cell; or (2) DNA molecules that result from the replication of those described in (1) above.

Protection Against Scientific Fraud

Section 493 of the PHS Act as amended by P.L. 99–158, the "Health Research Extension Act of 1985," provides that the Secretary of the DHHS must issue regulations requiring each *applicant organization to submit an assurance* that it: (1) *has established an administrative process to review reports of scientific fraud* related to biomedical and behavioral research conducted at or sponsored by the organization; and (2) *will report* to the Secretary any *investigation of alleged scientific fraud that appears substantial.* The development of these regulations will be publicized by communication with applicant organizations both directly and through the *Federal Register* and the *NIH Guide for Grants and Contracts.*

The PHS defines "scientific fraud" as: (1) serious deviation, such as fabrication, falsification or plagiarism, from accepted practices in carrying out research or in reporting the results of research; or (2) material failure to comply with Federal requirements affecting specific aspects of the conduct of research, e.g., the protection of human subjects and the welfare of laboratory animals.

Other Assurances

The three certifications described below are made by checking the appropriate boxes on the CHECKLIST page of the application and verified by the signatures on the FACE PAGE of the application. These three certifications do not apply to foreign applicant organizations.

1. **CIVIL RIGHTS.** Before a grant award can be made, a domestic applicant organization must certify that it has filed with the DHHS Office for Civil Rights an Assurance of Compliance (Form HHS 441) with Title VI of the Civil Rights Act of 1964 (42 USC 2000d). This provides that *no person in the United States shall, on the grounds of race, creed, color, or national origin, be excluded from participation in, be denied the benefits of, or be subjected to discrimination under any program or activity receiving Federal financial assistance.* The pertinent DHHS implementing regulations are found in 45 CFR 80.

End of Page 7 of NIH instructions.

----

2. **HANDICAPPED INDIVIDUALS.** Before a grant award can be made, a domestic applicant organization must certify that it has filed with the DHHS Office for Civil Rights an Assurance of Compliance (Form HHS 641) with Section 504 of the Rehabilitation Act of 1973, as amended (29 USC 794). This provides that *no handicapped individual in the United States shall, solely by reason of the handicap, be excluded from participation in, be denied the benefit of, or be subjected to discrimination under any program or activity receiving Federal financial assistance.* The pertinent DHHS implementing regulations are found in 45 CFR 84.

3. **SEX DISCRIMINATION.** Before a grant award can be made, a domestic applicant educational organization (or any domestic

non-educational organization which has applied for training grant support) must certify that it has filed with the DHHS Office for Civil Rights an Assurance of Compliance (Form HHS 639-A) with Section 901 of Title IX of the Education Amendments of 1972(20 USC 1681) as amended. This provides that *no person in the United States shall, on the basis of sex, be excluded from participation in, be denied the benefits of, or be subjected to discrimination under any education program or activity receiving Federal financial assistance.* The pertinent DHHS implementing regulations are found in 45 CFR 86.

The Assurance of Compliance Forms HHS 441, 641, and 639-A are available from the Office of Grants Inquiries, Division of Research Grants, National Institutes of Health, Bethesda, MD 20892.

GENERAL INSTRUCTIONS

Introduction

If a grant is awarded as the result of this application, the *applicant organization becomes a grantee* and assumes legal and financial accountability for the awarded funds and for the performance of the grant supported activities. The applicant organization is responsible for verifying the accuracy, validity, and conformity with the most current institutional guidelines of all the administrative, fiscal, and scientific information in the application, including the indirect cost rate. Deliberate withholding, falsification, or misrepresentation of information could result in administrative actions such as withdrawal of an application, the suspension and/or termination of an award, and debarment, as well as possible criminal penalties.

Read and follow the instructions carefully to avoid delays and misunderstandings. Before preparing an application, review the Public Health Service Grants Policy Statement. *A copy of this document is available at most applicant organizations,* or can be purchased from the Superintendent of Documents, U.S. Government Printing Office, Washington, D.C. 20402. To expedite delivery, cite the GPO stock number 017–020–00090–01. *Specific program announcements,* requests for applications (RFA), *and changes in policies and procedures are published in the* Federal Register *and in the* NIH Guide for Grants and

Contracts. *To be included on the mailing list for the* Guide, *write to the Office of Grants Inquiries, Division of Research Grants, National Institutes of Health, Bethesda, MD 20892. Also available from the Office of Grants Inquiries are descriptions of the peer review system that the PHS uses to review grant applications.*

End of Page 8 of NIH instructions.

Forms

Use Form PHS 398 to apply for all new, competing continuation, and supplemental research and research training grant and cooperative agreement support, except as shown in the table below:

Type of Application	Use Form Number
Small Business Innovation Research Program-Phase I	PHS 6246–1
Small Business Innovation Research Program-Phase II	PHS 6246–2
Individual National Research Service Award or Senior	
International Fellowship Award	PHS 416–1
International Research Fellowship Award	NIH 1541–1
Nonresearch Training Grant	PHS 6025
Grant to State or Local Government Agency	PHS 5161–1
Health Services Project	PHS 5161–1
Construction Grant	NIH 2575
Biomedical Research Support Grant	NIH 147–1
Medical Library Resource Improvement Grant	NIH 1887

Most of the above application forms have *corresponding forms* to be used when applying *for noncompeting continuation support* during an approved project period. The *form corresponding to PHS 398 is Form PHS 2590.*

The instructions provided in this kit pertain to applications for traditional, unsolicited, investigator-initiated, research project grants. Use the additional instructions and substitute pages included in this kit when applying for an Institutional National Research Service Award or a Research Career Development Award. Request additional instructions from the PHS components indicated below when using Form PHS 398 to apply for other specialized grants. These include but are not limited to:

Academic Investigator Award:
Appropriate component of the National Institutes of Health, Bethesda, MD 20892

Animal Resources Grant:
Division of Research Resources, National Institutes of Health, Bethesda, MD 20892

Biomedical Research Technology Resource, Resource Development, and Resource-Related Project Grants:
Division of Research Resources, National Institutes of Health, Bethesda, MD 20892

Clinical Investigator Award:
Office of Grants Inquiries, Division of Research Grants, National Institutes of Health, Bethesda, MD 20892

Conference Grant:
Office of Grants Inquiries, Division of Research Grants, National Institutes of Health, Bethesda, MD 20892

Consortium Grant:
Office of Grants Inquiries, Division of Research Grants, National Institutes of Health, Bethesda, MD 20892

First Independent Research Support and Transition Award:
Office of Grants Inquiries, Division of Research Grants, National Institutes of Health, Bethesda, MD 20892, or the Alcohol, Drug Abuse, and Mental Health Administration, Rockville, MD 20857

General Clinical Research Center Grant:
Division of Research Resources, National Institutes of Health, Bethesda, MD 20892

End of Page 9 of NIH instructions.

Investigator-Initiated Multicenter Clinical Trial Grant:
National Heart, Lung, and Blood Institute, Bethesda, MD 20892

Medical Library Resource Project Grant:
National Library of Medicine, Bethesda, MD 20894

Minority Access to Research Careers Training Grant:
National Institute of General Medical Sciences, Bethesda, MD 20892, or

the Alcohol, Drug Abuse, and Mental Health Administration, Rockville, MD 20857

Minority Biomedical Research Support Grant:
Division of Research Resources, National Institutes of Health, Bethesda, MD 20892

Minority School Faculty Development Award:
National Heart, Lung, and Blood Institute, Bethesda, MD 20892

Outstanding Investigator Grant:
National Cancer Institute, Bethesda, MD 20892

Physician Scientist Award:
Office of Grant Inquiries, Division of Research Grants, National Institutes of Health, Bethesda, MD 20892

Program Project and Center Grants:
Appropriate component of the National Institutes of Health, Bethesda, MD 20892, or the Alcohol, Drug Abuse, and Mental Health Administration, Rockville, MD 20857

Publication Grant:
National Library of Medicine, Bethesda, MD 20894

Research Scientist Development and Research Scientist Awards:
Appropriate Institute of the Alcohol, Drug Abuse, and Mental Health Administration, Rockville, MD 20857

Shared Instrumentation Grant:
Division of Research Resources, National Institutes of Health, Bethesda, MD 20892, or National Institute of General Medical Sciences, Bethesda, MD 20892

Short-Term Training Grant for Students in Health Professional Schools:
Office of Grants Inquiries, Division of Research Grants, National Institutes of Health, Bethesda, MD 20892

Small Grant:
Appropriate component of the National Institutes of Health, Bethesda, MD 20892 or Grants Management Office, National Institute of Mental Health, Rockville, MD 20857

Special Emphasis Research Career Award:
Division of Research Resources, National Institutes of Health, Bethesda, MD 20892, or National Institute on Aging, Bethesda, MD 20892

When responding to a specific program announcement or request for applications (RFA) published in the *NIH Guide for Grants and Contracts*, the *Federal Register*, or other public media, contact the issuing PHS component for additional instructions.

Submission

Use English only and *avoid jargon and unusual abbreviations. Type* the application, *single spaced,* and *stay within the margin* limitations indicated on the form and continuation pages. *Use standard size black type* that can be photocopied; *do **not** use photoreduction.* Draw all graphs, diagrams, tables, and charts in black ink. *Do **not** include photographs, oversized documents, or materials that cannot be photocopied in the body of the application; submit them in six collated sets in the Appendix. Mail or deliver the complete and signed typewritten original of the application and six signed, exact, clear, single-sided photocopies, in one package with the Appendix, to the Division of Research Grants,*

End of Page 10 of NIH instructions.

----

*Room 240, Westwood Building, 5333 Westbard Avenue, Bethesda, MD 20892. Do **not** bind or staple the sets, but secure them with rubber bands or paper clips. Do not photocopy the Checklist page* of the application **or** the *Personal Data form; submit the originals only.*

When submitting an application, *the principal investigator/program director may suggest an initial review group and/or a PHS component to which it could be appropriately assigned.* However, do **not** send such correspondence under separate cover; *attach* it *to the application at time of submission.* Although these *suggestions will be taken into consideration,* the *final determination will be made by the PHS.*

*Do **not** submit an incomplete application.* **An application will be considered incomplete and returned if it is illegible, if it fails to follow the instructions, or if the material presented is insufficient to permit an adequate review.** *Unless specifically required by these instructions (e.g. human subjects certification, vertebrate animals verification, changes in other support), do **not** send supplementary or corrective material pertinent to an application after the receipt date without its being specifically solicited or agreed to by prior discussion* *with an appropriate PHS staff member, usually the executive secretary of the initial review group.*

To avoid delays in assignment and review, submit a complete application as early as possible. The PHS uses the following review and award schedule:

Application Receipt Dates (Unless specified differently in additional instructions, a program announcement, or a request for applications)			Initial Review Group Dates	National Advisory Council or Board Dates	Earliest Possible Beginning Dates
Jan. 10 May 10 Sept. 10	Feb. 1 June 1 Oct. 1	Mar.1 July 1 Nov. 1	June-July Oct.-Nov. Feb.-Mar.	Sept.-Oct. Jan.-Feb. May-June	Dec. 1 Apr. 1 July 1
for *All** Institutional National Research Service Award applications.	for *All* NEW grant and Research Career Development Award applications. *All**Program Project and Center grant applications.	for COMPETING CONTINUATION and SUPPLEMENTAL research grant applications.			
*Includes NEW, COMPETING CONTINUATION, AND SUPPLEMENTAL					

Applications must be **received** *by the above dates.* To insure against problems caused by carrier delays, *retain a legible proof-of-mailing receipt from the carrier, dated no later than one week prior to the receipt date.* If the receipt date falls on a weekend, it will be extended to Monday; if the date falls on a holiday, it will be extended to the following work day. The receipt date will be waived only in extenuating circumstances. To request such a waiver, include an explanatory letter with the signed, completed application. **No request for a waiver will be considered prior to receipt of the application.**

As soon as possible after the receipt date, *usually within six weeks,* the *PHS will send the principal investigator/program director and the appli-*cant organization the *application's number and the name, address, and telephone number of the executive secretary of the initial review group to which it has been assigned.* If this information is **not** received within *that time, contact the Referral Office, Division of Research Grants,*

National Institutes of Health, Bethesda, MD 20892 (telephone 301–496–7447).

End of Page 11 of NIH instructions.

SPECIFIC INSTRUCTIONS-SECTION 1.

(Face Page)

Item 1. Title of Project. *Choose a title that is descriptive and specifically appropriate,* rather than general. *Do not exceed 56 typewriter spaces, including the spaces between words and punctuation. A NEW application must have a different title* from any other PHS project with the same principal investigator/program director. *A COMPETING CONTINUATION or REVISED application should ordinarily have the same title as the previous grant or application. If the specific aims of the project have changed significantly, choose a new title. A SUPPLEMENTAL application must have the same title* as the currently funded grant.

Item 2. Response to Specific Program Announcement. If the application is submitted in response to a published specific program announcement or request for applications (RFA), check the box marked "YES" and identify the title of the announcement or the number of the RFA. The term "specific program announcement" also includes specialized grants, such as a Research Career Development Award, an Institutional National Research Service Award, and those listed under "Forms" in the "General Instructions" section.

Item 3. Check the box *only* if the principal investigator/program director has never received independent research grant or contract support from the PHS.

Item 3a. Name of Principal Investigator/Program Director. Name the *one person* responsible to the applicant organization for the scientific and technical direction of the project. The *concept of co-investigator is not formally recognized.*

Item 3b. Degree(s). Self-explanatory.

Item 3c. Social Security Number. Self-explanatory.

Item 3d. Position Title. If the principal investigator/program director has more than one title, *indicate the one most relevant to the proposed project,* such as Professor of Biochemistry, Chief of Surgical Service, or Group Leader.

Item 3e. Mailing Address. Self-explanatory.

Item 3f. Department, Service, Laboratory, or Equivalent. Indicate the organizational affiliation, such as Department of Medicine, Materials Research Laboratory, or Social Sciences Institute. *If part of a larger component, indicate both,* e.g., Section on Anesthesiology, Department of Surgery; or Division of Laboratory Medicine, Department of Medicine.

Item 3g. Major Subdivision. Indicate the school, college, or other major subdivision, such as medical, dental, engineering, graduate, nursing, or public health, *If there is no such subdivision, enter "none."*

Item 3h. Telephone. Self-explanatory.

Item 4. Human Subjects. If activities involving human subjects are not planned **at any time** during the proposed project period, check the box marked "NO" at Item 4a. The remaining parts of Item 4 are then not applicable.

End of Page 12 of NIH instructions.

If activities involving human subjects, whether or not exempt from the regulations, are planned **at any time** during the proposed project period, check the box marked "YES" at Item 4a. *If the activities are designated to be exempt from the regulations, insert the exemption number(s)* corresponding to one or more of the six exemption categories listed in the "General Information" section. The remaining parts of Item 4 are then not applicable. ***Inappropriate designations of the non-involvement of human subjects or of exempt categories of research may result in delays in the review of an application. The PHS will make a final determination as to whether the proposed activities are covered by the regulations or are in an exempt*** category, based on the information provided in Section E of the Research Plan. *In doubtful cases, prior consultation with the Office for Protection from Research Risks, National Institutes of Health, Bethesda, MD 20892 is recommended.*

If the planned activities involving human subjects are not exempt, complete the remaining parts of Item 4. If the applicant organization has an approved Multiple Project Assurance of Compliance on file with the OPRR that covers the specific activity, insert at Item 4b the Assurance identification number and at Item 4a the latest date of approval by the institutional review board (IRB) of the proposed activities. This date must be not earlier than one year before the receipt date for which the application is submitted. **This information in Items 4a and 4b and the signatures on the Face Page fulfill the requirement for certification of IRB approval.**

To insure against delays in the review of the application, IRB review is best completed prior to submission of the application. However, *if the IRB review is unavoidably delayed* beyond the submission of the application, enter "pending" at Item 4a. *A follow-up certification of IRB approval from an official signing for the applicant organization must then be sent to and received by the Executive Secretary of the initial review group within 60 days after the receipt date for which the application is submitted.* Any modifications in the Research Plan section of the application required by the IRB must be submitted with the follow-up certification. Occasionally PHS initial review may be scheduled to occur before the end of the 60-day grace period. *In these special cases of accelerated review, the follow-up certification will be requested earlier.* **Otherwise, *it is the responsibility of the applicant organization to submit the follow-up certification.* The PHS does not guarantee that it will remind the applicant organization or the principal investigator/program director to provide this missing information. *If certification of IRB approval is not received prior to the scheduled PHS initial review date, the application will be considered incomplete and deferred to the next review cycle.***

If the applicant organization does not have on file with OPRR an approved Assurance of Compliance, insert "NONE" in item 4b. In this case, the applicant organization, by the signatures on the Face Page, is declaring that it will comply with 45 CFR 46 by establishing an IRB and submitting an Assurance of Compliance and certification of IRB approval within 30 days of a specific request from OPRR.

Item 5. Vertebrate Animals. If activities involving vertebrate animals are not planned **at any time** during the proposed project period, check the box marked "NO" at Item 5a. Item 5b is then not applicable.

If activities involving vertebrate animals are planned **at any time** during the proposed project period, check the box marked "YES" at Item 5a. If applicant organization has an approved Animal Welfare Assurance on file with OPRR, insert at Item 5b the Assurance identification number and at Item 5a the date of approval by the institutional animal care and use committee(IACUC) of those sections of the application related to the care and use of animals. **This information in Items 5a and 5b and the signatures on the Face Page fulfill the requirement for verification of IACUC approval.**

To insure against delays in the review of the application, IACUC review is best completed prior to submission of the application. However, *if the IACUC review is unavoidably delayed* beyond the submission of the application, enter "pending" at Item 5a. *A follow-up verification of IACUC approval from an official signing for the applicant organization*

End of Page 13 of NIH instructions.

---

must then be sent to and received by the Executive Secretary of the initial review group within 60 days after the receipt date for which the application is submitted. Any modifications of the Research Plan section of the application required by the IACUC must be submitted with the follow-up verification. Occasionally PHS initial review may be scheduled to occur before the end of this 60-day grace period. *In these special cases of accelerated review, the follow-up verification will be requested earlier.* **Otherwise, it is the responsibility of the applicant organization to submit the follow-up verification. The PHS does not guarantee that it will remind the applicant organization or the principal investigator/program director to provide this missing information. If verification of IACUC approval is not received prior to the scheduled PHS initial review date, the application will be considered incomplete and deferred to the next review cycle.**

If the applicant organization does not have on file with OPRR an approved Animal Welfare Assurance, insert "NONE" in Item 5b. In this case, the applicant organization, by the signatures on the Face Page, is declaring that it will comply with PHS policy regarding the care and use of animals by establishing an IACUC and submitting an Animal Welfare Assurance and verification of IACUC approval when requested to do so by OPRR.

Item 6. Dates of Entire Proposed Project Period. *Request no more than five years of support* for the entire proposed project period; *do not exceed three years for foreign applicant organizations.* To *select an appropriate beginning date* for a NEW or SUPPLEMENTAL application, *consult the review and award schedule* in these instructions. For a COMPETING CONTINUATION application, choose a beginning date immediately following the termination date of the currently funded grant. *Submit a SUPPLEMENTAL application only for a period within* the project period of the currently funded grant, not extending beyond it. Make the ending date of the supplement's first budget period coincide with the ending date of the budget period that is to be supplemented, regardless of the supplement's beginning date. If supplemental funds are being requested also for the future years of a currently funded grant, make the future years' budget periods coincide with the relevant budget periods of the currently funded grant.

Item 7a. Direct Costs Requested for First 12-Month Budget Period. Enter the direct costs from page 4.

Item 7b. Total Costs Requested for First 12-Month Budget Period. Enter *the sum* of (1) the total direct costs on page 4 and (2) the indirect costs for the first 12-month budget period calculated on the Checklist.

Item 8a. Direct Cost Requested for Entire Proposed Project Period. Enter the direct costs from page 5.

Item 8b. Total Costs Requested for Entire Proposed Project Period. Enter *the sum* of (1) the total direct costs on page 5 and (2) the indirect costs for the entire proposed project period calculated on the Checklist.

Item 9. Performance Sites. Indicate where the work described in the Research Plan will be conducted. Include any affiliation with the Veterans Administration or any other Federal agency. If there is more than one performance site, *list all the sites* and provide an explanation on the Resources and Environment page of the application. *One of the sites indicated must be the applicant organization or be identified as off-site* *in accordance with the conditions of the applicant organization's indirect cost rate negotiation agreement.* This information must be in agreement with the indirect cost information on the Checklist page of the application. *State if a consortium/contractual arrangement is involved* with one or more collaborating organizations for the relatively independent conduct of a portion of the work described in the Research Plan.

End of Page 14 of NIH instructions.

Item 10. Inventions (Competing Continuation Application Only). If no inventions were conceived or reduced to practice during the previous project period, check the box marked "NO." The remaining parts of Item 10 are then not applicable.

If any inventions were conceived or reduced to practice during the previous project period, check the box marked "YES," list their titles in the progress report section of the Research Plan, and submit copies in the Appendix. Indicate whether or not they have been previously reported to the PHS or to the official responsible for patent matters in the applicant organization. It is important that the patent official report these inventions to the Patent Branch, Office of the General Counsel, DHHS, Westwood Building, Bethesda, MD 20892. *Failure to report promptly prior to publication may result in the loss of valuable invention rights.* Statutes preclude obtaining valid patent protection after one year from the date of a publication that discloses the invention.

Item 11. Applicant Organization. Name the **one** organization that will be legally and financially responsible for the conduct of activities supported by the award.

Item 12. Type of Organization. Check the appropriate box. *If the applicant organization is public, specify whether it is Federal, State, or local.* A Federal organization is a cabinet-level department or independent agency of the Executive Branch of the Federal Government or any component part of such a department or agency that may be assigned the responsibility for carrying out a grant-supported project. *A Federal organization must submit with the completed application a certification of eligibility in accordance with the PHS Grants Administration Manual, Chapter 1–515. A State organization* is any agency or instrumentality of a

State government of any of the United States or its territories. A *local organization* is any agency or instrumentality of a political subdivision of government below the State level.

A *private nonprofit organization* is an institution, corporation, or other legal entity no part of whose net earnings may lawfully inure to the benefit of any private shareholder or individual. *A private nonprofit organization must submit proof of its nonprofit status if it has not previously done so.* Acceptable proof to be submitted with the completed application may be: (a) a reference to the organization's listing in the most recent Internal Revenue Service cumulative list of tax exempt organizations; (b) a copy of a currently valid Internal Revenue Service tax exemption certificate; (c) a statement from a State taxing authority or State attorney general certifying that the organization is a nonprofit organization operating within the State, and that no part of its earnings may lawfully inure to the benefit of any private shareholder or individual; or (d) a certified copy of the certificate of incorporation or other document that clearly establishes the nonprofit status of the organization.

A *for-profit organization* is an institution, cooperation or other legal entity which is organized for the profit or benefit of its shareholders or other owners. *A for-profit organization is considered to be a small business if* it is independently owned and operated, if it is not dominant in the field of operation of the application, and if it employs fewer than 500 persons.

Item 13. Entity Identification Number. Enter the number assigned to the applicant organization by the DHHS for payment and accounting purposes. If a number has not yet been assigned, enter the organization's Internal Revenue Service employer identification number.

Item 14. Organizational Component to Receive Credit Towards a Biomedical Research Support Grant. This item is *not applicable to Federal, foreign, or for-profit applicant organizations, nor to applications for Institutional National Research Service Awards and other training grants. For all other applications, identify the major component that is to receive credit towards eligibility for a Biomedical Research Support Grant should an award be made.*

End of Page 15 of NIH instructions.

The component to receive credit must be the one responsible for the research and for administration of the award. *For an application from a basic science department or division that is shared by two or more schools of a university, designate the school having primary interest in the substance of the application.*

Complete information regarding this item is contained *in the Biomedical Research Support Grant Information Statement and Administrative Guidelines.* Copies of this statement may be obtained from the Division of Research Resources, National Institutes of Health, Bethesda, MD 20892. Enter one of the following codes and identifications:

Academic Institutions

Code Identification

01	School of Medicine
03	School of Dentistry
05	School of Osteopathy
07	School of Pharmacy
09	School of Nursing
11	School of Veterinary Medicine
13	School of Public Health
14	School of Optometry
15	School of Allied Health
20	Other Academic

Nonacademic Institutions

Code Identification

30	Hospital
52	Health Department
60	Research Organization

Item 15. Official in Business Office to be Notified if an Award is Made. Self-explanatory.

Item 16. Official Signing for Applicant Organization. Name an individual *authorized to act for the applicant organization* and to assume the obligations imposed by the requirements and conditions for any grant, including the applicable Federal regulations.

Item 17. Principal Investigator/Program Director Assurance. Self-explanatory.

Item 18. Certification and Acceptance. Self-explanatory.

(Form Page 2)

Description. Follow instructions on page 2.

Key Personnel. *List all individuals, salaried or not salaried,* including the principal investigator and collaborating investigators *at the applicant institution or elsewhere,* who participate in scientific development/execution of the project. *This category will generally include individuals with professional degrees,* i.e., Ph.D., M.D., D.D.S., D.V.M., D.O., B.S.N., or B.S.E., but *in some projects this may also include individuals with other degrees at the masters and baccalaureate levels.* For every individual *include all degrees and Social Security Number* (SSN). When requesting Social Security Number from key personnel, explain to them that *provision of Social Security Number is voluntary* and the information will be used only for program management purposes. (See Instructions: General Information, page 1.)

(Form Page 3)

Table of Contents. Self-explanatory.

(Form Page 4)

End of Page 16 of NIH Instructions.

Detailed Budget For First 12-Month Budget Period. *List only the direct costs* requested in this application. Do not include any items that are treated by the applicant organization as indirect costs according to a Federal rate negotiation agreement except for those indirect costs included in consortium/contractual costs. For a SUPPLEMENTAL application, show only those items for which additional funds are requested, prorating the personnel costs and other appropriate parts of the detailed budget if the first budget period of the application is less than 12 months.

Personnel. *Whether or not salaries are requested,* list the *names and roles* of all applicant organization personnel to be involved in the project during the 12-month budget period. *Starting with the P.I., list all key personnel first and then support personnel.* Key personnel are those individuals who participate in the scientific development/execution of the projects. This will *generally include individuals with professional degrees,* i.e., Ph.D., M.D., D.D.S., D.O., D.V.M., B.S.N., or B.S.E., but *in some projects this may also include individuals with other degrees at the masters and baccalaureate levels. Support personnel* are those individuals who *provide administrative or technical assistance* to the project, i.e., dishwashers, animal caretakers, histopathology technicians, electron microscopy technicians, and in some instances research technicians or associates.

Column 1 indicates whether the type of appointment at the applicant organization is full-time or part-time for each individual. *A full-time 12-month appointment is coded 1.0. If an individual has outside commitments or concurrent appointments with other organizations, enter only that portion of 1.0 which is allocable to this* applicant *organization.* If the 12-month year is divided into *academic and summer periods,* identify and *enter on separate lines* the types of appointment for each period.

For example:

Half-time appointment for 12 months $(0.5 \times 12/12) = 0.5$
Full-time appointment for 6 months $(1.0 \times 6/12) = 0.5$
Half-time appointment for 9 months (academic year) $(0.5 \times 9/12) = 0.38$
Full-time appointment for 3 months (summer) $(1.0 \times 3/12) = 0.25$

Column 2 indicates the *percentage of each appointment at the applicant organization to be devoted to this* project. Enter on the appropriate separate lines the percentages for the academic and summer periods. If an individual engages in other institutional responsibilities, such as teaching, the *total* percentage devoted to *all* research activities by the individual must be less than 100%.

Column 3 is the *effort on the project.* This is calculated for each line by multiplying Column 1 by Column 2 and *expressing the result as a decimal.*

Enter the dollar amounts for each position for which funds are requested. The maximum salary that may be requested is calculated by multiplying the individual's base salary, defined below, by the percentage of the appointment to be devoted to the project (Column 2). If a lesser amount is requested for any position, explain on page 5 (for example, endowed position, institutional sources, other support). Enter on the appropriate separate lines the salaries requested for the academic and summer periods. The monthly base for summer salaries is calculated by dividing the base salary for the academic period appointment by the number of months of that appointment.

Base salary is defined as *the compensation that the applicant organization pays for the individual's appointment, whether that individual's time is spent on research, teaching, patient care, or other activities.* Base salary excludes any income that an individual may be permitted to earn outside of duties to the applicant organization. *Base salary may not be increased as a result of replacing institutional salary funds with grant funds.*

End of Page 17 of NIH instructions.

Fringe benefits may be requested provided such costs are treated consistently by the applicant organization as a direct cost to all sponsors.

Calculate the totals for each position and *enter the subtotals in each column* where indicated.

The applicant organization has the option of having specific salary and fringe benefit amounts for individuals omitted from the copies of the application that are made available to non-Federal reviewers. If the applicant organization elects to exercise this option, *use asterisks* on the original and copies of the application to indicate those individuals for whom salaries and fringe benefits are being requested; the *subtotals must still be shown.* In addition, *submit one copy of page 4 of the application, completed in full* with the asterisks replaced by the salaries and fringe benefits requested. This budget page will be reserved for PHS staff use only.

Consultant Costs. *Whether or not costs are involved, provide the names and organizational affiliations of any consultants,* other than those involved in consortium/contractual arrangements, who have agreed to serve in that capacity. Include consultant physicians in connection with patient care. *Briefly describe and justify on page 5 the services to be performed, including the number of days of consultation, the expected rate of compensation, travel, per diem,* and other related costs.

Equipment. *List separately each item of equipment with a unit acquisition cost of $500 or more.* If funds are requested to purchase items of equipment that appear to duplicate or to be equivalent to items listed on the Resources and Environment page or items used in preliminary studies, *justify* the reasons for the duplication on page 5.

Supplies. *Itemize supplies in separate categories* such as glassware, chemicals, radioisotopes, etc. *Categories in amounts less than $1,000 do not have to be itemized.* However, *if animals are involved, state how many are to be used, their unit purchase cost, and their unit care cost.*

Travel. State the *purpose* of any travel, giving the *number of trips* involved, the *destinations,* and the *number of individuals* for whom funds are requested, bearing in mind that PHS policy requires that less than first class air travel be used. Justify foreign travel in detail on page 5, describing its importance to the accomplishment of the project.

Patient Care Costs. If inpatient and outpatient charges incident to the research are requested, on page 5 provide the *names of the hospitals or clinics to be used* and the *amounts* requested for each. State whether each hospital or clinic has a currently effective DHHS-negotiated patient care rate agreement, and if not, what *basis* is *used for calculating charges.* If there is "limited" patient care activity that does not require the establishment of a DHHS-negotiated rate, an institutional patient care rate may be provisionally approved by the PHS awarding component. Indicate in detail the basis for estimating costs in this category, including the number of patient days, estimated cost per day, and cost per test or treatment. *Patient care costs do **not** include travel, lodging, and subsistence or donor/volunteer fees; request these costs in the "Other Expenses" category. Request consultant physician fees in the "Consultant Costs" category.* Patient care costs will be provided to foreign organizations only in exceptional circumstances.

Alterations and Renovations. *The costs of construction per se are not permissible charges.* If the costs of *essential alterations of facilities,* including repairs, painting, removal, or installation of partitions, shielding, or air conditioning, are requested, *itemize them by category and justify them fully on page 5.* When applicable, indicate the square footage involved, submit a line drawing of the alterations being proposed. Cost for alterations and renovations are not allowed on grants made to foreign applicant organizations.

End of Page 18 of NIH Instructions.

Consortium/Contractual Costs. Consortium arrangements may involve costs such as personnel, supplies, and any other allowable expenses, including indirect costs, for the relatively independent conduct of a portion of the work described in the Research Plan. Contractual arrangements for major support services, such as the laboratory testing of biological materials, clinical services, etc., are occasionally also of sufficient scope to warrant a similar categorical breakdown of costs. For either of the above arrangements, enter the total direct costs and indirect costs, if any, separately for each participating organization. *Use photocopies of pages 4 and 5 to itemize and justify separate detailed budgets for the first 12-month budget period and for the entire proposed project period for each participating organization. Itemize any indirect costs and provide the basis for the rate in the "Other Expenses" category of these supplementary budget pages. Insert the supplementary budget pages after pages 4 and 5 and number them sequentially.*

Other Expenses. *Itemize by category and unit cost* such other expenses as publication costs, page charges, books, computer charges, rentals and leases, equipment maintenance, minor fee-for-service contracts, etc. *Reimbursement is allowable for tuition remission in lieu of all or part of salary for student work on the project.* State on page 5 the percentage of tuition requested in proportion to the time devoted to the project. *Reimbursement is allowable for donor/volunteer fees and for travel, lodging, and subsistence costs incurred by human subjects participating in the project, including travel of an escort, if required.* This reimbursement is applicable to all classes of human subjects, including inpatients, outpatients, donors, and normal volunteers, regardless of employment status. Detail such costs on page 5.

(Form Page 5)

Budget for Entire Proposed Project Period. Self-explanatory.

(Form Additional Pages)

Biographical Sketch, Other Support, Resources and Environment Pages. Self-explanatory.

SPECIFIC INSTRUCTIONS-SECTION 2.

AN APPLICATION MAY BE RETURNED IF SECTION 2 FAILS TO OBSERVE THE PAGE LIMITATIONS. Only in rare cases involving interdependent multiple subprojects will the PHS determine that applications exceeding the page limitations are acceptable. The page limitations may not apply to the specialized grant applications listed in the General Instructions section. Request and follow the additional instructions for those applications.

Include sufficient information in Section 2 to facilitate an effective review without reference to any previous application. Be specific and informative and avoid redundancies. Reviewers often consider *brevity and clarity in the presentation to be indicative of a principal investigator/program director's focused approach to a research objective and ability to achieve the specific aims of the project.*

Introduction. *Use* an introduction *for a REVISED or SUPPLEMENTAL application only.* **Do not exceed one page.**

- **Revised Application.** Acceptance of a REVISED application automatically withdraws the prior version. *Summarize* any substantial additions, deletions, and *changes* that have been made. *Include responses to* criticisms in the *previous summary statement. Highlight* these *changes* within the text of the Research Plan by appropriate bracketing, indenting, or changing of typography. *Incorporate* in the Progress Report/Preliminary Studies any *work done since the prior version was submitted.* **A revised application will be returned if substantial revisions are not clearly apparent.**

End of Page 19 of NIH instructions.

- **Supplemental Application.** A SUPPLEMENTAL application will **not** be accepted until after the original application has been funded. *Provide a statement* describing how the supplement, or the lack of it, will influence the specific aims, experimental design and methods of the current grant. Include a statement describing any changes intended in the allocation of funds within and among budget categories for the remainder of the project period of the current grant.

Research Plan. Organize Sections A-D of the Research Plan to answer these questions. (A) What do you intend to do? (B) Why is the work important? (C) What has already been done? (D) How are you going to do the work? ***Do not exceed 20 pages for Sections A-D.*** You may use any page distribution within this overall limitation; however, the PHS recommends the following format and distribution:

A. **Specific Aims.** State the *broad, long-term objectives* and describe concisely and realistically *what the specific research* described in this application *is intended to accomplish* and any hypotheses to be tested. ***One page* is *recommended.***

B. **Background and Significance.** Briefly sketch the *background* to the present proposal, critically *evaluate existing knowledge,* and specifically *identify the gaps* which the project is intended to fill. State concisely the *importance of the research* described in this application by relating the specific aims to the broad, long-term objectives. ***Two to three pages* are recommended.**

C. **Progress Report/Preliminary Studies. A progress report is required for COMPETING CONTINUATION and SUP-PLEMENTAL applications; for NEW applications a report of the principal investigator/program director's preliminary studies is useful but optional.**

For COMPETING CONTINUATION and SUPPLEMENTAL applications, give the *beginning and ending dates* for the period covered since the project was last reviewed competitively. List all *key personnel* who have worked on the project during this period, their *titles, dates of service, and percentages of their appointments* devoted to the project. *Summarize* the *previous* application's *specific aims* and provide a *succinct account of* published and unpublished results indicating *progress* toward their achievement. Summarize the *importance of the findings.* Discuss any *changes in the specific aims* since the project was last reviewed competitively. *List* the titles and complete references to all *publications,* manuscripts **accepted** for publication, patents, invention reports, and other printed materials that have resulted from the project since it was last reviewed competitively. Submit six collated sets of **no more than ten** such items as an Appendix.

NEW applications may use this section to provide an account of the principal investigator/program director's *preliminary studies* pertinent to the application and/or any other *information that will help to establish the experience and competence of the investigator to pursue the proposed project.* The titles and complete references to appropriate *publications* and manuscripts **accepted** for publication may be listed, and six collated sets of **no more than ten** such items of background material may be submitted as an Appendix. ***Six to eight pages* are recommended *for* the *narrative portion* of the Progress Report/Preliminary Studies.**

D. **Experimental Design and Methods.** *Outline* the *experimental design and* the *procedures* to be used to accomplish the specific aims of the project. Include the *means by which the data will be collected, analyzed, and interpreted.* Describe any new methodology and its *advantage over existing methodologies.* Discuss the *potential difficulties and limitations* of the proposed procedures and *alternative approaches* to achieve the aims. Provide a *tentative sequence or timetable* for the investigation. Point out any *procedures, situations, or materials that may be hazardous* to personnel and the precautions to be exercised. **Although no specific number of pages is recommended for this section of the application, the *total for Sections A-D may not exceed 20 pages.***

End of Page 20 of NIH instructions.

E. **Human Subjects.** If you have marked Item 4a on the Face Page of the application "YES," and designated no exemptions from the regulations, *address the following six points.*

1. Provide a detailed description of the proposed involvement of human subjects in the work previously outlined in the experimental design and methods section. Describe the *characteristics of the subject population,* including their anticipated number, age, ranges, sex, ethnic background, and health status. Identify the *criteria for inclusion or exclusion.* Explain the *rationale for the involvement of special classes* of subjects, if any, such as fetuses, pregnant women, children, human *in*

vitro   fertilization, prisoners or other institutionalized individuals, or others who are likely to be vulnerable.

2. Identify the *sources of research material* obtained from individually identifiable living human subjects in the form of specimens, records, or data. Indicate whether the material or data will be obtained specifically for research purposes or whether use will be made of existing specimens, records, or data.

3. Describe *plans for the recruitment of subjects* and the *consent procedures* to be followed, including the circumstances under which consent will be sought and obtained, who will seek it, the nature of the information to be provided to prospective subjects, and the method of documenting consent. State if the institutional review board (IRB) has authorized a modification or waiver of the elements of consent or the requirement for documentation of consent. The consent form, which must have IRB approval, should be submitted to the PHS only on request.

4. Describe any *potential risks*—physical, psychological, social, legal, or other—and assess their likelihood and seriousness. Where appropriate, describe *alternative treatments* and procedures that might be advantageous to the subjects.

5. Describe the *procedures for protecting against or minimizing any potential risks,* including risks to confidentiality, and assess their likely effectiveness. Where appropriate, discuss *provisions for ensuring necessary medical or professional intervention in the event of adverse effects* to the subjects. Also, where appropriate, describe the provisions for monitoring the data collected to ensure the safety of subjects.

6. Discuss *why* the *risks* to subjects *are reasonable in relation to the anticipated benefits* to subjects and in relation to the importance of the knowledge that may reasonably be expected to result.

If you have marked Item 4a on the Face Page of the application "YES" and designated exemptions from the human subjects regulations, provide sufficient information to allow a determination that the designated exemptions are appropriate.

If a test article (investigational new drug, device, or biologic) is involved, *name* the *test article* and state whether the 30-day interval has elapsed or has been waived and/or whether use of the test article has been withheld or restricted by the Food and Drug Administration.

Although no specific page limitation applies to this section of the application, be succinct.

F. **Vertebrate Animals.** If you have marked Item 5 on the Face Page of the application "YES," *address the following five points.*

End of Page 21 of NIH instructions.

----

1. Provide a detailed description of the *proposed use of the animals* in the work previously outlined in the experimental design and methods section. *Identify the species, strains, ages, sex, and numbers of animals* to be used in the proposed work.

2. *Justify* the *use* of animals, the *choice of species,* and the *numbers used.* If animals are in short supply, costly, or to be used in large numbers, provide an *additional rationale* for their selection and their numbers.

3. Provide information on the *veterinary care* of the animals involved.

4. Describe the *procedures for ensuring that discomfort, distress, pain, and injury will be limited* to that which is unavoidable in the conduct of scientifically sound research. Describe the use of analgesic, anesthetic, and tranquilizing drugs and/or comfortable restraining devices where appropriate to minimize discomfort, distress, pain, and injury.

5. Describe any *euthanasia method* to be used and the reasons for its selection. State whether this method is consistent with

the recommendations of the Panel on Euthanasia of the American Veterinary Medical Association. If not, present a justification for not following the recommendations.

Although no specific page limitation applies to this section of the application, *be succinct*.

G. **Consultants/Collaborators.** *Attach an appropriate letter* from each individual confirming his or her role in the project. Include *Biographical Sketch* pages for each consultant and collaborator.

H. **Consortium/Contractual Arrangements.** Provide a *detailed explanation* of the programmatic, fiscal, and administrative arrangements made between the applicant organization and the collaborating organizations. Provide a statement that the applicant organization and the collaborating organizations have established or are prepared to establish written inter-organizational agreements that will ensure compliance with all pertinent Federal regulations and policies. Attach *confirming letters* or copies of *written agreements*.

If consortium/contractual activities represent a significant portion of the overall project, *explain why the applicant organization*, rather than the ultimate performer of the activities, *should be the grantee*. The major purpose of this requirement is to ensure that the applicant organization intends to perform a substantive role in the conduct of the project, as prescribed by PHS grants policy.

I. **Literature Cited.** Do not scatter literature citations throughout the text. *List* them *at the end of the Research Plan.* The list may include, but not replace, the list of publications in the Progress Report required for COMPETING CONTINUATION and SUPPLEMENTAL applications. Each literature citation must include the names of all authors, the name of the book or journal, volume number, page numbers, and year of publication. Providing *titles* is *useful but optional*. Make every attempt to *be judicious* in compiling a *relevant* and *current* list of literature citations; it need not be exhaustive. ***Do not exceed four pages.***

Checklist. Self-explanatory. This is the last page of the application.

End of Page 22 of NIH instructions.

SPECIFIC INSTRUCTIONS-SECTION 3

Appendix

AN APPLICATION MAY BE RETURNED IF THE APPENDIX FAILS TO OBSERVE THE SIZE LIMITATIONS. **The size limitations may not apply to the specialized grant applications listed in the General Instructions section. Request and follow the additional instructions for those applications.**

Include six collated sets of the *appendix* material in the application package. *Do not mail* this material *separately. Identify each* of the *sets with* the *name* of the principal investigator/program director *and the project title.*

Submit six collated sets of photographs, oversized documents, or materials that do not photocopy well. For COMPETING CONTINUATION and SUPPLEMENTAL applications, submit six collated sets of **no more than ten** publications, manuscripts **accepted** for publication, patents, invention reports, and other printed materials that have resulted from the project since it was last reviewed competitively. NEW applications may also have appended to them six collated sets of similar background material documenting preliminary studies.

Six collated sets of *supplementary background graphs, diagrams, tables, and charts directly pertinent to the application* may also be submitted as appendix material. However, *keep such material to a minimum;* if it is essential to an evaluation of the application, incorporate it in the Research Plan. *The Appendix is* **not** *to be used to circumvent the page limitations in the Research Plan. The Appendix will* **not** be duplicated with the rest of the application.

End of Page 23 of NIH instructions.

NOTE: The application for a non-competing renewal, form PHS 2590 was also revised 9/86. This form is to be used by grantees (i.e., those who have had an application approved and funded) to submit an *annual Budget Report and Progress Report* to NIH. Non-competing renewal applications must be submitted 2 months before the start of each new budget period.

Appendix II

Sample Outline for Section 2 of NIH-R01 Application
(PHS Form 398: Revised 9/86)

This section of the grant application includes the Research Plan.

(*Note:* This is not the only possible outline; it is only a sample outline; *your* outline should fit the needs of *your* project—*but must follow NIH instructions.*)

Section 2

I.   *Introduction*—1 Page (Only for revisions or supplements)

    A.   Summary of substantial additions, deletions, and changes (Highlight changes by brackets, indents, or change of typestyle)

        1. Addition: Page y, paragraph x describes . . . . .
        2. Addition: Page v, paragraph w describes . . . . .
        3. Deletion: Page x, paragraph z has been deleted because . . . . .
        4. Change: Page m, paragraph n has been changed to reflect . . . . .

    B.   Responses to criticisms in previous summary statement

        1. Response to pink sheet paragraph x
        2. Response to pink sheet paragraph y

    C.   Work done since prior version of application was submitted

        1. Set of experiments # 1: completed since prior submission
        2. Set of experiments # 2: begun since prior submission

II.   **Research Plan**—Maximum of 20 pages total for items A-D

A.   Specific Aims—1 Page

Summarize broad, long-term objectives; what the research is intended to accomplish; hypotheses to be tested.

1. Specific Aim 1
2. Specific Aim 2
3. Specific Aim 3

B.   **Background and Significance**—2–3 Pages

1. Background (Refer to pertinent references in the bibliography, Literature Cited, item I.)
2. Critical evaluation of existing knowledge
3. Gaps that this project is intended to fill
4. Importance of the research—relate Specific Aims to broad, long-term objectives

   a) Specific Aim 1 will . . . . towards the broad, long-term objectives
   b) Specific Aim 2 will . . . . towards the broad, long-term objectives
   c) Specific Aim 3 will . . . . towards the broad, long-term objectives

C.   **Progress Report**—6–8 Pages

(For competing continuations and supplements)

[**Preliminary Studies**—Optional for **NEW** applications in place of Progress Report]

(Include small but readable and well-labeled figures, tables, and photos or refer to them and provide them in the Appendix.)

(Cite your own publications in the text and list them in the appropriate section at the end of the Progress Report/Preliminary Studies.)

1. Beginning and ending *dates* for period covered since last competitive review.

2. List *key personnel.*

   (Give titles, dates of service, % of their appointments devoted to the project.)

3. *Progress*

   (Summarize previous Specific Aims, give succinct account of progress toward their achievement and explain importance of the findings.)

   [**NEW applicants:** USEFUL but OPTIONAL: Describe preliminary studies pertinent to the application and/or give other information that will help establish your experience and competence to pursue the proposed project.]

   a) Specific Aim 1 (from previous application)

      (1) Summary of Specific Aim 1 (from previous application)
      (2) Progress toward achievement of Specific Aim 1 (from previous application)
      (3). Importance of findings related to achievement of Specific Aim 1 (from previous application)

   b) Specific Aim 2 (from previous application)

      (1) Summary of Specific Aim 2 (from previous application)
      (2) Progress toward achievement of Specific Aim 2 (from previous application)
      (3) Importance of findings related to achievement of Specific Aim 2 (from previous application)

   Repeat for each Specific Aim in previous application.

   c) Discuss any changes in Specific Aims since project was last reviewed competitively.

4. **Publications**—Give titles and complete references.

(Submit 6 collated sets of NO MORE THAN 10 such items in the appendix.)

[NEW applicants: List any pertinent publications and submit 6 collated sets of NO MORE THAN 10 such items in the appendix.]

a) Published materials

  (1) Original research reports

    (1). Hokum, J. and Pokum, L., ... 1987
    (2). Hokum, J. and Pokum, L., ... 1986
    (3). Hokum, J. and Pokum, L., ... 1985

  (2) Review articles
  (3) Books
  (4) Abstracts

b) Manuscripts **accepted for publication**

  (1) Original research reports
  (2) Review articles
  (3) Books
  (4) Abstracts

c) Patents
d) Invention reports
e) Other printed materials

D. **Experimental Design and Methods**—About 8–11 Pages (Maximum length of items A–D must not exceed 20 Pages.)

(Refer to pertinent references in the bibliography, Literature Cited, item I.)

1. Experimental Design to accomplish the Specific Aims (If applicable, describe overall Experimental Design.) (Include all pertinent control experiments.)

a) Experimental Design for Specific Aim 1
b) Experimental Design for Specific Aim 2
c) Experimental Design for Specific Aim 3

2. Procedures to carry out the Experimental Design (Include pertinent controls for procedures.)

a) For Specific Aim 1
b) For Specific Aim 2
c) For Specific Aim 3
d) General procedures that apply to more than one Experimental Design

----

Or (alternatively) combine 1 and 2 above.

1. Experimental Design and procedures to accomplish the Specific Aims (If applicable, describe overall Experimental Design.) (Include all pertinent control experiments.)

a) Experimental Design and procedures for Specific Aim 1

(1) Experimental Design for Specific Aim 1
(2) Procedures for Specific Aim 1

b) Experimental Design and procedures for Specific Aim 2

(1) Experimental Design for Specific Aim 2
(2) Procedures for Specific Aim 2

c) Experimental Design and procedures for Specific Aim 3

(1) Experimental Design for Specific Aim 3
(2) Procedures for Specific Aim 3

d) General procedures that apply to more than one Experimental Design

(Note: If you use this form, the remaining topics (3 to 8 below) under D. will have to be re-numbered 2 to 7)

----

3. Explain means by which data will be collected, analyzed, and interpreted (You may need—or prefer—to discuss this and the next 3 items separately for each Specific Aim.)
4. For any new methodologies: Explain advantage over existing methodologies.
5. Discuss potential limitations and difficulties of proposed procedures.
6. Discuss alternative approaches to achieve the Aims.
7. Give a tentative sequence or timetable for the studies.
8. Point out procedures, situations, or materials that may be hazardous to personnel. For each case, specify precautions to be exercised.

E. **Human Subjects**—For items E through I below, see the main part of this book.

F. **Vertebrate Animals**

G. **Consultants/Collaborators**

H. **Consortium/Contractual Agreements**—See NIH instructions.

I. **Literature Cited**—*4 Pages maximum*

III. **Checklist**—*Form provided in Application Kit; required as last page of Application*

Appendix III

General Checklist

This checklist was adapted from a list I received from a federal agency that funds proposals in the social sciences. It was a list of reasons why some proposals at that agency are not funded. I have reworded the statements and made some minor changes and additions to the list.

A. Are the Research Goals Appropriate and Clear?

A1. Is the topic [or purpose(s)] appropriate for support by the granting agency?
If in doubt, call or write the agency to ask.
[For an RFP (Request for proposal): Is the topic responsive to the scope of the announcement?]

A2. Are the purposes of the study clear and sufficiently detailed? Are the hypotheses explicit?

A3. Are the research goals worthy of support?

A4. Have the compiled data been analyzed fully and appropriately?

A5. Where pertinent, have you included specific end-points, applications, or products in the research goals?

B. Is the Study Design Good?

B1. Have you determined that the research proposed has not been done by others?
Don't waste your time.—Perhaps the study design was tried and judged inadequate by others (in so far as it is possible to assess this). Don't re-invent the wheel!

B2. Is there sufficient attention given to related research by others?

B3. Is the study design carefully related to the purposes of the project?

B4. Will the study design provide the data needed to achieve the aims of the project?
Will the study yield enough data (cases) to support the analysis?

B5. Is there evidence of coherent direction in the study? (Not just parts thrown together.)

B6. Is the proposal well coordinated and clearly related to a central focus?

B7. Is the sampling design appropriate? Have you justified the sample size?

B8. Are the data unbiased?
Is there recognition of the problems of bias and ways to correct the bias?

B9. Is the methodology sufficiently detailed?

B10. Have you spelled out
a. The major dependent and independent variables?
b. How the data will be obtained and analyzed?
c. Whether the data contain enough information to support the proposed analysis?

C. Are Staff, Time, and Budget Appropriate?

C1. Are specific tasks clearly related to personnel, time, and budget?

C2. Is there sufficient time commitment by the Principal Investigators?
(Avoid small allocations of time among a large number of investigators.)

C3. Are the scientific disciplines of the research team (including consultants) appropriate for the topics to be investigated?

D. Is the Overall Presentation Good?

D1. Have you spelled out a specific plan of research rather than expected the reviewers to trust in your past reputation?

D2. Have you accounted for the possibility that the reviewers have not read about your past research?

D3. Is there a balanced presentation in the proposal? Does the proposal focus on particular data sets and techniques of analysis without obscuring the overall research goal? Does the proposal relate each specific focus to the overall goal?

(Have you started with a problem or topic and looked for data sets that address the issues rather than started with a data set and looked for a research problem that might be appropriate for that data set?)

E. Administrative Detail

E1. Is the budget realistic for the work proposed?

E2. Is the budget justification sufficiently detailed to allow reviewers to relate each phase and level of the project to the budget?

E3. Have you provided letters that outline willingness to participate and extent of commitment for all consultants, collaborators, and subcontractors?

E4. Have you
  a. Filled out and obtained signatures for the cover page? If you wait till the last minute the appropriate official may be out of town.
  b. Entered the appropriate page numbers in the Table of Contents after printing out the final copy?
  c. Made sure the abstract reflects the contents of the application?
  d. Provided the necessary information and forms concerning
     (1) Human studies
     (2) Humane treatment of vertebrate animals
     (3) Other assurances (Recombinant DNA, Civil rights, Handicapped individuals, Sex discrimination, Protection against scientific fraud)
     (4) Personal data form on ethnic origin, etc. (Optional)
     (5) Other grant support
     (6) Resources and Environment (Facilities and Equipment) Include support services and description of work ambience. (Who is available for collaboration and exchange of ideas?)
     (7) Checklist (for NIH applications) Have you numbered it as the last page of the application?
  e. Provided a STAMPED self-addressed postcard (to receive acknowledgement of application receipt)?
  f. Marked your calendar at 6 weeks post-submission to be sure you have received review board assignment?

Appendix IV

Sample Budget Justification

The following is part of a sample budget justification for the sample budget shown in part 2 of this book, section 1, Administrative and Financial Information. This is followed by the budget justification from the proposal for which the Summary Statement is shown in Example B, Appendix V—a proposal that the reviewers considered to be "an extremely well-written grant proposal." The examples of budget justifications shown here are not the only way to write a budget justification. But they illustrate a format that I thought to be effective after listening to about 600 budget discussions (3 meetings per year x 2 years x 100 proposals per meeting = 600!).

Budget Justification

Example A

1. Personnel $145,777

(a) Dr. Jones, Principal Investigator (salary + fringe) . . . $68,185

Dr. Jones has planned this project, including the specific experiments to be carried out. He will be responsible for managing the project and for analyzing and interpreting the data with the help of the co-investigator. He and the co-investigator will jointly develop manuscripts for publication as is warranted. Dr. Jones has specific expertise in . . . . He will spend 100 percent of his time on this project year round. He has a long track record in the field of . . .

(b) Dr. Smith, co-investigator (salary + fringe). $39,892

Dr. Smith is an established investigator in the field of . . . and will provide the "hands on" experience with respect to . . . . She will be responsible for carrying out the ... aspect of the experiments described in the methods section of the proposal. This project cannot be carried out without a person with the expertise and competence of Dr. Smith for successful resolution of the experiments. Dr. Smith has been with the University of ... for 6 years and has collaborated with Dr. Jones for the last 3 years. They have been a very successful team and have published 11 papers in well-reviewed journals during their collaboration.

> Note that Dr. Smith's salary is based on $45,800 for full time. She has a three-quarter-time appointment at the university during the academic year and plans to devote seventy-five percent of her time to this research project. ($3/4 \times 9/12 = 0.56 \times 0.75 = 0.42 \times \$45,800 = \$19,236$). During the three summer months, she will work full time at the university and devote one hundred percent of her time to this project. ($1.0 \times 3/12 = 0.25 \times 1.0 = 0.25 \times \$45,800 = \$11,450$). Fringe benefits have been calculated at thirty percent.

(c) Mr. West, Research Assistant (salary + fringe) $22,100

Mr. West will devote one hundred percent effort to this project on a year-round basis. Mr. West has been working with Dr. Jones for the last 9 years. He has developed unique expertise in the field of . . . . Mr. West has been a co-author on 15 publications during his time in Dr. Jones's laboratory. His full-time effort is essential for carrying out the experiments on ... which are an integral part of the total research project.

(d) Technician (To be named) (salary + fringe) $15,600

In addition to Mr. West, the research assistant, a medium level technician is essential for carrying out this project. The laboratory currently does not have someone in this category. The intention is to hire a person with a B.A. degree who has reasonably extensive experience in carrying out . . . experiments. We will specifically look for a person who has had hands-on experience working with rats in a system similar to the one in which we propose to work in this project.

2. Consultant Costs $0

Dr. Northstar, consultant, is a full professor at the University of . . . ,
department of . . . . She is a nationally known expert in . . . and is
currently writing a book on this subject. She has agreed to be a
consultant at no charge, for the . . . part of the project; she will
advise on . . . and will also provide help with data analysis (see
attached letter).

3. Equipment $32,560

(a) Zeiss microscope, model XYZ $29,710

We have been using a microscope that belongs to Dr. M in the
department of . . . . Dr. M will be leaving the University of . . . at
about the time that this project will begin if it is funded. He will take
his microscope with him to the University of . . . . Because a good
quality microscope is essential to carrying out this research project,
we are requesting money to buy a model XYZ Zeiss microscope.

(b) Diamond Knife. $2,500

Dr. M has recently converted from using glass knives to using a
diamond knife. He will be taking both his diamond knife and the
glass knife cutter with him when he leaves this department.
Therefore, we are requesting $2,500 to purchase a diamond knife
for cutting thin sections of . . . for these experiments.

(c) Embedding oven $350

We have been using Dr. M's embedding oven. He will take this
piece of equipment to the University of . . . when he leaves in June,
1988. We are therefore requesting $350 to purchase an embedding
oven.

4. Supplies $9,384

(a) Rats (including maintenance)

etc.

For additional details about budget justification see Example B below.

Budget Justification

Example B

This budget justification is from a grant proposal, that reviewers considered to be "an extremely well-written grant proposal." Example B, Appendix V is the summary statement for that proposal.

1. Personnel . . . . S . . . . .

(a) PI and Co-Investigator . . . . S . . . . .

Dr. . . . and Dr. . . . have planned this project, and will, for the most part, plan the specific experiments to be carried out. We will be entirely responsible for analyzing and interpreting the biochemical data; we will also plan the morphological experiments, but since neither of us have "hands-on" experience in this area, the work will of necessity be done by someone experienced in morphological techniques and the anatomy of the . . .

(b) Research Associate. . . . . S . . . . .

This is the person who will provide the "hands-on" experience, and will (with the help of the research assistant) be responsible for carrying out all the morphological aspects of the experiments described in the "Methods" section of the proposal. It should be specifically noted that this project cannot be carried out without a morphologist of this level of competence and someone to help with the more routine aspects of the lengthy experimental work-up. A search cannot be initiated for this individual unless and until funding is obtained. The research associate would be responsible for carrying out and helping to interpret the morphological experiments. This individual would have to be experienced in both light and electron microscopy and be familiar with . . . anatomy in particular. He/she would presumably have had three or more years of postdoctoral experience in . . . morphology.

(c) Research Assistant . . . . $ . . . . .

This individual will assist in carrying out both the morphological and biochemical experiments. He is familiar with tissue work-up, sectioning, and photographic techniques, but will also be able to assist with handling of animals, as well as the more routine aspects of the biochemical assays. He will be primarily responsible to the Research Associate morphologist, but will also be directly responsible to the PI and Co-investigator in helping to set up certain experiments and run the necessary assays.

2. Consultant $0

Dr. . . . at the . . . Hospital, Department of . . . , is a known expert in . . . syndrome and is currently finishing a chapter on this subject. He has kindly agreed to be a consultant, at no charge, and will also provide . . . material from . . . victims, as available (see attached letter). In addition, he will help us procure such material from other sources.

3. Equipment $23,805

(a) Zeiss Microscope $21,605

(b) Diamond Knife. $2,000

The . . . Morphology Unit is a well-equipped, but heavily used, facility. Most equipment necessary to carry out this project is available through the Unit; however, Dr. . . . , the Unit head, has indicated that because of the heavy use required to carry out this project, a separate light microscope and diamond knife will be essential. Fluorescence optics will be necessary for . . . experiments to localize and quantify various . . . , e.g., ... It is estimated that this microscope will be used substantially on a daily basis by both the Research Associate Morphologist and the research assistant. In addition, it will be used frequently by the PI and the Co-Investigator to review the results of experiments and discuss the interpretations with the Research Associate morphologist.

(c) Embedding oven $200

Although embedding ovens are available at the . . . , we have been advised by the Morphology Unit to have our own for the purposes of optimal curing of plastic sections.

4. Supplies $11,739

(a) Animals. $2,687

We consider that a full-time Morphologist with a full-time Research Assistant will be capable of carrying out about two experiments (each having ten to twelve morphological samples and an equivalent number of biochemical samples) per week, for three weeks of every month. The fourth week will be used to record and assess the results, including taking and processing photographs. We are thus calculating costs on the basis of thirty-eight weeks for experiments, taking into account three weeks vacation time per year.

(1) Eggs $979

We estimate two-and-one-half dozen eggs per week at $6 per dozen plus $8 delivery charge = $874 at current prices. With 12 percent inflation by the beginning of the project period, this cost would be $979 for the first year.

(2) Other Animals $1,708

The second experiment each week will involve cow . . . . half of the time and in vitro experiments in newborn and young rats during the remaining weeks.

- Cow (organ) $1,140

  $2 per . . . x 20 . . . + $20 delivery charge = $60 per week x 19 weeks = $1,140.

- Rats (Cost and care) $568

  Current price of one litter of rats (newborn) $18.65. We project $20 by the beginning of the project period. One litter per week for 19 weeks

= $380. Animal room charge for maintenance of
one cage of rats at $188/year/cage = $188. Total
for rats and care = $568.

(b) Medium and Serum $920

(1) Medium $570

We estimate a total of twenty-four chick embryo . . . cultures
per week for the total of morphological and biochemical
samples. These samples require 20 ml of medium per flask,
i.e., one 500-ml bottle per week. (Cow . . . will be maintained
in re-usable glass flasks and will require only small amounts
of medium.) We project $15 per bottle by the beginning of
the project period. $15 x 38 weeks = $570.

(2) Serum $350

The current price of fetal calf serum, which is essential for the
maintenance of chick embryo . . . in culture, is $29.20 per
100-ml bottle. Because of the enormous fluctuations of the
price of this product in the past year, we make no attempt to
adjust this figure. We estimate 12 bottles per year. $29.20 x 12
= $350.

(c) Chemicals, Glassware, Plasticware $1,812

Chemicals $600

These include antibiotics, buffers, assay reagents for biochemical experiments and radioactive precursors for uptake and
incorporation studies. We estimate $600.

Falcon Flasks $912

We have found 75 sq cm flasks to be optimal for . . . cultures.
24 per week at $1 per flask for 38 weeks = $912.

Counting vials and scintillation fluid $300

We will try to be as conservative as possible in this area, but
the project will necessitate a small number of incorporation
and uptake studies. We estimate $300 in this category.

(d) Microscopy Supplies $3,450

(1) Fixatives $1,500

Glutaraldehyde, paraformaldehyde, osmium tetroxide, de-hydrating agents, embedding compounds and stains for light microscopy. We estimate $1500.

(2) Glass for microtome knives, etc. $750

This includes also, embedding molds, disposable beakers, disposable gloves, slides, cover slips, and vials which will be required for light microscopy.

(3) Dissecting instruments
     and microtomy equipment $1,000

For example, micro-dissecting scissors costs approximately $100. We estimate $1000 in this category.

(4) Electron microscopy supplies. $200

This category includes grids, grid holders, and stains for electron microscopy.

(e) Photo Supplies $2,870

(1) Black-and-white film. $456

2 rolls per experiment, $3 per roll, 2 experiments per week x 38 weeks = $456.

(2) Color slides: $304

1 roll per week x $8 per roll for film and processing x 38 weeks = $304

(3) Paper for printing black-and-white photos. $1,710

We plan to use multigrade resin paper, 50 sheets per experiment (including test sheets). 2 experiments per week = 100 sheets per week. $45 per 100 sheets x 38 weeks = $1,710.

(4) Photochemicals $400

For processing black-and-white film and prints. We estimate $400 per year.

5. Travel $2,500

Because of the nature of the proposed work, which involves . . . as a model of . . . , it will be important for the Research Associate to go to both the . . . meeting and the . . . meeting. In addition, it will be important for the PI to attend conferences specifically concerned with the latest development on . . . syndrome once a year in order to keep up with both the clinical and research areas related to this disease. In November, 19xx, a . . . syndrome symposium (II) took place in . . . . . Another . . . Symposium is scheduled in early 19xx (see . . . Newsletter, vol . . . page . . . , Sept., 19xx)

The total figure for travel is based on $800 for this year's . . . travel budget. (This figure was arrived at by the . . . Committee at . . . , calculated on the basis of Super-Saver fares and double room occupancy). Assuming similar costs for the other two meetings, in the same geographic area, and allowing a small increment for inflation, we are estimating $2500 in the travel category for the first year.

6. Other Expenses $3,280

(a) Publication costs $1,000

These include drafting, photography, photocopy charges, etc. Publications resulting from this project will of necessity involve numerous photographic plates. The current page charge for half tones, for example, in Journal of Cell Biology is $70 per page for short papers and $100 per page for longer papers.

300 reprints for a 6-page article currently cost at least $150.

We estimate at least one major publication per year:

Drafting $200
Photographs $150
Page charge (6 x $70) $420
Reprints (500) $230

Total $1000

(b) Users' fee for the Morphology Unit $2,280

Because of increased expenses and decreased funding, the Morphology Unit at . . . has instituted a $3-per-hour "use fee" for all users. The items included in the users' fee do not cover any supplies requested above; they do include service contracts, and use of available instruments, liquid nitrogen, etc.

The budgeted amount is based on twenty hours of use per week.

7. Budget for Subsequent Years

(a) Each category is increased by 10 % per year to account for inflation.

(b) No additional equipment is requested in years 02 and 03.

(c) "Other Expenses" is increased by $1000 in year 03 for sharpening the diamond knife.

Appendix V

Sample Summary Statements ("Pink Sheets")

The Summary Statement is prepared by the Executive Secretary of the Study Section and is based on the reviewers' reports and the discussion of all the Study Section members. (Each proposal has at least a primary and secondary reviewer; sometimes there is also a tertiary reviewer and additional outside reviewers or reviews by mail.)

This Appendix contains some sample Summary Statements (edited for reasons of confidentiality) for a number of grant proposals submitted to NIH with a variety of outcomes. (An example of reviewers' reports for a National Science Foundation (NSF) grant proposal is given in Appendix VIII: More About National Science Foundation Applications.) I have put in italic type (and in some cases, boldface italic type) some of the key words and phrases that may help to direct your thinking when you write your grant proposal. Note the dates, the comments, and the priority scores! If you study the samples carefully, you will get a good idea of what reviewers look for in an application. Perhaps, with the help of this book, your Summary Statement will also contain the sentence shown in boldface in "Example B." When you write and edit your proposal, remember that reviewers are generally very overworked people who are reviewing proposals in their "spare time"—sometimes late at night, or on a commuter train. Use good psychology, good organization, and clear presentation to make the reviewer's job as easy as possible. If your grant proposal is written so that all information needed by the reviewer is easy to find and unambiguous, the reviewer is likely to view your proposal more favorably—all other things being equal.

Example A

Excerpts from a summary statement for a proposal with a priority score of 181 (very good in 1979). This project was funded for 5 years with the budget reduced as indicated.

SUMMARY STATEMENT

Degree: Ph.D.

Requested Start Date: 04/01/79

Recommendation: APPROVAL   Priority Score: 181

Special Note: NO HUMAN SUBJECTS

NO RECOMBINANT DNA RESEARCH IS INVOLVED

Project Year	Direct Costs Requested	Direct Costs Recommended	Previously Recommended	Grant Period
03	113,873	96,117		4/1/79
04	126,253	101,408		4/1/80
05	139,533	107,109		4/1/81
06	155,590	114,406		4/1/82
07	173,518	122,236		4/1/83

RESUME: A *competent* biochemist requests continued support for studies on the . . . as a model system of a . . . tissue and as a system for a study of . . . in the tissue. *The problem is complex but important,* the *program well organized,* and the *principal investigator has* **demonstrated by his published work** in this field that he is capable of conducting this program. Approval is recommended with some reduction in the budget.

DESCRIPTION: The principal investigator wished to continue studies on . . . .

CRITIQUE: This is a long but *well organized, detailed presentation* of an immensely complex subject. Working with a small group, but *collaborating effectively* with a number of other investigators, the principal investigator has made *reasonable progress* over the past three years *in spite of moving his laboratory* in . . . 1976 and in spite of the complexity of the problem. He is a competent biochemist who *has been able to develop the necessary techniques of cell biology to follow this problem.* The general question of the regulation of . . . and the specific problem of the regulation of the appearance of . . . *are of fundamental importance.* It is of considerable interest to elucidate the role of the . . . , and to determine if it is involved in the modification of . . . . The specific aims delineated in the application are *highly ambitious* and cover a *wide spectrum of initiatives.* Of particular importance are the problems of the . . . in the . . . and determination of the physiological function of the . . . . The *difficulty in achieving the overall objectives of the project are complicated by* the fact that the applicant is studying the control of . . . whose role is not known, whose distribution is only vaguely suspected, and whose induction can be modified by widely differing compounds. *There is also some concern* that the model system . . . is not . . . typical . . . and that the influence of the . . . environment produces anomalous effects. Nevertheless, the *principal investigator's work has been well received, he has been **productive, publishing generally in critically-reviewed journals,** and has clearly *demonstrated the intellectual capacity* to attack this most difficult problem. Approval is recommended with a reduced budget.

INVESTIGATOR: . . . Ph.D.,received his B.A. at . . . University and his Ph.D. in . . . at the University of . . . . He took a three year post-doctoral at . . . , with . . . , a well-known scientist, who introduced him into the field of . . . . Since . . . , he had held appointments in various branches of . . . and is now . . . . *He has published some twenty papers* dealing with . . . and their effect upon the . . . , and in the case of . . . , upon the human. *A number of papers have recently been submitted for publication and are included with this application.*

RESOURCES AND ENVIRONMENT: These are adequate.

BUDGET: The following reductions are recommended. Personnel: *Delete the Research Assistant* . . . since there **does not appear to be a strong argument** for both a full-time Research Associate and a Research Assistant.

Travel: Allow Domestic and Foreign Travel ($500 and $850 in the first year.) Reduce travel in future years to $1,000.

Example B

Excerpts from a summary statement for a well-written grant proposal that does not have sufficient preliminary data to convince the reviewers of the feasibility of the study.

RESUME: This proposal outlines histological and biochemical studies of the . . . of victims of . . . disease. Effect on high . . . associated with the disease, will be studied in animal . . . . The *proposal is weakened by the absence of preliminary data* demonstrating the . . . pathology presumed to accompany . . . disease. The . . . *biochemical studies are enthusiastically approved* but the *morphological studies are discouraged until an expert in . . . ultrastructure can be recruited.* Approval is recommended for the requested time and reduced amount.

CRITIQUE: **This is an extremely well-written grant proposal** that suggests a great many *sophisticated biochemical experiments* on *in vivo* and *in vitro* animal models and even some attempts at . . . . *All the experimental manipulations hinge on* there actually being pathology of the . . . , *which has yet to be demonstrated.* There is said to be . . . in . . . cases but this may only be a manifestation of the increased . . . that is a symptom of the disease. *There is also no evidence,* cited in this proposal at least, of . . . impairment in the affected patients with . . . syndrome. *Neither has it been demonstrated* that there are definite morphological changes in the . . . itself, . . . which are highly selectively damaged in the . . . , appear to be normal in . . . , and the only hint of pathology is apparently some . . . . No biochemical analyses have been done on affected . . . to see if the elevated . . . levels have affected the . . . cycle, the formation of . . . or . . . . *The whole grant proposal is written around the supposition that* the latter . . . systems are affected in . . . tissue in . . . syndrome, and that because the . . . is more easily studied under experimental conditions of high . . . than . . . tissue, the . . . is an ideal model for . . . syndrome.

It would seem to be a first priority of the proposed project to thoroughly investigate the human material, both . . . and . . . for details of structural damage and for problems in the . . . systems. *If it can be demonstrated* that either one of these approaches show pathology in the . . . , then the animal . . . experiments will certainly be valid and address the question of . . . . The *recruitment of a good electron microscopist is essential* for the morphological studies although not crucial to the whole application, for if the biochemical assays indicate a defect, then *the biochemical experi-*

ments alone will likely lead to a better understanding of the role of increased . . . in artificially produced . . . syndrome . . . simply because we need to know more concerning . . . in the vertebrate . . . . The *principal investigator is known for the unique contributions from her lab* concerning . . . . *and* . . . , *and has developed some impressive in vitro experimental designs.* For example, most recently, *she has been successful with . . . . We do not doubt . . . capabilities to produce meaningful results and a strong research program in* . . . On the other hand, Dr. . . . 's *expertise in ultrastructural studies . . . has not been demonstrated to date,* and there is *some concern that this part of the proposal cannot be attempted without a competent electron microscopist.* If the pathology in . . . syndrome or . . . is manifest only as subtle changes in . . . , *they might not be unequivocally detected by the anatomical approaches proposed* here. The use of . . . and . . . methods to demonstrate . . . in . . . or in . . . *are interesting approaches but again no expertise in these areas is offered by any member of this grant application.* In sum, the proposal contains *interesting and worthwhile experiments* in the principal investigator's principal area of expertise and are *sure to lead to meaningful information* concerning . . . . *However, the research is not necessarily addressing the question of . . . syndrome and may not actually be what the title of the application suggests—namely, a model for . . . syndrome.* Approval is recommended particularly for the biochemical aspects of the proposal. It would seem most appropriate to *consider support for the work after preliminary experiments by the principal investigator have indicated the presence of clear pathology* in the human . . . material. Current grant supports from the . . . Institute should be sufficient to allow such *pilot studies.*

Example C

Another example of a summary statement for a successful application with high priority score, which was funded for 5 years.

SUMMARY STATEMENT

Review Group: Application Number:

Meeting Date:

Investigator: Degree: Ph.D.

Position:

Organization:

City, State:

Project Title:
Recommendation: APPROVAL   Priority Score: 146

Special Note: NO HUMAN SUBJECTS

Project Year	Direct Costs Requested	Direct Costs Recommended	Previously Recommended	Grant Period
04	75,188	57,983		7/1/80
05	99,268	78,896		7/1/81
06	112,514	85,871		7/1/82
07	120,701	93,388		7/1/83
08	130,749	101,596		7/1/84

RESUME: A *most capable investigator* requests five years continued support for studies related to . . . . Various agents will be tested for their effects on the levels of . . . and effective compounds will be further assessed for the effect on a variety of . . . characteristics related to . . . . The *concepts are sound* and the *experiments well planned* using both *in vivo* and *in vitro* approaches. Approval is recommended.

DESCRIPTION: In this application the principal investigator proposes to investigate . . .

CRITIQUE: The *prior* three-year *award* (two-year reporting period) *has been productive.* It was shown that . . . . Recent studies using . . . , also revealed . . . . During this period there were *four publications and two papers in press.*

This is an *extremely interesting proposal* and addresses *important problems* of . . . . The *applicant is an established investigator* in the fields of . . .

She recently moved her interest into the . . . aspects of the . . . . The ten specific *aims listed are straightforward and logical, and all should produce new data* concerning the effect of . . . . She bases her expanded studies on . . . responses of the . . . which may be influenced by . . . 1) . . . 2) . . . 3) . . . 4) . . . . It is interesting that she addresses the source of the . . . Therefore, it is proposed to conduct studies with . . . and to monitor their . . . compared to controls. It would also be appropriate to monitor . . . .

Throughout the application, the principal investigator considers the . . . collectively and, particularly with the isolation procedures, it appears that after isolation of the . . . , levels in the total tissue will be studied without regard to the component layers. It is only in the latter part of the application that the effect of some of these . . . influences in the component layers is considered. It would appear to be advisable to divide the . . . into its components after excision. The *proposed studies on . . . may not be as straightforward as the applicant proposes. It is not clear* whether . . . or . . . will be used. One of the major factors which could effect . . . is . . . , a component of the vehicle in . . . .

A few suggestions should be noted for improvement of this otherwise excellent project. For comparing the efficacy of a drug, . . . will be used as a control. The . . . *may not be a suitable control* since . . . . The effect of . . . *should be examined.* The assessment of the . . . is reasonable, but the . . . studies under the influence of a number of these compounds *could also be further expanded* to look at . . . . Certainly the studies as planned should produce some interesting data on . . . . The methodology is relatively standard, save for a change in . . . . *A weakness in the proposal is the lack of any indication of the numbers of determinations* for each procedure or drug or *in vivo* treatment regimen. The principal investigator's *prior studies and those reported in the proposal indicate, however, that she is a most **careful worker*** and that, despite the lack of prescribed numbers, she will produce some interesting and reliable data. Approval is recommended.

INVESTIGATORS: ..., Ph.D., ... University, 1971, currently .... Her emphasis has been on ... research as interfaced with ... both as related to ... and to .... She is *extremely competent and active* in this field.

Mr.... M.S., ... University, has experience with ... and ....

RESOURCES AND ENVIRONMENT: These are *very good. Collaboration* on biochemical techniques with Drs.... should be useful.

BUDGET: The following reductions are recommended:

Personnel: *Delete the Research Technician.* Adequate assistance is otherwise requested. Supplies: *Reduce* from ... to ... since neither ... nor assays will be performed each week.

Travel: *Reduce* from $1200 to $600.

Example D

A summary statement for a proposal with a high priority score which involved a *site visit.*

SUMMARY STATEMENT

Degree: Ph.D.

Requested Start Date: 09/01/75

Recommendation: APPROVAL   Priority Score: 156

Special Note: Project Site Visit
              Executive Secretary's note

Project Year	Direct Costs Requested	Direct Costs Recommended	Previously Recommended	Grant Period
10	75,511	75,111		9/1/75
11	83,797	83,797		9/1/76
12	91,765	91,765		9/1/77
13	100,576	100,576		9/1/78
14	110,217	110,217		9/1/79

RESUME: Past performance assures continued excellent productivity in this important study of . . . and in the . . . and other tissues. His budget requests are reasonable and justified and the full period of time re-quested should be allowed. Consideration should be given in future applications to separating the two areas of investigation covered in this grant.

PROJECT SITE VISIT: A site visit was held to learn the scope of the applicant's current interests and relative priority of the various aspects of the project. The reviewers assembled at . . . for a pre-site-visit meeting. By 9:30 Dr. . . . joined the reviewers for a discussion of the project followed by a tour of the laboratories. After lunch, the reviewers met to write a report. No separate site-visit report has been written.

DESCRIPTION: The application is concerned with the role of . . . .

CRITIQUE: The *strengths of this proposal* lie (a) in the increased background and fundamental knowledge of . . . *(an area much needing investigation)* , which will be revealed by the studies, and (b) in that the approach to . . . was developed in the PI's . . . laboratory and the *application is a logical continuation of the work of a leader in this* field. The weakness lies in that the *area covered by the application is rather diffuse,* encompassing *too large an area of investigation.* It is recognized that when the applicant applied for a second grant it was made a supplement to his existing grant, combining two areas. Hence, in the writing of this application an emphasis was placed on the . . . aspect to the detriment of that part of the application concerning the . . . effect on . . . . *The application as written, essentially consists of two separate parts which, in reality, warrant different priorities.*

It is hoped that the . . . screening of . . . will be pursued only until sufficient specificity, or lack of same, is demonstrated in each system and that full, in-depth studies will not be made with each available . . . . *It is recommended that this be brought to the attention of the applicant.*

The *aims* of the proposal are *very logical,* progressing from the . . . established over the last five years by this investigator. The chosen approach is also *valid* and most *adequate* to achieve the ends anticipated in the proposal. The procedures are ones which have been utilized in the applicant's laboratory for a number of years and offer *no technical problems.* The *applicant has more than adequately demonstrated his competence* previously with the techniques and methodology. The research will undoubtedly produce new data concerning . . . , and will shed new light on this phenomenon; in addition, the *expected data should confirm various hypotheses* concerning the mechanism of . . . and its inhibition or acceleration. The proposed *work has significance* in the area of providing a . . . basis for the understanding of . . . processes in addition to basic knowledge of . . . per se and the understanding of . . . processes in the . . . . The proposal may set the groundwork for potential clinical therapeutic application in the treatment of . . . with regard to . . . . The . . . and data gathered in the proposed study should cast some light on this problem.

*Past **progress*** on the award ***has been most substantial,*** with the principal investigator establishing . . . as a real phenomenon. The *contribution made by the applicant is very significant* not only in the . . . , but also in other tissues. The applicant's *laboratory is possibly the only one pursuing these studies and this should be encouraged.*

INVESTIGATOR: The principal investigator has shown himself to be *able, competent and experienced* as evidenced by the *past publications* in a variety of research areas. *He is a leader in the . . . field* and is most *familiar with the necessary techniques.* The *senior technician* has also been *associated with the project for several years.*

RESOURCES AND ENVIRONMENT: The facilities and equipment are more than adequate for this study. The environment is entirely appropriate for good interchange of ideas with others and *the connection with Dr. . . . is excellent and beneficial.*

BUDGET: Most *reasonable* and presented at as low a level conceivably possible. *All items are justified on the basis of the proposal.* The full five years of support are needed in order to achieve the aims of this proposal.

EXECUTIVE SECRETARY'S NOTE: The reviewers recognize that the applicant wrote an all-encompassing application since two previous applications had been combined into one grant. This raised certain *problems in assessing the application* since some areas of the proposal were considered to have a higher priority than others. The current reviewers, therefore, wish to express disagreement with the philosophy of blending two diverse areas of interest into one application. This action encourages applicants not to submit proposals which attempt to *coalesce different areas of interest, often to the detriment of the application as a whole.*

Example E

A summary statement for a grant proposal with a poor priority score.

SUMMARY STATEMENT

Degree: Ph.D.

Requested Start Date: 07/01/77
Recommendation: APPROVAL   Priority Score: 363

NO HUMAN SUBJECTS

Project Year	Direct Costs Requested	Direct Costs Recommended	Previously Recommended	Grant Period
01	76,971	39,010		7/1/77
02	94,749	48,055		7/1/78
03	96,090			

RESUME: Support is requested for a study of . . . . Animals will be used for this study . . . . The *aims are worthwhile,* the *investigator is competent,* but a number of the aspects of the *protocol* are *not well formulated.* Approval for two years is recommended to give the principal investigator the *opportunity to demonstrate the feasibility* of this project especially the ability to acquire a sufficient number of . . . .

CRITIQUE: The *aims* of this project *are important.* The interrelationships of . . . disease certainly should be investigated, and the use of animal models is a viable approach to this problem. Although the aims are laudable, the **research plan is vague** *and has weaknesses.* The prior . . . results noted by Dr. . . . are of interest. However, in the appendix article the differences between . . . *are not analyzed* with respect to the degree of . . . or necessity for . . . , which could be accounting for these differences. Moreover, the increased . . . are only documented for two patients. Dr. . . . plans to use . . . kits for the measurements of . . . . *These are not always ideal,* and he notes that a bioassay also will be used in some cases. His experimental protocol utilizing controls seems adequate, but it is unclear from his description of his procedures, how often the various parameters will be measured, at what time intervals, and when the animals will be sacrificed. *Will* the 2–3 months of initial *observations be sufficient to document* the . . . , and, moreover, how long will it take in these animals before . . . ? It is at this time that these . . . analyses would be most productive . . . . He does not approach the interesting problem based on his own observation, of why the . . . does not reduce . . . . **Simply determining the levels of the four parameters and vaguely intimating that . . . will be examined, is not a sufficient research plan.**

There is some *concern about aspects of the methodology.* For the . . . experiments, the principal investigator notes that it takes approximately *x* animals with pooled blood samples to get enough volume to carry out the procedure. If this be the case, *one must question* how many blood samples will be available to prove or disprove the hypothesis. In order to obtain sufficient blood for a single determination of . . . , approximately *x* animals will be required; to determine the . . . activity, *y* ml of whole blood is required. The need for such levels of animals and blood samples *will complicate the overall experimentation.* It is only planned to measure . . . However, other . . . have an effect on . . . and some of the previous work would indicate that . . . is equally promising. *Certain manipulations should be carried out that are not mentioned.* Certainly, . . . examinations in the . . . would be important and could be correlated to the . . . parameters. Also, efforts to measure . . . might be very illuminating.

Approval is recommended for two years. The *time is reduced because there is some considerable doubt that he will be able to get sufficient numbers* of . . . . Two years should be sufficient to *demonstrate the feasibility* of this project.

INVESTIGATORS: . . . , Ph.D., is Professor and Director of the Laboratory . . . . He has worked extensively in . . . . His *bibliography is extensive* in this regard. He is *fully capable* of carrying out the proposed studies.

Dr. . . . is Associate Professor in the College of . . . . *His role would be* to handle and study the . . . from which specimens would be taken in the protocol. This would be done under a subcontract to the University of . . . . His bibliography includes numerous articles on . . . .

Dr. . . . , M.D., University of . . . , is Associate Professor of . . . , . . . University Medical School. *He would supervise* the . . . work proposed for the later years of the study. His bibliography indicates *extensive experience* on topics of . . . .

RESOURCES AND ENVIRONMENT: Excellent

BUDGET: For the two years recommended for approval, the following changes in the budget are recommended.

Personnel: *Delete* support for Dr. . . . , **since this position is *not justified*** and does not appear necessary to carry out this project. *Delete* a research assistant. One research assistant on this project should be sufficient. Furthermore, there is a research assistant *on another grant* who probably could be called upon when needed.

Travel: Reduce from $1,600 to $600.

Other Expenses: Reduce from . . . to . . . , since this is a feasibility study and there is some question about the availability of . . . . If such . . . become available in sufficient number, the amount for this category should be increased.

Example F

A summary statement for a proposal with a very low priority score.

SUMMARY STATEMENT

Degree: Ph.D.

Requested Start Date: 12/01/77

Recommendation: APPROVAL   Priority Score: 400

Special Note: NO HUMAN SUBJECTS

Project Year	Direct Costs Requested	Direct Costs Recommended	Previously Recommended	Grant Period
01	63,903	37,011		12/1/77
02	70,803	57,138		12/1/78
03	77,000	63,702		12/1/79

RESUME: Although there is a need to establish the role of . . . in . . . , and the possible role of . . . in preventing the . . . , the principal investigator *has approached the problem superficially.* Nonetheless, *to encourage the investigator to examine in depth his initial observation* that . . . , approval is recommended with a reduction in the budget.

DESCRIPTION: The specific aims of this project are . . . .

CRITIQUE: In preliminary studies the principal investigator has observed that . . . . He is of the opinion that this system may be . . . . He has further observed that . . . . There has been *considerable interest recently* in the role of . . . . However, *it remains to be clearly established* whether the . . . has the suggested role. In support of the evidence for a role of . . . in the . . . and the beneficial effect of . . . in the treatment of . . . , *he cites largely unpublished work* in . . . (p. X). Reference is also made to a paper presented to the . . . meeting in 1974. *Because of the unpublished nature of this work,* **it is difficult to evaluate** whether . . . has, in fact, a therapeutic effect.

Nevertheless, there is *clearly a need* for careful investigation to study . . . .

The *preliminary evidence supporting the . . . is weak and unconvincing.* A claim has been made that . . . ; *however,* **the values reported are based on a difference of two large numbers.** In the second assay procedure where . . . was used, ... This may not be applicable to . . . which contains almost . . . concentration of . . . . Also, *it is difficult to see how in the presence of such large concentrations of . . . , . . .* will accumulate in . . . .

The principal investigator's assessment of the current status of information of the role of . . . in . . . processes is *superficial* and in many places *inexact* (p. Y). In describing the role of . . . , he does not mention that . . . . *His explanation* of how . . . may occur during . . . *begins with a typographical error (or, possibly worse, a misunderstanding of inter-, intra-, and extracellular),* and then proceeds to a *distorted view* of how . . . . He rather *one-sidedly* invokes . . . as the cause of . . . , when there is abundant evidence from . . . and others that . . . . Other *cited literature is given a one-line evaluation* **slanted toward his own view** of things.

The *application* is, in places, rather **carelessly prepared** and, *occasionally, even* **incomprehensible.** For example, on page Y, section B, there seems to be a **confusion** between the prefixes inter-, extra-, and intra-. The term . . . is *used incorrectly* on page Z. These should be termed . . . . The term . . . is *not appropriate.* In the discussion of his observations that . . . can prevent . . . , it is **surprising that he does not discuss the work of** . . . who have shown that . . . have similar effects. With regard to the effect of . . . , the mechanism . . . is *not well worked out* and the . . . involvement *may not be as straightforward as implied* in this application.

On the positive side, there is some need to critically examine the role of . . . .

Approval is recommended.

INVESTIGATORS: . . . , received a Ph.D. . . . from the University of . . . , and is currently a Research Associate in the Department of . . . , College of Medicine . . . . He has *fourteen publications listed in his bibliography; two of these are in preparation; some of them are in journals such as Science and J. of . . . .*

Dr. . . . , Assistant Professor in the Department of . . . is listed on page 2 as Co-investigator on this application but *no biographical sketch* is provided.

RESOURCES AND ENVIRONMENT: Dr. . . . is apparently moving into a new . . . square foot space this month. *Facilities are probably good.*

BUDGET: The following *reductions* are recommended.

Personnel: *Because of the limited scope, delete* the 100% Research Assistant . . . , the . . . Laboratory Assistant . . . and Secretary . . . .

Equipment: *Reduce* from . . . to . . . .

Supplies: *Reduce* from . . . to . . . .

Travel: *Reduce* Domestic Travel from $800 to $600 and *delete* Foreign Travel.

Example G

Excerpts from a primary reviewer's report. The Study Section voted to defer this grant.

Grant Number

Name of PI

Primary Reviewer

Secondary reviewer

1977

Title: . . .

DESCRIPTION: This is a three-year proposal to study the effects of . . . in . . . tissue, particularly as it relates to certain disease states.

The thesis upon which this proposal is based is that a variety of events leading to . . . damage with impairment of . . . may be related to . . . damage. Apparently *preliminary work in Dr. . . . 's laboratory has indicated* the existence of . . . in a variety of . . . tissues. *However, no data are given.* Dr. . . . *conjectures* that . . . may be caused by destruction mediated by . . . accumulated over the . . . . He bases this on observations by others that . . . level increases in . . . , and draws the analogy that an increase of . . . might predispose to . . . .

The *specific aims are vague* but relate to refinement of analyses of . . . , as well as . . . , in the various . . . tissues. The levels of these 2 . . . will also be measured under a variety of . . . conditions, once baseline levels are established. Levels of . . . and . . . will also be measured. Models of . . . and . . . will be induced and changes in . . . will be determined. Lastly, some histopathology *is alluded to* (last sentence, para. 2, p. X). Experiments will utilize . . . and similar laboratory animals.

CRITIQUE: This proposal is based on *recent interesting findings* about the role of . . . in . . . tissues. *Unfortunately, the **proposal is vague,*** and ***much of the methods section,*** *after the initial description of a variety of published . . . assays,* **is really more of a discussion section** *than a* *section on methodology.** In addition, *Dr. . . .* **does not seem to be up to date** on recent developments in this area. He mentions in his background section that no data on . . . or on . . . is yet in the scientific . . . literature (para. 4, P. XX); thus, *he is unaware* of the paper by . . . (1975) entitled . . . . *Nor is a reference given to* . . . *by* . . . , *in October 1976* . . . , entitled . . . , which addresses itself specifically to this question. Likewise, the *discussion of* . . . *and* . . . *in the methods section refers to "extensive investigation of"* . . . , *but only a single reference to a paper by* . . . *is given. No reference is made to* a voluminous amount of work from . . . laboratory on the involvement of . . . in the . . . and its possible involvement in . . . . The **proposal has not been well thought out, is sloppily written and has apparently not been proofread.**

Sentences such as the last one on page Y make no sense at all . . . .

I found it *difficult* in several places *to understand what Dr.* . . . *was trying to say.* For example, he says that . . . . The next sentence is . . . (last para., p. YY). **It is difficult to decide whether the problem is writing or logic.**

The two-paragraph section on . . . and . . . on page Z is a discussion of some *vague ideas* on possible involvement of . . . in . . . but *not a single specific experiment is mentioned,* nor is any specific methodology given. The same is true for the methods section entitled . . . on page ZZ, and the section on . . . on the same page. In the methods section on . . . , he proposes three types of experiments, but **no methodology is given,** nor is there any statement of any awareness on his part of how much material is necessary to do a single determination of either . . . or . . . . *Are the* proposed experiments feasible without using an inordinately large number of animals? How many . . . are necessary to do a single . . . determination?

There are certainly *some interesting possibilities* in this grant and there is no question but that there is a great need to study the possible involvement of . . . and . . . in . . . . However, I can only *characterize this grant proposal as "FUZZY."*

INVESTIGATOR: . . . , M.D., . . . School of Medicine, 19 . . . , is currently instructor of . . . at School of Medicine in . . . He has an *appreciable*

---

* It should be kept in mind that at the time of this review the grant application format was different from the currently used format.

bibliography but a number of the entries are abstracts or talks presented at meetings. There are **no publications of which he is the sole author.**

RESOURCES AND ENVIRONMENT: These are probably good.

BUDGET: The *budget seems high* for the proposed work and **no justification** is given for any of the budgetary items.

Dr. . . . *is asking . . . for a . . . but in the facilities available he says that he already has a . . . .*

He is asking for a . . . but there is a . . . available.

He is asking for a . . . , but there is *no budget justification* given and it is not clear to me that he couldn't do with the . . . one instead.

I doubt that he needs $ . . . for . . . .

It seems to me that there would be a . . . that he can use until he gets some data.

The *supplies category is awfully high* as well . . . and . . . miscellaneous items should be cut to . . . .

REVIEWER'S RECOMMENDATION: Either approval with a pretty low degree of enthusiasm, or disapproval???

Example H

Summary statement for a grant proposal that was disapproved.

SUMMARY STATEMENT

Requested Start Date: 1981

Recommendation: DISAPPROVAL

Special Note: HUMAN SUBJECTS-PROTECTION ADEQUATE

RESUME: Continued support is requested to . . . . *The proposal's technical aspirations constitute both its strength and its weakness.* The method of . . . would provide some technical improvements over the more conventional techniques of . . . . However, it is *not apparent that the increased technical sophistication would be justified by the theoretical importance* of the proposed experiments. *Nor is it likely, based on past performance of Dr. . . . (the Principal Investigator), that these experiments would reach fruition.* Disapproval is recommended.

CRITIQUE: The salient feature of the proposed *experiments* is that they are *technically difficult and sophisticated* . . . . Dr. . . . claims that the accuracy of this technique would be . . . . However ingenious this technique of . . . might be, *it would surely take a long time to achieve* prior to the . . . of . . . useful data. However, the technical sophistication of the . . . technique is the only feature of this proposal *which distinguishes it from previously reported investigations* on the effect of . . . on the activity of . . . .

Based on past performance, it is unlikely that Dr. . . . would bring these experiments to a successful conclusion. It is a regrettable but sobering fact that **since 1971 Dr. . . . has appeared as the senior author on only one non-technical, refereed, full-length paper, and this paper was unrelated to any of the proposed experiments.** In previous reviews, Dr. . . . was forewarned concerning his *lack of productivity;* most recently in 1978. Since that warning, one abstract . . . has been produced in collaboration with Dr. . . . , who spent two years with Dr. . . . as a postdoctoral fellow working on the problem of . . . .

A preliminary manuscript received late in the review period did little to assure the reviewers that any of the proposed experiments can be successfully carried out by the Principal Investigator. The sample . . . furnished with this manuscript show that at least . . . can be measured with more than adequate accuracy with the . . . , but . . . are another problem. There is an apparent . . . artifact. Even worse, *the investigator shows a total lack of seasoned judgment* in correlating . . . data with . . . . We are told that this . . . but no . . . is given . . . . A check made in the . . . during . . . would be appropriate. *There is no indication that this investigator has even thought about this procedure.* Even worse we are told that past interpretations of . . . are incorrect, all based on apparently one . . . .

INVESTIGATORS: Dr. . . . is currently a . . . . After completing his doctoral dissertation at . . . , he took a postdoctoral fellowship with Dr. . . . at the University . . . . In 19.., he moved to his present institution. His work during the past nine years has been characterized by a range of interests: investigations of . . . . *His publication record has probably suffered as a consequence of his technical and multifaceted interests.*

Examples I, J, and K

On the following pages are three consecutive summary statements received by the same investigator. This investigator was a mature researcher who, however, had never been a Principal Investigator and was also entering a new field of study. All three requests were funded.

Example I

SUMMARY STATEMENT
(Privileged Communication)

Application Number: 1 . . . R23. . . . ..C1
Dual Review: . . .

Review Group: . . . STUDY SECTION

Meeting Date: FEB/MARCH 1979

Investigator: . . .   Degree: Ph.D.

Position:

Organization: . . .

City, State: . . .   Request Start Date: 09/01/79

Project Title: Biochemical Aspects of . . .

Recommendation: Approval   Priority Score: 185

Special Note: Norm Score: 209

No Human Subjects
No Recombinant DNA Research Involved

Project Year	Direct Costs Requested	Direct Costs Recommended	Previously Recommended	Grant Period
01	10,000	10,000		
02	10,000	10,000		
03	10,000	10,000		

RESUME: A well qualified and experienced biochemist *requests modest funds* to investigate the processes involved in . . . . This is a *significant and worthwhile project* that merits enthusiastic support. Approval is recommended for the time and amount requested. However, it *should be conveyed to the investigator that this application, or an expanded version of it, is sufficiently ambitious and wide- ranging to merit full support at a level commensurate with a regular research grant application.*

DESCRIPTION: The overall purpose of the proposed research is the investigation of factors that are involved . . . .

Laboratory Animals: . . . .

CRITIQUE: Experiments described by the principal investigator are *very ambitious in range.* Several studies involve the use of developing . . . as a means of correlating a particular property with the appearance of . . . : 1. Histological studies will be done to determine . . . . 2. . . . activity will be monitored so as to follow . . . . In addition, . . . will be evaluated. 3. . . . incorporation will be followed with the hope of isolating a specific . . . . The first two sets of experiments should be relatively straightforward, whereas the third one requires the ability to isolate . . . .

A particularly strong point for this application is the documentation of a number of preliminary results. **These appear to be *of good quality.*** For example, one group of results concern . . . studies on . . . . Dr. . . . has measured . . . . Dr. . . . believes that this may be related to a requirement for . . . .

Dr. . . . has also begun an examination of . . . . The . . . preparation was obtained by . . . . Primary fractionation on . . . showed a number of . . . bands. The pattern was completely different from those of . . . . Dr. . . . *appears to be aware of the problem* that . . . . However, he has omitted the . . . steps and modified the technique in other ways so that apparently the . . . appears to be good by . . . .

In summary, this is a very *ambitious application that is* **backed up by promising preliminary results.** The *proposed work is directed to a significant area of . . . research.* The principal investigator is *well trained* to carry out many of the areas of research proposed.

INVESTIGATOR: Dr. . . . received his Ph.D. in . . . in 19.. from . . . University where he worked with Dr. . . . on . . . . He took two postdoctorals, one between 19.. and 19.. with Dr. . . . . The second, . . . between 19.. and 19.. with Dr. . . . , where his work was on . . . . He then went to . . . University between 19.. and 19.. where he carried out studies on . . . . Between 19.. and 19.. he was a . . . in the laboratory of Dr. . . . at . . . where his work was mainly on the . . . . In 19.., he joined the . . . as an . . . where he is carrying out research on . . . as well as . . . studies. He also holds a position of . . . at . . . .

RESOURCES AND ENVIRONMENT: These appear to be *adequate* for the proposed research.

BUDGET: At $10,000 per year, the maximum for an R23 Award, the *budget is very reasonable.*

Example J

SUMMARY STATEMENT
(Privileged Communication)

Application Number: 1 R01 . . . -01
Dual Review: . . .

Review Group: . . . Review Group

Meeting Date: FEB/MARCH 1982

Investigator: . . .   Degree: Ph.D.

Position:

Organization: . . .

City, State: . . .   Request Start Date: 09/01/82

Project Title: . . .

Recommendation: Approval   Priority Score: 169

Special Note:
No Human Subjects

Project Year	Direct Costs Requested	Direct Costs Recommended	Previously Recommended	Grant Period
01	76,907	76,907		
02	82,300	82,300		
03	90,510	90,510		

RESUME: Dr. . . . has proposed studies whose goals are the characterization of the components and their functions of the . . . . *Several components of these studies seem desirable.* These include characterization of the . . . , determination of the presence of . . . , and a cross comparison to determine differences in . . . distribution in different . . . . Approval is recommended for time and budget with *high enthusiasm.*

DESCRIPTION: The . . . is the . . . .

The investigators have already shown that . . . .

One project is to determine whether . . . .

Additional aims are to study . . . .

Laboratory animals: . . . .

CRITIQUE: This is a **carefully organized research plan that follows logically from extensive preliminary data** collected by the principal investigator. The project is a very important one, for little information is now available on the paths for transfer of material between . . . and the functions of the . . . . The proposal includes both *projects which will undoubtedly succeed* and provide important information, such as the . . . and more speculative projects on the functions of . . . . However, the *more speculative projects are based on* **substantial preliminary data** and are worth pursuing.

A *major potential problem* in this research, the *contamination of material from . . . , is serious.* **The principal investigator is fully aware of such criticism and has diligently attempted to deal with it. This is a major strength in the proposal.** Nonetheless, *questions remain.* In particular, the separation . . . may require further analysis. The *principal investigator might be encouraged,* in so far as possible, to carry out . . . analysis on the material obtained by the . . . procedure of . . . . The alternative mode of preparation of . . . is an important complementary method. This should ensure more complete . . . .

INVESTIGATOR: Dr. . . . received his Ph.D. from . . . University in . . . in 19.. . He did postdoctoral work with Dr. . . . at . . . and spent . . . years at . . . with Dr. . . . . Dr. . . . was a . . . with . . . at . . . University from 19.. to 19.. . His training ranges from . . . to . . . . Dr. . . . has been an . . . at . . . since 19.. . The principal investigator is *very well trained* in . . . techniques and is *well able to carry out the proposed experiments.*

RESOURCES AND ENVIRONMENT: Equipment and Laboratory *facilities are very adequate* for the proposed research and the **scientific environment is excellent.**

BUDGET: The budget is appropriate for the proposed research.

Example K

SUMMARY STATEMENT
(Privileged Communication)

Application Number: 2 R01 . . . -04
Dual Review: . . .

Review Group: . . . Review Group

Meeting Date: FEB/MARCH 1985

Investigator: . . .   Degree: Ph.D.

Organization: . . .

City, State: . . .   Request Start Date: 09/01/85

Project Title: . . .

Recommendation: Approval   Priority Score: 149

Human Subjects: 10-No Human Subjects Involved

Animal Subjects: 30-Animals Involved—No IRG Comments or concerns
noted

Project Year	Direct Costs Requested	Direct Costs Recommended
04	97,404	97,404
05	115,138	115,138
06	122,840	122,840
07	134,350	134,350
08	144,015	144,015

OUTSIDE OPINION:

RESUME: An experienced research worker requests five years of support to extend his studies on the . . . . The *investigator has pioneered work in this area and has made significant contributions to its development.* He proposes to extend studies on the structure and function of the . . . and to determine . . . . These studies may assist in understanding the nature of . . . . Approval is recommended in time and amount.

DESCRIPTION: The . . . in normal . . . .

Animals: . . . .

CRITIQUE: Because the functions of . . . depend on a supply of . . . , it is important to understand how the . . . works. It is logical to assume that the . . . . *The present proposal is important* because so little is known about the chemical composition and functions of the . . . . Dr. . . . has previously analyzed . . . and characterized some of the . . . .

Of various . . . , the investigator is particularly interested in . . . . His main interest lies in the elucidation of the role of . . . . *Experiments are designed to answer several key questions* such as: Can . . . ? Can . . . ? Does . . . ? Can . . . ? Affirmative answers to these questions are necessary but not sufficient to establish that . . . plays a role in . . . . In addition to the *in vitro* experiments, *in vivo* experiments are essential in which . . . of the . . . is quantitatively determined at . . . . In view of the *research capacity* of Dr. . . . 's laboratory, this project alone would take all his time and efforts. *Overcommitment to diversified problems as stated may not be rewarding in the long run.* His *publication record and progress report* indicate that his expertise and background are strong in . . . . The *investigator is therefore encouraged to emphasize* in his approach quantitative aspects of . . . .

The investigator seeks to extend his studies of . . . to determine if it can . . . . Mimicking the . . . found adjacent to . . . would appear important for this experiment. The investigator also seeks to determine whether . . . may participate in a . . . . Drs. . . . and . . . have postulated . . . . The investigator should note that this is a quantitatively rare process as measured by Drs. . . . and . . . and *could not expect to be detected by his proposed procedures.* In addition, based upon . . . *it is difficult to imagine how . . . could successfully* . . . . The *investigator is encouraged to scrutinize his preliminary data with these considerations in mind.*

The investigator will further pursue . . . . The use of . . . methods is proposed in order to preserve . . . . *However, this method may not remove all traces of . . . whose presence could complicate interpretation of the results. Validity of the measurements will depend upon demonstration that such interference is not present.*

The investigator proposes to investigate whether . . . can be . . . . It will be necessary to prepare each of the . . . , and the *investigator proposes trying new procedures* rather than reproducing the lengthy conventional ones. *For the sake of efficiency it would nevertheless seem more reasonable to use the worked out published procedures rather than to develop totally new ones for such restricted purposes—purposes which are also somewhat peripheral to the stated central objectives of the research.*

It is proposed to evaluate the mechanism of . . . . The . . . *approaches outlined seem straightforward in approach and well designed to elicit the information desired.* It is with the . . . and . . . approaches that *some caution is due.* At least *four other laboratories* and their collaborators seem to be *uniquely capable* in performing studies involving these skills. The **investigator would be well advised to concentrate on those areas to which he can make some unique contributions.**

. . . is suggested to have . . . . The investigator proposes to further study its . . . properties by . . . measurements and by . . . followed by . . . . Hopefully, this will help in understanding how its . . . is important in its . . . properties. The determination of . . . is proposed via use of . . . . *The investigator presents the theory behind the approach but* **does not appear to be familiar with analogous work which has been published** *on the . . . [J. . . . (19..)]. The . . . chemistry is far from trivial and is not undertaken lightly.* Considerable experience in . . . , the . . . desired by the investigator has been obtained by the laboratory of . . . , and by that of . . . . *These investigators may help the applicant evaluate* what kind of commitment would be involved in cost and time of . . . and in amounts of . . . required.

The search for . . . represents a *fruitful approach* to understanding the functions of the . . . . This is an area pioneered by the investigator and which is worthy of renewed attention. The investigator proposes the use of novel . . . in order to definitively . . . .

The origins of the . . . will be sought using . . . . *This would appear to be a difficult problem* to undertake, although the choice of animal seems reasonable based upon techniques available for dealing with the . . . . This is to be coupled with investigation of the . . . . *Either of these two topics would be sufficiently broad and open-ended to warrant full-scale multi-year studies in themselves. The investigator will certainly need to ask pointed questions and focus narrowly on principal vs. peripheral objectives.*

It is of interest to extend these studies to models of . . . , and the investigator proposed use of the . . . . *However, at the 1984 . . . meeting, the validity of this model was questioned. The investigator may wish to restrict these studies to the better developed models.*

INVESTIGATOR: Dr. . . . received his B.A. in . . . from . . . College, and his Ph.D. in . . . at . . . . He received postdoctoral *training in several fine laboratories* and was . . . at . . . from 19..-19.. . Since that time he has been . . . at . . . . *During the last grant period he has published 10 papers with 2 more in press and another submitted for publication.*

RESOURCES AND ENVIRONMENT: These are adequate for performance of the research proposal.

BUDGET: The proposed *budget is reasonable and justified.* Approval is recommended in time and amount.

Examples L and M

Example L is the Summary Statement for a proposal that was approved but *not* funded. It is followed by Example M, the Summary Statement for the *same* investigator's revised proposal which *was* funded. Note the change in priority score, percentile rank and recommended funding.

Example L

SUMMARY STATEMENT
(Privileged Communication)

Application Number: 2 R01 . . . -07
Dual Review:

Review Group: . . . Study Section

Meeting Date: OCT/NOV 1984

Investigator: . . .   Degree: Ph.D.

Organization: . . .

City, State: . . .   Request Start Date: 06/01/85

Project Title: . . .

Recommended: Approval   Priority Score: 160

Percentile: 40.4

Human Subjects: 10-No Human Subjects Involved

Animal Subjects: 10-No Live Vertebrate Animals Involved

Project Year	Direct Costs Requested	Direct Costs Recommended
07	141,687	117,417
08	145,811	124,391
09	155,905	134,485
10	166,707	0
11	178,264	0

ADMINISTRATIVE NOTE

RESUME: Dr. . . . 's *interesting and productive studies* on the . . . will be related to the . . . . Future results *may be expected to generate information on key steps* in the regulation of . . . , *but the newer directions of research have only been briefly described.* Dr. . . . *is highly qualified* to pursue these studies. To facilitate an early review of the detailed plans for new departures, support is recommended for only three years at this time.

DESCRIPTION: The regulation of . . . .

CRITIQUE: This is a **well written, carefully documented proposal** to continue a productive line of research on an **important subject:** the physical basis of . . . in the . . . of . . . . This *research promises to continue to make important progress* in the understanding of . . . in systems containing . . . . This application proposes to extend this study to another similar . . . , and the *prospects for success appear good.* This is **very timely research,** since previous models for . . . have recently been questioned, resulting in increased attention to possible changes in these . . . .

Dr. . . . has been a leader in the study of . . . for the past ten years and **progress in the current period was excellent, resulting in nine papers in refereed journals of high quality.** Previous studies were about evenly divided between studies of . . . and studies of . . . in . . . , and the proposed work shifts more emphasis toward the . . . studies and toward studies of . . . .

Most of the . . . analysis will be done with . . . previously characterized by Dr. . . . . These *experiments are well designed,* and Dr. . . . *discusses clearly* the need to distinguish between changes in . . . and changes in the . . . properties of . . . . *Nevertheless, it remains a difficult problem that cannot always be solved, and inevitably results in some ambiguity in data interpretation.* The *problem of the role of . . . in . . . requires a more global view* of the various . . . . Dr. . . . intends to put together all of the . . . , but the parameter monitored will in most cases be *restricted to . . . .*

A *universal concern* in . . . studies is . . . . Dr. . . . states that this can be an advantage, but **his arguments are not convincing.** Comparisons with . . . data will help, but . . . is a very gross measure containing contributions over all the . . . .

The project increases the emphasis on . . . measurements to provide . . . information to complement the . . . measurements. This should help provide a more complete picture of the . . . interactions in this system.

In general, it remains to be seen whether . . . are important in . . . , so that the proposed increased emphasis on . . . is important.

Proposed studies on . . . are only briefly sketched, but the *collaboration with Dr. . . . looks promising.* Similarly, the . . . studies in *collaboration with Dr. . . . should continue to be interesting.* Proposed studies are similar to those on . . . , although these are at a much earlier stage. *This part of the project has become much more interesting recently,* in light of evidence obtained from others that suggest the importance of . . . . The importance of . . . was recently described, but *the proposed new work is only briefly alluded to.*

INVESTIGATORS: Dr. . . . obtained his Ph.D. in . . . from the University of . . . in 19.., did postdoctoral work with . . . at . . . University from 19.. to 19.. and then joined the Department of . . . at . . . , where he is now a . . . . He has an **impressive publication record** in the field of . . . , particularly in the study of . . . . **No one is better qualified than he to carry out the proposed research.**

Dr. . . . , Research Associate, obtained his Ph.D. in . . . recently from . . . University. During the past year he has worked directly with Dr. . . . on . . . .

BUDGET: The request is one-third higher than the current award; *addition of another staff person is difficult to justify,* and therefore funds for a research assistant ($ . . .) may be *omitted.* The *price of the . . . appears high—*$X,000 should prove adequate. Other categories are appropriate. The **new directions of this project are not described in sufficient detail, and therefore support should be limited to three years at this time.**

ADMINISTRATIVE NOTE: **A parallel application is pending** before the . . . program of the NSF (# . . .).

Example M

Example M is the Summary Statement for the revised proposal written in response to the Summary Statement given in Example L.

SUMMARY STATEMENT
(Privileged Communication)

Application Number: 2 R01 . . . -07A1
Dual:

Review Group: . . . Study Section

Meeting Date: June 1985

Investigator: . . .   Degree: Ph.D.

Organization: . . .

City, State: . . .   Request Start Date: 12/01/85

Project Title: . . .

Recommended: Approval   Priority Score: 131

Percentile: 9.3

Human Subjects: 10-No Human Subjects Involved

Animal Subjects: 10-No Live Vertebrate Animals Involved

Project Year	Direct Costs Requested	Direct Costs Recommended
07A1	146,310	146,310
08	154,762	154,762
09	166,806	166,806
10	179,814	179,814
11	193,863	193,863

ADMINISTRATIVE NOTE:

RESUME: Dr. . . . , *a leader in the study of* . . . , **has been highly productive** of important contributions. The work will be extended to . . . . The **work is sound and innovative,** *and the* **results have broad implications for** . . . . *Continued support is enthusiastically endorsed.*

DESCRIPTION: This is a revised continuation application. The previous version was highly recommended for approval last fall but it was not supported. The . . . .

CRITIQUE: Dr. . . . **has quite successfully dealt with the earlier questions in the review.** *New data are cited* in the application and provided in additional manuscripts *to show that* . . . *is capable of* . . . . The evidence also indicates that . . . . Dr. . . . also plans to . . . , to provide a second . . . . This strategy will require the difficult use of the . . . which consists of . . . . In any investigation which requires the use of . . . , the question of . . . introduced by . . . always arises. Dr. . . . **is keenly aware of potential pitfalls, and is prepared to deal with them.** A subtle . . . is introduced . . . ; this . . . has been well characterized. It is this . . . that leads to . . . . Other new data show that the loss of . . . is related to . . . . This . . . is related to the extent of . . . . *The arguments are convincing that the* . . . *are indeed advantageous.*

Previous studies carried out by Dr. . . . and collaborators have *yielded a powerful and clever approach* to investigate the . . . . This is based on the unique . . . . Dr. . . . *has had remarkable success* in exploiting the . . . that take place . . . . **Ten full papers have been published in refereed journals for work that was carried out in the last three years. Two additional manuscripts are listed as pending. This is a very productive record. The quality of the papers is generally high.**

The present proposal describes *a* **sharply focused research** direction and shows a **well planned** and **carefully thought out project.** Studies currently underway in Dr. . . . 's laboratory have emphasized . . . , but with a leaning toward . . . . The proposed work will have a heavy emphasis on correlation of . . . studies with . . . . This *shift of emphasis is both timely and well justified* because sufficient knowledge is now on hand about the behavior of . . . .

Evidence is accumulating to suggest that . . . . The proposed involvement of . . . is likely to be valid, but its precise roles remains to be elucidated.

How well the . . . of . . . that was first demonstrated by the applicant, and has since been extensively investigated by him, would fit into the overall scheme *remains to be seen. It is likely that some very interesting information will be forthcoming* from Dr. . . .'s laboratory.

The proposed *work specifically related to . . . is less well developed, and the potential success in this component is somewhat less certain.*

Some efforts during the next period will be spent on . . . . This *represents a new direction* for Dr. . . . . *This expansion is logical* because . . . . *His collaborator,* Dr. . . . , has expertise in the . . . and *will contribute significantly* to the proposed work in which the . . . methodologies successfully used for . . . will be applied to . . . . *A significant paper has been published from this collaboration* in which . . . .

INVESTIGATORS: Dr. . . . obtained his Ph.D. in . . . from the University of . . . in 19.., did postdoctoral work with . . . at . . . University from 19.. to 19.., and then joined the Department of . . . at . . . , where he is now a . . . . He has an **impressive publication record** in the field of . . . , particularly in the study of . . . . **No one is better qualified than he to carry out the proposed research.**

Dr. . . . , Research Associate, obtained his Ph.D. in . . . recently from . . . University. During the past year he has worked directly with Dr. . . . on . . . .

BUDGET: The request is similar to the previous application but is now **thoroughly justified,** and no changes are needed.

ADMINISTRATIVE NOTE: A **parallel proposal is pending** before *the NSF (# . . .)*

Example N

This is an example of a proposal with a very poor priority score that was not funded.

SUMMARY STATEMENT
(Privileged Communication)

Application Number: 1 R01 ... -01
DUAL REVIEW: ...

Review Group: ... STUDY SECTION

Meeting Date: FEB/MARCH 1987

Investigator: Degree: Ph.D.

Organization: ...

City, State: ...   Requested Start Date: 07/01/87

Project Title: THE ...   OF THE ....

Priority Score: 421

Percentile: 94.6

Recommended : APPROVAL

Human Subjects: 10-NO HUMAN SUBJECTS INVOLVED

Animal Subjects: 30-ANMLS INV.-VERIFIED, NO IRG CONCERNS OR COMMENT

Project Year	Direct Costs Requested	Direct Costs Recommended
01	122,817	88,042
02	130,095	95,320
03	139,313	104,538

RESUME: This . . . study will examine . . . changes in the . . . associated with the disruption of . . . in . . . . *The proposal was found* **conceptually weak.** The **experimental design lacks in precision, and some experiments are seriously flawed.** *Despite these weaknesses,* it was felt that the *study may add some new information* on . . . . Approval with a 'modest reduction in budget was therefore recommended.

DESCRIPTION (**adapted from the investigator's abstract**): The long-term objective of the proposed studies is . . .

CRITIQUE : This is a **well-organized and concisely written** proposal to study . . . changes in the . . . associated with the disruption of . . . in . . . and . . . exposed to . . . . The **proposal addresses an interesting question,** i.e., whether the changes in . . . that are observed in . . . during . . . and can be correlated with . . . . The investigator speculates that the disappearance of . . . may be due to . . . . Since some . . . changes in other . . . have been described in the literature, a closer look at . . . in this respect is justified, and the *study can* thus *contribute to the overall picture of* . . . . Although the proposed *studies would inevitably come short of establishing* the direct causal relationship between . . . and . . . , they *nevertheless may result in interesting observations* which could lead to further exploration of this relationship. The part of the proposal that deals with monitoring . . . represents *a definite strength of the project. These studies have been carefully designed* and will provide a comprehensive picture of the state of the animals in regard to . . . . The **observations will not have much independent value or novelty,** however, since the . . . changes of these parameters *have been extensively studied.* Nevertheless, the significance of this part of the proposal is in relationship to . . . studies that will be performed on the same animals.

Another major strength of the proposed research is that the . . . analyses will be performed in animals with clearly defined and monitored deficits. The . . . analyses are relatively simple and take advantage of computerized . . . programs which are described in detail. *Most of the proposed techniques are feasible and capable of yielding the desired descriptive information.* The investigator is a *well-trained* . . . with experiences in both . . . and . . . techniques. *However, he has had only limited experience in* . . . . Dr. . . . , co-investigator, is an experienced . . . and appears to be *fully competent* to carry out the . . . experiments and . . . .

The project has also a number of weaknesses. The described studies represent *a* **data-gathering search with no underlying hypotheses**

and *little explanation of how the collected data will be interpreted.* Furthermore, there are **no preliminary results** suggesting that . . . may occur. *In the absence of such preliminary data, the **entire project may be a futile search*** which will yield little, if any, new information since most of the . . . aspects of the . . . have already been described in . . . . There are *several serious concerns* in regard to the . . . part of the proposal. This part **lacks essential details** and therefore *in several instances, one **could only guess what exactly is planned to be studied.*** For example, it was *not clear how* . . . in experiment B under Specific Aim 1 are possible from . . . that will be taken at regular intervals. It appears that the *resolution achieved with such a technique is not sufficient to identify* the location and concrete boundaries of . . . . It *is not clear* then how the comparisons of . . . and . . . are possible with this technique. In experiment C under Specific Aim 1, number and size of . . . will be determined in three unspecified . . . . *What happens if . . . is found? What exactly will be measured and how? How will the individual . . . be identified?* There is *no description* of these aspects. All this leaves an **impression that very little thought has been given to experimental design.**

There are also *flaws in the design of specific experiments.* Experiment D includes . . . analysis where the investigator plans to study distribution of . . . and examine the possibility of . . . of different . . . . As stated, there is *no indication that the investigator has prior experience with . . .* and *whether any of these procedures have already been established in his laboratory. Controls, . . . , possible problems* that can be encountered in . . . , or even the *exact organization* of these experiments are *not discussed, nor are the probable outcome and interpretation of results.* A *similar criticism* applies to . . . , which is *only mentioned briefly.* Further, experiments combining . . . and . . . *cannot be successfully completed using the described procedures.* The purpose of these experiments is to identify . . . . The . . . giving rise to the particular . . . will be identified by . . . . The . . . *are not described.* It *is probably not possible* to . . . . Moreover, it is *not discussed how* the . . . sites *will be controlled, which is of crucial importance* in . . . with its closely situated . . . and functionally diverse . . . . *No other . . . experiments have been planned.* Therefore, it is *not clear how the goal of this part of the project will be achieved.* In another set of studies the . . . investigator plans to . . . . *No details of these experiments are given.* It is mentioned, however, that all results will be . . . using a computer . . . . The . . . demonstration of the . . . content within each of these . . . *will also be impossible to obtain from these experiments since the . . . used is not compatible with . . . .* This will be done on normal . . . and, as could be guessed, will involve description of . . . and probably some kind of measurement. *What exactly will be achieved in this study and how the results can be related to those in other parts of the proposal is not discussed.* The final part of the proposal involves . . . with *unidentified goals, unspecified* . . . and . . . .

In summary, *the* **proposal is incomplete.** The **essential details are omitted both with regard to the methodology and with respect to how results are to be interpreted.** Moreover, the *proposal is conceptually weak, lacks focus, and logical design of experiments is nonexistent.* Some of the *techniques proposed appear inadequate to achieve the specific aims.* The outcome of other experiments, i.e., . . . , can be *compromised by the lack of experience of the investigator in this methodology.*

INVESTIGATORS : . . . is Associate Professor of . . . in the Department of . . . at . . . Medical School. He received a Ph.D. in . . . from . . . in 19.. . *He published 20 original papers and 6 chapters.* He *has been involved for years in cooperative studies with* Dr. . . . on . . . .

Dr. . . . is a Research Associate in the . . . at . . . Medical School. He received a Ph.D. in . . . from the University of . . . . He *has co-authored 6 papers and 1 book chapter.*

BUDGET: Appears somewhat excessive. Dr. . . . 's involvement in the project can be reduced to 50% ($1X,XXX) and the research assistant can be *deleted* ($1X,XXX). Supplies can be *reduced* by $4XXX .

Example O

This is the Summary Statement for a proposal that was funded at its third submission. This third submission was revised using the advice set forth in a workshop given by the author of this book—advice that is, to a large extent, set forth in the present edition of this book.

SUMMARY STATEMENT
(Privileged Communication)

Application Number: 1 R01 . . . -01A1

Review Group: . . . Study Section

Meeting Date: June 1987

Investigator: . . .   Degree: Ph.D.

Organization: . . .

City, State: . . .   Request Start Date: 12/01/87

Project Title: . . .

Recommended: Approval   Priority Score: 127

Percentile: 3.6

Human Subjects: 10-No Human Subjects Involved

Animal Subjects: 30-ANMLS INV.-VERIFIED, NO IRG CONCERNS OR COMMENT

Project Year	Direct Costs Requested	Direct Costs Recommended
01A1	123,282	123,282
02	127,441	127,441
03	133,324	133,324

RESUME: This is an *excellent proposal* from a **very strong research group.** The research is *highly likely to produce very important data.* The proposal is recommended for approval with *strong enthusiasm.*

DESCRIPTION: (**Adapted from investigator's original abstract.**) This research project deals with the study of . . . .

CRITIQUE: This *amended application* was originally submitted as an R01 application. The next submission was expanded and submitted as a FIRST award application. That application was *reviewed very favorably, but did not have a sufficiently high priority score to receive funding.* At that time there were concerns expressed in the review that the investigator may be too senior for the First award funding mechanisms. In addition, there were some *potential methodological limitation concerns* identified. **This revised application has addressed all of the concerns in the previous review in a satisfactory manner.**

This proposal represents a natural extension of previous studies of this group. The overall goal is to study . . . with special emphasis on dealing with the mechanisms which affect . . . . The proposal *outlines a **logical series of experiments*** dealing with . . . . They will use . . . , a . . . model of . . . . In all cases, . . . will be measured. In addition, . . . will be measured using a . . . .

The research is *highly significant,* in that these will be the first studies measuring . . . and . . . simultaneously. The studies deal with the fundamental mechanisms which govern . . . . The *studies will help to develop a novel . . . for measuring . . .* using a . . . means. These measurements will then be compared with the . . . method for measuring . . . .

The methodology is appropriate for the proposed research and, in fact, **the unique methodology is a strength of the proposal.** A problem of the previous application was that there was concern about several limitations of the proposed methodology. However, the *investigators have added a substantial amount of text indicating that they are well aware of these limitations and do, in fact, have a* **great deal of insight into the ways of solving any potential problems that arise.** It is now clear that the research will *provide a substantial amount of new and important data.*

INVESTIGATORS: Dr. . . . is . . . in . . . at . . . . He obtained his Ph.D. degree in . . . from . . . . Dr. . . . lists *a number of publications in both the . . . and* the . . . *literature.* He is a **well-trained** investigator who is *very likely to successfully accomplish the goals* of the project. Also participating will be Dr. . . . , . . . in . . . . He is a **well known and capable** investigator **in this area of research.** Dr. . . . is a . . . in . . . . He received an M.D. degree from . . . and has been a . . . in this department since . . . . *Other collaborators* include: . . . . These collaborators *add important expertise* to the project. Together, this *investigative team is extremely well qualified* to carry out the proposed research.

BUDGET: The budget is appropriate as requested.

Appendix VI

NIH Information

A. ABBREVIATIONS OF NIH INSTITUTES AND OTHER FUNDING COMPONENTS

CA	NCI	National Cancer Institute
EY	NEI	National Eye Institute
HL	NHLBI	National Heart, Lung and Blood Institute
AG	NIA	National Institute on Aging
*	NIDCD	National Institute of Deafness and Other Communication Disorders
DK	NIDDK	National Institute of Diabetes, and Digestive and Kidney Diseases
AI	NIAID	National Institute of Allergy and Infectious Diseases
HD	NICHD	National Institute of Child Health and Human Development
DE	NIDR	National Institute of Dental Research
ES	NIEHS	National Institute of Environmental Health Sciences
GM	NIGMS	National Institute of General Medical Sciences
NS	NINCDS	National Institute of Neurological and Communicative Disorders and Stroke

AR	*NIAMS*	*National Institute of Arthritis, Musculoskeletal and Skin Diseases*
RR	*DRR*	*Division of Research Resources*
TW	*FIC*	*Fogarty International Center*
LM	*NLM*	*National Library of Medicine*
NR	*NCNR*	*National Center for Nursing Research*

B. OTHER ABBREVIATIONS

DHHS	Department of Health and Human Services
DRG	Division of Research Grants
IRG	Initial Review Group (also called Scientific Review Group)
NIH	National Institutes of Health
NRSA	National Research Service Award (Fellowship)
OD	Office of the Director (of NIH)
OPRR	Office of Protection from Research Risks, OD
ORDA	Office of Recombinant DNA Activities, NIAID
PHS	Public Health Service
RCDA	Research Career Development Award
RFA	Request for Applications (Announcement requesting grant applications for a research area)
RFP	Request for Proposals (Announcement requesting contract proposals for a project)
R-29	The first Independent Research and Transition Award (Also called "First Award." For new investigators. See *NIH*

GUIDE FOR GRANTS AND CONTRACTS 15, #4, March 28, 1986 and *15, #6*, May 23, 1986.)

SBIR   Small Business Innovation Research

SRB   Scientific Review Branch (DRG)

SRG   Scientific Review Group (Performs initial scientific merit review of grant applications and contract proposals—called Initial Review Group (or Study Section) when pertaining to grant applications)

C. DRG STUDY SECTIONS

Note that many Study Sections have subcommittees; thus, there are many more operative Study Sections than those listed below.

STUDY SECTION	CODE
Adolescent Family Life	*(AFL)*
Allergy and Immunology	*(ALY)*
Bacteriology and Mycology	*(BM)*
Behavioral and Neuroscience-Fellowships	*(BNS)*
Behavioral Medicine	*(BEM)*
Biochemical Endocrinology	*(BCE)*
Biochemistry	*(BIO)*
Biomedical Sciences-Fellowships	*(BI)*
Bio-Organic and Natural Products Chemistry	*(BNP)*
Biophysical Chemistry	*(BBCB)*
Bio-Psychology	*(BPO)*

Cardiovascular and Pulmonary	*(CVA)*
Cardiovascular and Renal	*(CVB)*
Cellular Biology and Physiology	*(CBY)*
Chemical Pathology	*(CPA)*
Clinical Sciences-Fellowships	*(CLN)*
Diagnostic Radiology	*(RNM)*
Endocrinology	*(END)*
Epidemiology and Disease Control	*(EDC)*
Experimental Cardiovascular Sciences	*(ECS)*
Experimental Immunology	*(EI)*
Experimental Therapeutics	*(ET)*
Experimental Virology	*(EVR)*
General Medicine A	*(GMA)*
General Medicine B	*(GMB)*
Genetics	*(GEN)*
Hearing Research	*(HAR)*
Hematology	*(HEM)*
Human Development and Aging	*(HUD)*
Human Embryology and Development	*(HED)*
Immunobiology	*(IMB)*
Immunological Sciences	*(IMS)*

Mammalian Genetics	*(MGN)*
Medicinal Chemistry	*(MCHA)*
Metabolic Pathology	*(MEP)*
Metabolism	*(MET)*
Metallobiochemistry	*(BMT)*
Microbial Physiology and Genetics	*(MBC)*
Molecular and Cellular Biophysics	*(BBCA)*
Molecular Biology	*(MBY)*
Molecular Cytology	*(CTY)*
Neurological Sciences	*(NLS)*
Neurology A	*(NEUA)*
Neurology B	*(NEUB)*
Neurology C	*(NEUC)*
Nursing Research	*(NURS)*
Nutrition	*(NTN)*
Oral Biology and Medicine	*(OBM)*
Orthopedics and Musculoskeletal	*(ORTH)*
Pathobiochemistry	*(PBC)*
Pathology A	*(PTHA)*
Pathology B	*(PTHB)*
Pharmacology	*(PHRA)*

Physical Biochemistry	*(PB)*
Physiological Chemistry	*(PC)*
Physiology	*(PHY)*
Radiation	*(RAD)*
Reproductive Biology	*(REB)*
Reproductive Endocrinology	*(REN)*
Respiratory and Applied Physiology	*(RAP)*
Safety and Occupational Health	*(SOH)*
Sensory Disorders and Language	*(CMS)*
Social Sciences and Population	*(SSP)*
Special Programs	*(SSS)*
Surgery and Bioengineering	*(SB)*
Surgery, Anesthesiology, and Trauma	*(SAT)*
Toxicology	*(TOX)*
Tropical Medicine and Parasitology	*(TMP)*
Virology	*(VR)*
Visual Sciences A	*(VISA)*
Visual Sciences B	*(VISB)*

D. SPECIFIC SOURCES OF NIH INFORMATION

1. *Research Grants Policy*

    - Dr. Kathryn Bick, Deputy Director for Extramural Research and Training, Office of the Director, (301) 496–1096
    - Dr. George Galasso, Associate Director for Extramural Affairs, Office of the Director, (301) 496–5356
    - Mr. Jeff Grant, Grants Policy Officer, Office of the Director, (301) 496–5967
    - Dr. William H. Goldwater, NIH Extramural Programs Management Officer, (301) 496–2241
    - Dr. Samuel H. Joseloff, Chief, Office of Grants Inquiries, Division of Research Grants, (301) 496–7441

2. *Research Training Policy*

    - Dr. William Pitlick, Research Training and Research Resources Officer, Office of the Director, (301) 496–9748

3. *Receipt and Assignment of Applications*

    (Referral Section, Referral and Review Branch, Division of Research Grants)

    - Dr. Patricia Straat, Chief, (301) 496–7447
    - Dr. Julius Currie, Assistant Chief, (301) 496–7447
    - Dr Eugene Zebovitz, Assistant Chief, (301) 496–7447
    - Dr. Julius Currie, Assistant Chief, (301) 496–7447
    - Ms. Jean Malcolm, Head, Project Control, (301) 496–7324

4. *Scientific Merit Review of Applications*

    a) *Division of Research Grants*

    - Dr. Jerome Green, Director, (301) 496–7461
    - Dr. Donald H. Luecke, Deputy Director, (301) 496–7461
    - Dr. Anthony Demsey, Associate Director for Referral and Review, (301) 495–7023
    - Dr. Faye Calhoun, Deputy Chief for Review, Referral and Review Branch, (301) 496–7023
    - Appropriate Section Chief, Executive Secretary, or Grants Technical Assistant

b) *Awarding Bureau, Institute*

- Associate Directors for Extramural Programs (or Equivalent Positions)

  —Ms. Barbara Bynum, National Cancer Institute, (301) 496–5147
  —Dr. Frances A. Pitlick, National Heart, Lung, and Blood Institute, (301) 496–7416
  —Dr. Walter Stolz, National Institute of Arthritis, Diabetes, and Digestive and Kidney Diseases, (301) 496–7277
  —Mr. Arthur Broering (acting), National Library of Medicine, (301) 496–4621
  —Dr. Miriam Kelty, National Institute on Aging, (301) 496–9374
  —Dr. John Diggs, National Institute of Allergy and Infectious Diseases (301) 496–7291
  —Dr. Steven Hausman, National Institute of Arthritis and Musculoskeletal and Skin Diseases (301) 496–7495
  —Dr. Antonia C. Novello, National Institute of Child Health and Human Development, (301) 496–1848
  —Dr. Marie U. Nylen, National Institute of Dental Research, (301) 496–7723
  —Dr. Anne Sassaman, National Institute of Environmental Health Sciences, (919) 541–7723
  —Dr. Jack A. McLaughlin, National Eye Institute, (301) 496–5983
  —Dr. Elke Jordan, National Institute of General Medical Sciences, (301) 496–7061
  —Dr. John Dalton, National Institute of Neurological and Communicative Disorders and Stroke, (301) 496–9248
  —Dr. James O'Donnell, Division of Research Resources, (301) 496–6023
  —Dr. Bettie Graham, Fogarty International Center, (301) 496–6688
  —Dr. Janet Heinrich, National Center for Nursing Research, (301) 496–0526

- Appropriate Executive Secretary, Program Staff Member, Grants Management Officer, or Grants Technical Assistant

5. *General Information*

  a) *Research Involving Human Subjects or Animals*

  - Dr. Charles McCarthy, Director, Office for Protection from Research Risks, (301) 496–7005

- Dr. Charles MacKay, Deputy Director, Office for Protection from Research Risks, (301) 496–7005

b) *Privacy Act*

- *Ms. Barbara E. Bullman, NIH Privacy Act Officer, (301) 496–2832*
- *Appropriate NIH Component Privacy Act Coordinator*

c) *Freedom of Information Act*

- *Ms. Joanne Belk, NIH Freedom of Information Act Officer, (301) 496–5633*
- *Appropriate NIH Component Freedom of Information Act Coordinator*

d) *Public Information*

- *Mr. Storm Whaley, Associate Director for Communication, Office of the Director, (301) 496–4461*
- *Ms. Anne Thomas, Director, Division of Public Information, Office of the Director (301) 496–5787*

e) *Publications and Single Copies of Application Kits*

- *Dr. Samuel H. Joseloff, Chief, Office of Grants Inquiries, Division of Research Grants, (301) 496–7441*

6. *Information about Small Business Innovation Research (SBIR)*

a) *SBIR Program*

- Ms. Lily O. Engstrom, SBIR Program Coordinator, National Institutes of Health, Bldg. 31, Room 1B54, Bethesda, MD 20892; (301) 496–1968.

b) *Review of SBIR Grant Applications*

- Dr. Jeanne Kettley, Special Review Section, Division of Research Grants, NIH, Westwood Bldg., Room 2A16; (301) 496–7558.

E. *NIH: AN AGENCY OF THE PUBLIC HEALTH SERVICE*

The Public Health Service (PHS) is part of the Department of Health and Human Services (DHHS).

DHHS; (202) 245–6296.

Public Health Service (PHS), Rm. 725H, HHH Bldg., 200 Independence Ave. SW, Washington, D. C. 20201; (301) 443–2403.

Public Health Service, Office of Communications; (202) 245–6867.

The Public Health Service has 7 agencies. They are

- Agency for Toxic Substances and Disease Registry (ATSDR); (404) 488–4590.
- Alcohol, Drug Abuse and Mental Health Administration (ADAMHA); (301) 443–3783.
- Center for Disease Control (CDC); (404) 639–3286.
- Food and Drug Administration (FDA); (301) 443–4177.
- Health Resources and Services Administration; (301) 443–2086.
- Indian Health Service; (301) 443–1083.
- National Institutes of Health; (301) 496–4461.

Appendix VII

Brief Comments on Proposals Submitted to the National Science Foundation (NSF)

By Bruce Trumbo
Professor of Statistics and Mathematics,
California State University, Hayward

With some revisions for the second edition

By Sherwin S. Lehrer
Senior Staff Scientist
Boston Biomedical Research Institute
and Principal Associate, Department of
Neurology, Harvard Medical School

(Dr. Lehrer was a member of an NSF Review
Panel from 1986 to 1988.)

Almost all of the general principles and many of the specific suggestions in Dr. Reif-Lehrer's manuscript would apply to the writing of an effective proposal for submission to any agency or foundation. Because the National Science Foundation (NSF) is another major source of support for scientific research, the editors have asked me to discuss briefly some respects in which NSF differs from NIH. I have chosen to emphasize two differences that I think have particular impact on the planning and writing of proposals.

DIFFERENCES IN MISSION

The first important difference between NSF and NIH is that Congress has given them different scientific missions. NSF does not make grants for research mainly oriented toward clinical medicine, but does support basic research in almost all scientific fields, such as sociology, physics, biology, economics, psychology, chemistry, mathematics, engineering, and so forth. The foundation also makes grants to support science education but this discussion is restricted to grants made from the Research Directorates.

Some projects involving basic scientific research also have potential clinical applications and so may fall within the missions of both agencies. There is nothing wrong with submitting proposals to both NSF and NIH, as long as each proposal clearly indicates the existence and nature of the other. **You must , of course, re-structure the text to conform to the appropriate format for each agency.** In such cases, each agency gives a separate review to the proposal it receives and cooperates with the other to avoid double funding, or perhaps to arrange joint funding. (If your research may overlap more than one section at NSF, send a single proposal directed to one section and in the cover letter give your suggestions for possible joint review by other sections. The final decision on program assignment is up to NSF.)

PROGRAMS AND PROPOSALS

The NSF booklet, *Grants for Research and Education in Science and Engineering* (revised January, 1987), describes the basic procedures for applying for all general research grants (most of the proposals to NSF and most of the funds granted by NSF fall into this general or nonselected category). Because of the varying patterns of research activity across the broad spectrum of scientific work supported by NSF, however, it is not possible to be as specific about the details of how a proposal is handled at NSF as Dr. Reif-Lehrer has been about NIH. A proposal by a mathematician may involve the principal investigator, one graduate student, and occasional use of a small computer. A proposal by a group of astronomers or high energy physicists may involve detailed administrative considerations and scheduled use of a multimillion dollar facility. Clearly the details of processing and reviewing proposals must differ from section to section within NSF. It is important for writers of proposals to be aware of deadlines and of any special proposal-writing suggestions of the NSF section that handles their area of science. Most NSF sections distribute such information widely, for example, through the NSF Bulletin, in professional journals, to university research offices and to present grantees. A brief phone call or letter to the appropriate NSF section may help to define the relevance of a particular proposal to a particular program, but remember that NSF program officers are not paid to be consultants in grantsmanship.

In addition to general research grants, NSF supports a variety of cooperative international and exchange programs. NSF also establishes special programs from time to time to meet specific needs—support for a conference in an expanding research area or for a particular kind of instrumentation, for example. Other current NSF programs include Research Opportunities for Women, Biological Instrumentation Program, etc. and a number of fellowships.

These programs are announced in brochures that give the details for application. Unfortunately, sometimes the legislative, budgetary, and legal considerations that go into establishing these programs leave little time between formal announcement in a brochure and the deadline for applying. However, the fact that a particular program is under consideration at NSF is generally not a secret from the scientific community it will serve (and which has doubtless been lobbying for it), even though the most specific details are available only in the formal announcement. Moreover, many such programs continue essentially unchanged through several fiscal years. (At a university the spring schedule of classes is not often available the previous summer, but clever students generally find no real surprises in the schedule when it is published.) Thus, the scientist who knows his research needs and capabilities, and who pays some attention to trends of NSF support can often consider in advance the general thrust of possible proposals for special program funds. It is important, however, to read carefully the brochure describing a specific program to determine the purposes for which it has been established, the exact eligibility and contractual requirements, and so forth, before deciding to apply. Far-fetched rationalizations that attempt to squeeze a proposal (however sound scientifically) into an ill-fitting mold waste the time of proposers, reviewers, and program officers alike. Remember also that different agencies have different formats for proposal submission.

For example, NSF tends to be somewhat less formal than NIH in terms of the Research Plan; but the budget pages are prescribed and are different from those of NIH. In addition, NSF likes to cost-share with the grantee institution. Also, at NSF, indirect costs are included in the total award and are not negotiated separately.

DIFFERENCES IN METHODS OF PROPOSAL REVIEW

A second major difference between NSF and NIH is the review process. The use of Initial Review Groups by NIH is described in detail in the main manuscript. NSF uses a variety of review procedures, less uniform than the NIH process with its review groups. Some NSF programs arrange panel meetings of reviewers, typically with the presumption that each panel member has studied the proposals before the panel meeting. Often panel members or other reviewers have submitted written reviews before the panel meets. Thus, the essence of an NSF panel meeting is usually a round table discussion focusing initially on many individual reactions to each proposal, often with the experts in the field summarizing the proposal first. Sometimes panels are asked to rank proposals or to sort them into several categories as to merit, but anything approaching the detailed score-keeping approach used at NIH is rare in an NSF panel meeting. Even when NSF reviewers meet in face to face discussions, their interaction is likely to be structured somewhat more loosely than at an NIH Study Section, with each review panel having its own flavor, set by the Program Director.

Most NSF programs use mail reviews. Typically the program director will initially select several outside reviewers for a proposal, following guidelines to ensure balance. Reviewers are asked to comment on all aspects of the proposal and to rate it as Excellent, Very Good, Good, Fair, or Poor, where each category is carefully defined by NSF in terms of scientific merit, capability of the investigator and the availability of resources. Additional reviews are often sought to reconcile differences in reviewer reaction or to pursue issues raised by the first round of reviewers. Based on the relative merit determined by the panel and/or mail reviews, the panel recommends funding or "declination" of the project. For projects recommended for funding, the Program Director attempts to fund as many proposals as possible with the available funds. Often, the panel recommends a revised, smaller budget, consistent with the requirements of the reviewed project, which may then permit funding of more projects.

Copies of reviewers comments (but not their names) are sent to the principal investigator after final action on the proposal has been taken. These comments can be educational for both successful and unsuccessful applicants.

Because the *initial* impression of each panel reviewer and the *only* impression of a mail reviewer is the solitary one of a fellow scientist reading the proposal, it can be argued that the NSF review system places a heavy responsibility on the proposer to communicate ideas in a clear and organized way and to document the budget adequately. Some

reviewers will be researchers in the same narrow subfield as the proposer and others will be viewing the proposal from some scientific distance.
It is important for proposal writers to give attention both to explaining
exactly what is proposed and to showing its place and importance in the
context of the field as a whole.

This latter point takes on added significance when one reflects upon the
fact that the program director, who cannot possibly be an expert in the
narrow subfield of each proposal he or she handles, selects the reviewers
based largely on information contained in the proposal. Through clear
understanding of the essence and importance of the proposal and a
bibliography that is neither skimpy and loaded nor padded and expan-
sive, the proposer can help to ensure that the first round of reviewers
will provide the balanced body of opinion and evaluation needed for
a prompt and fair decision. In addition, "proposers are invited to suggest names of individuals who, in their opinion, are especially well
qualified to evaluate the proposal objectively." (NSF 83-57, rev. 1/87,
p. 9)

CONCLUSION

These observations are based on personal experience with NSF as (at
different times in the past) applicant, reviewer, and program director.
They have no official status.

One further personal reaction may be in order. I have had a few opportunities to compare the NSF and NIH review processes for essentially
identical proposals. In each of these instances the procedural differences
mentioned here, while important, were of far less practical significance
than the astonishing similarities in results. The same issues were
discussed, the same objections offered, and same strengths noted, the
same budget items questioned, and the same conclusions reached.

The main manuscript begins with the comment that a good proposal
requires, above all else, a good idea. By bad presentation it is possible to
obscure a good idea from reviewers either at NSF or NIH. A routine or
mediocre idea will look no better than routine or mediocre when viewed
through either pair of spectacles.

Appendix VIII

More About National Science Foundation (NSF) Applications

(Including an example of the reviewers' reports for a grant proposal submitted to the NSF)

Note: In this appendix, *Grants For Research and Education in Science and Engineering* (Document: NSF 83–57; Revised 1/87) will be referred to simply as the NSF Instructions.

Where to get information about preparing an NSF application

The NSF grant application form and instructions for preparation and submission of the application are contained in *Grants For Research and Education in Science and Engineering* (Document: NSF 83–57; Revised 1/87. See Appendix XI, Resources).

Copies of the NSF *Grant General Conditions* may be obtained from Forms and Publications, National Science Foundation, Washington, D.C. 20550.

Information about the NSF grant process, proposers, and grantees is available in the NSF *Grant Policy Manual* NSF 77–47 (See Appendix XI, Resources).

Watch for NSF announcements in the *NSF Bulletin* (See Appendix XI, Resources).

Before formal submission of a grant application, you may wish to discuss your proposal with NSF staff by letter, telephone or in person. This is especially important if you are thinking of applying to one of the special programs sponsored by NSF; first talk to NSF staff to determine the purpose, the exact eligibility, any contractual requirements, etc.

Because the scope of projects reviewed by NSF Panels is broader than that of projects reviewed by NIH Review Groups, the details of processing and reviewing proposals differs more from section to section at NSF than at NIH. *Get specific information from the section relevant to your proposal before you begin to write.*

NSF relies much more heavily on written reviews than NIH does. Additional reviewers are often sought to reconcile differences in reviewer reaction or to pursue issues raised by the first round of reviewers.

Call NSF for information: (202) 357–9498. Also see NSF listing in Appendix XI, Resources.

What NSF is looking for

The mission at NSF is to support the most meritorious research, whether basic or applied. NSF is interested in proposals in Science, Engineering, and Science-education. NSF supports basic research in almost all scientific fields: Biology, Chemistry, Economics, Engineering, Mathematics, Physics, Psychology, Sociology, etc. However, NSF will not normally support biomedical research with disease-related goals.

NSF also accepts proposals for specialized equipment (See page 1 of the NSF Instructions, not included in this book.)

Items not supported by NSF are listed on page 1 of the NSF Instructions.

Permissible categories of applicants are described on Page 2 of the NSF Instructions. **Unaffiliated persons *may* apply.**

NSF is interested in the potential of the proposed research to contribute to better understanding or improvement of the quality, distribution, or effectiveness of the Nation's scientific and engineering research, education, and human resource base.

What to submit to NSF

Regular proposals

Regular proposals may be submitted to NSF at any time. However, Panels meet on specific dates, 2 to 3 times/year. You may want to "aim" for one of these meetings (Call the relevant program director). Some NSF programs set target dates or deadlines for submission. Watch the *NSF Bulletin* and other relevant periodicals. (See Appendix XI, Resources.)

Renewal applications

Two ways to apply for renewals of NSF grants

1. "Traditional" Renewal. Like a new grant application + "Results from prior work."

2. "Accomplishment-Based Renewal (ABR)." Project description is replaced by reprints (See page 1, col. 1, item 2 in the NSF Instructions.)

   (This method may **not** be used for consecutive renewals.)

General instructions

Allow **6 months for review and processing** of your application.

A proposal should follow the points in the NSF Instructions insofar as they are applicable.

A *single* copy of NSF Form 1225, Information about principal investigators/project directors (Appendix II in the NSF Instructions) is required.

Form 1225 *must be received* before the proposal is reviewed, but filling in the requested *information is optional.*

- If you don't want to give the information, check in the bottom box of each column.
- Attach Form 1225 on top of the cover page of the copy of your proposal that has the original signatures.
- Notice that your *name does not appear* on this form.

Use the **Cover Sheet** provided in Appendix III, page 18 in the NSF Instructions.

A **table of contents** is required.

The **project summary** should be 200 words or less. (See page 4, col. 1 in the NSF Instructions.) The project summary should be typed or printed on a separate sheet of paper (put your name, social security number, and project title at the top). It follows the Table of Contents in the application.

A **progress report** is required for renewal applications. Assume that the reviewers DO NOT have access to any previously submitted applications or materials.

The NSF **Project Description** is similar to items A, B, and D of section 2, Research Plan of the NIH application.

A **bibliography** is required. Failure to adhere to appropriate standards of attribution and citation in an NSF grant application can result in disqualification of a proposal.

Biographical sketches are required for senior personnel.

Use a copy of Form 1030, Summary Proposal **Budget,** (page 19, Appendix IV in the NSF Instructions) for the budget for each year and also for the **Cumulative Budget.** Thus, for a 3-year proposal, you need 4 copies of the form.

The **Budget Justification** should follow immediately after the Cumulative Budget.

Other support. Use Appendix VI, page 22 in the NSF instructions.

Statement about **residual funds** (if appropriate)

Appendices. Include material about **facilities** and **equipment, special considerations,** and **special information** and **supporting documents.**

You *may* provide a list of names of well-qualified, objective **reviewers** for your proposal.

Appropriate **certifications** are required for human subjects, recombinant DNA, special provisions for research in Greenland or Antarctica, animal care, etc. Most are listed on the application Cover Sheet, Appendix III, page 18 in the NSF Instructions.

Pages should be **numbered at the bottom** and have a 1-inch margin at the top.

Be sure your name, social security number and project title appear on each sheet of the application.

Mailing an NSF proposal

Usually 10 to 20 copies of the completed application are required (See Appendix VIII in the NSF Instructions). Most engineering proposals require 10 copies; science and engineering education proposals require 15 copies.

The *original* signed copy of the proposal should be printed only on one side of each sheet.

Additional copies may be copied double-sided.

Proposals should be **stapled** in the upper left-hand corner, but otherwise unbound.

Reprints, appendices, and other **materials** to be considered with the application **must be attached** (collated) to the individual copies of the proposal. Materials should be assembled in a standard sequence given in the NSF Instructions, page 3, col. 1, last paragraph of What to Submit.

Check your final application against the checklist on page 16, col. 2 (Appendix I) in the NSF Instructions.

Include a **self-addressed, stamped** postcard so that you will get acknowledgement of receipt of your application by NSF.

Send proposals to

Division of Administrative Services
National Science Foundation
Washington, D.C. 20550

If you must mail your proposal in more than 1 package, mark, ON EACH PACKAGE, the total number of packages.

See note about impending changes in procedure for submission of grant applications in main part of this book under "Mailing the Application."

After you mail the Proposal

You should receive an acknowledgement of receipt of your proposal (your postcard) within 10 days.

Subsequently, you will receive the official acknowledgement of receipt which will show the number assigned to your proposal.

Send additional supporting materials if appropriate.

After the review, you will receive copies of all the reviewer reports, excluding the names of the reviewers.

Notification of award is by letter addressed to your organization. You get a copy.

If your application is declined, you may request the reasons for the action from the Program Officer. (See page 10, col. 1, item III in the NSF Instructions for more information about this and about requesting reconsideration of actions.)

Information about extensions and additional support is given on page 13 in the NSF Instructions.

NSF encourages communication between Principal Investigators and Program Officers concerning progress on NSF-supported projects.

Reviewers' Reports for a National Science Foundation (NSF) grant proposal

First Reviewer's Report

This proposal outlines . . . and . . . studies involving . . . and other . . . on . . . with a view to testing an . . . and a . . . model. The investigator favors the . . . model and the proposed studies are to be carried out with heavy emphasis on a previously proposed model (ref. . . . of the bibliography.)

The applicant recognizes the importance of . . . in the regulation of a number of biological processes and ultimately wishes to relate . . . and the . . . behavior of . . . to its . . . function. It is somewhat puzzling that the framework for the proposed studies is a rather formal one with *little regard to current . . . information on . . . .* Thus . . . is referred to as . . . (second paragraph, page . . .) and only passing mention is made of the important recent studies establishing the . . . of . . . which show it to be a rather . . . with . . . —a . . . quite similar to that recently established for . . . . *No mention is made of . . . studies* that have shown that it is possible to distinguish . . . changes within . . . as . . . .

The proposed *studies would have more value if specific experiments had been spelled out* relating the . . . to . . . .

Mention is made of the use of . . . but no information seems to be provided concerning the value of such . . . in interpreting the results again in relation to . . . changes within the . . . . While the proposed studies involving . . . may constitute a valuable complement to studies carried out in various laboratories involving . . . methods, the lack of correlation with . . . changes would make the *interpretation of the results difficult.* The use of a model in which distinctions among . . . are not incorporated may create further difficulties.

The investigator has had a broad experience in the field of . . . . The biographical sketch refers to over 105 publications. The list of more recent publications shows continued interest in . . . studies utilizing sophisticated techniques. **The publication record** does not show extensive previous involvement with . . . , particularly with respect to the experimental approach.

The budget appears reasonable except that the reduction of travel to $ . . . per year is recommended.

Rating : Good

Second Reviewer's Report

It is rather disconcerting that the PI apparently has an *incomplete know-ledge of the wealth of information* that has been derived on . . . (See . . .). Using this and the information provided by other investigators, the *PI could greatly increase the effectiveness of his proposed studies by nar-rowing in on* . . . where significant . . . could be expected. In this regard the suggestion to use . . . would be impossible. Further, the . . . that he proposes to use as . . . may be difficult to obtain and it might be more effective to use . . . which has also been shown to dramatically effect . . . . *It detracts from the strength of the proposal that important studies on* . . . *are apparently not recognized.*

The investigator seems *well qualified* to conduct the . . . experiments and to do the necessary . . . to make a contribution to this area, although his **productivity in the last x years has been modest.** *One does not get a sense of confidence in the investigator's ability to produce* the . . . necessary . . . for the successful completion of these studies. Some **pre-liminary data would have been very helpful** in this regard.

Understanding the mechanism of . . . is, however, a very **relevant and meritorious area of research.** The proposed studies should contribute to the efforts of many in this area.

Rating : Good

Appendix IX

Sample Outline for an NSF Proposal

Note: This is not the only possible outline; it is only a sample outline

Please do not use the outline provided in this book *instead of reading the instructions. It is your responsibility to read and meticulously follow the instructions of the granting agency to which you are applying. The information in this book is intended as a guide to, not a substitute for, the original instructions.*

Outline of NSF Proposal Preparation Guidelines
NSF 83–57, Revised 1/87

Note: In this outline, *Grants For Research and Education in Science and Engineering* (Document: NSF 83–57; Revised 1/87) will be referred to simply as the NSF Instructions.

I. General information to be presented in the proposal

    A. Objectives and scientific or educational significance of the proposed work

    B. Suitability of the methods to be employed

    C. Qualifications of the investigator and the grantee organization

    D. Effect of the activity on the infrastructure of science, engineering, and education in these areas

    E. Amount of funding required

    F. Merits of the proposed project

    G. Other miscellaneous information and assurances

II. **Specific Information to be presented in the proposal**

(Assemble the specific items listed in this outline in
the sequence given below.)

A. Information about Principal Investigators

  1. Use **Form 1225** (Appendix II, page 17 of NSF Instructions).
  2. Submit a single copy; you *must* submit the form; filling in
     the information is optional.

B. **Cover page**

  1. Use Form 1207 (Appendix III, page 18 of NSF Instructions).
  2. Indicate the specific organizational unit most appropriate
     to consider your proposal (upper-left box of cover page).
     For list of NSF Programs, refer to Appendix VIII, pages 26 to
     29 of NSF Instructions.
  3. **Title**

     a. Brief
     b. Scientifically valid
     c. Intelligible to a scientifically literate reader
     d. Suitable for use in the public press
     e. Is subject to editing by NSF

  4. Proposed **duration for which support is requested**

     a. Consistent with nature and complexity of proposed
        activity
     b. Maximum of 5 years

  5. Specification of **desired start date** for project (See page 3
     of NSF Instructions.)

  6. Endorsement **signatures**

     a. Principal Investigator
     b. Official authorized to commit the grantee organization
        in business and financial affairs
     c. Additional signatures, if required by the proposing orga-
        nization

7. Submitting organization boxes
(See page 3 of NSF Instructions)

   a. Small businesses
   b. Minority businesses
   c. Woman-owned businesses

C. **Table of contents**

1. Required
2. Must show

   a. Location of each section of proposal
   b. Major subdivisions of the project description such as

      (1) Summary of previous work
      (2) Statement of proposed research or science education activity
      (3) Methods and procedures to be used

D. **Project Summary**

1. Write the project summary **last.**
2. The project summary follows the Table of Contents in the application.

   a. No form provided; use a plain white sheet of paper.
   b. 200 words
   c. Put your name, social security number and project title at the top of the sheet.

3. NSF specifies: summary (Not an abstract of the proposal)
4. Self-contained description of the activity that would result if the proposal is funded

   a. Statement of **objectives**
   b. **Methods** to be employed
   c. **Significance** of the proposed activity to the advancement of knowledge

5. Should be informative to other persons working in same or related fields

6. Try to **make understandable** to scientifically literate readers

E. Results from prior NSF support **(Progress Report)**
(If PI has received an NSF award in the past 5 years)
If you are a new applicant, use this section to provide preliminary results (pilot experiments).

1. NSF award number, amount and period of support
2. Title of prior project
3. Summary of results of completed work
(Maximum of **4 single-spaced pages**)
4. List of publications that acknowledge the NSF award
5. For renewals: Description of the relation of the completed work to the proposed work

F. **Project description** (Research Plan)

(Maximum of **15 single-spaced pages** or 30 double-spaced pages—or discuss justification with appropriate program officer **before** submission of proposal)

1. Detailed statement of work to be undertaken

   a. **Objectives** for the period of the proposed work
   b. Expected **significance**
   c. **Relation to longer-term goals** of the investigator's project
   d. Relation to the **present state of knowledge in the field** (The "**gaps**" in the present state of knowledge that your research project is intended to fill.)
   e. Relation to **work in progress** by the investigator under other support
   f. Relation to work in progress elsewhere (**Background**)
   g. Outline of **general plan of work**

      (1) **Broad design** of activities to be undertaken
      (2) Adequate description of **experimental methods**
      (3) Adequate description of **experimental procedures**

   h. List any substantial **collaborations** with individuals not listed in the budget.

(1) Describe the collaboration.

(2) Document with **letter from each collaborator.**

2. For **proposals for equipment:** Describe the project for which the equipment will be used.

   a. Be succinct.
   b. Give less detail than in a regular grant application.
   c. Emphasize the intrinsic scientific or educational merit of the activity.
   d. Describe the importance of the equipment to the project for which it will be used.
   e. For auxiliary users, provide only a brief summary.

3. For proposals that involve **use of vertebrate animals**

   a. Explain choice of species.
   b. Give number of animals to be used.
   c. Discuss necessary exposure of animals to discomfort, pain, or injury.

G. Special **guidelines** for Proposals to the Directorate for **Engineering**

   1. See page 4 of NSF Instructions.
   2. In addition to information in regular proposals, also include a separate section that describes the impact of the proposed research.

      a. Potential new discoveries or advances that may result from the research
      b. Specific contributions the work will make toward expanding or developing the knowledge and technology base

H. **Bibliography**

   1. Pertinent literature references
   2. Citations should be complete

I. **Biographical sketches**

(For definitions of categories of personnel, see Appendix V, page 21 of NSF Instructions.)

1. Senior Personnel

    a. Curriculum Vitae for each senior scientist—list only academic essentials
    b. Publications for last 5 years (include "In Press")

2. Other Personnel

    a. Exceptional qualifications that merit consideration.
    b. Provide biographical sketches for

       (1) Post-doctoral associates
       (2) Other professionals
       (3) Graduate students (Research assistants)

J. **Budget**

1. Use **Form 1030,** page 19, Appendix IV of NSF Instructions.

    a. Photocopy Form 1030 AFTER filling in items that remain the same for each budget year but BEFORE filling in items that change from year to year.
    b. You will need 1 copy of Form 1030 for each year of support you are requesting + 1 copy for the cumulative budget.
    c. See page 20 of NSF Instructions regarding summary proposal budget.

       (1) **Budget for each year** of requested support
       (2) **Cumulative budget** for full term of requested support

2. **Budget categories**

    a. **Salaries and wages** (See Appendix V for definition of categories of personnel.)

(1) Name (See page 5 of NSF Instructions.)

(2) Time for which funding is requested

    (a) Principal Investigator, faculty, and other senior associates: Academic-year, summer, or calendar-year person-months

    (b) Post-doctoral associates and other professionals

        (i) Full-time-equivalent person-months

        (ii) Rate of pay (hourly, monthly, or annual)

    (c) Graduate and undergraduate students, secretarial, clerical, technical employees

        (i) Total number of persons

        (ii) Total amount of salaries/year in each category

(3) Salaries

(4) Other considerations

    (a) Salaries requested must be consistent with the institution's regular practices.

    (b) For regulations about salary compensation, see page 5, col. 2, paragraphs 3–6 of the NSF Instructions.

    (c) For confidentiality of senior personnel salary data, see page 5, col. 2, paragraph 2 of the NSF Instructions.

    (d) Tuition remission for graduate students may be listed as a "Fringe Benefit" or under "Other Direct Costs."

b. **Fringe benefits**—If charged as direct costs

c. **Equipment**

(1) Defined as > $500 acquisition cost and service life > 2 years

(2) General purpose office equipment is not eligible!

(3) NSF has an Equipment Donation and Discount

agreement with certain manufacturers. For information, call (202) 357–9666.

(4) Items < $1,000 need not be listed separately.

(5) Items > $1,000

(a) Describe each item.

(b) Give estimated cost, including tax. (Provide a formal written estimate from the company; ask them to include a statement about anticipated price increases by the probable purchase date.)

(c) Justify

(i) The need for each item requested should be clearly explained in the body of the proposal.

(ii) Show that the item is not already available.

(iii) Show that you have obtained the best discount available.

(iv) For items > $1000

a) You must have PRIOR written approval from NSF or the grantee's Organizational Prior Approval System (OPAS) (see page 6, col. 1 in NSF Instructions).

b) Indicate such approval in budget or in subsequent correspondence.

d. **Domestic travel**

(Includes U.S. Possessions, Puerto Rico, and Canada)

(1) Type and extent of travel

(a) Purpose (e.g., Name of meeting; whether you will present a paper)

(b) Place

(c) Dates

(d) Approximate expense (Including subsistence)

(i) Personnel travel costs

a) Field work

b) Attendance at meetings/conferences which enhance investigator's ability to

        i)   Perform the work
       ii) Plan extensions of the work
     iii) Disseminate the results of the work

   c) Other travel associated with the proposed work

  (ii) Consultant(s') travel costs

(2) Relation to proposed activities
(3) Justification

e. **Foreign travel**

(1) Except for grantees with Organizational Prior Approval Systems (OPAS), each foreign trip not specifically included and authorized in the grant budget requires advance written approval by NSF to use grant funds.
(2) Use U.S. Flag carriers when available.
(3) Country to be visited
(4) Dates of visit (if known)
(5) Estimated cost (Use round trip economy air fare)
(6) Justify in connection with proposed project.
(7) For rules about travel of dependents, see page 6, col. 2, paragraph 3 of the NSF Instructions.

f. **Participant support costs**

(For participants in NSF-sponsored conferences/workshops)

(1) Transportation
(2) Per Diem
(3) Stipends
(4) Other related costs
(5) No indirect costs permitted in this category
(6) See also section IV, pages 10 to 12 of NSF Instructions.

g. **Other direct costs** (Justify all costs unless obvious.)

(1) **Materials and supplies**

(a) Expendable materials and supplies
(b) Estimated costs
(c) Justify (Give more details when costs are substantial.)

(2) **Publication costs**

(a) Preparing results for publication

(i) Cost of report

a) Typing
b) Photocopying

(ii) Illustrations

a) Graphic art work
b) Photographs of graphic art work
c) Photographs of equipment
d) Light and electron micrographs

(b) Publication charges (except cost for prior or early publication)

(i) Page charges
(ii) Reprints
(iii) Other journal costs

(3) **Consultant services**—Provide information about consultant(s')

(a) Expertise
(b) Primary organizational affiliation
(c) Daily compensation rate (may not exceed that of a U.S. Government GS-18 employee)
(d) Number of days of expected service
(e) Consultant(s') travel costs should be listed separately under "Travel."

(4) **Computer services**

(a) Computer time (hours)
(b) Costs (Provide established computer service rates at the proposing institution: Cost per hour.)

(i) Computer-based information retrieval

a) Scientific
b) Technical
c) Educational

(ii) Leasing automatic data-processing equipment
(iii) Charge for hard copies

(c) Justify need.
(d) Purchase of computer hardware and software should be listed under equipment.
(e) See also, chapter IV, page 12, col. 1 of NSF Instructions, "Supercomputer facilities support and access."

(5) Aircraft rental
(6) Space rental at research establishments away from the grantee institution
(7) Minor building alterations
(8) Payments to human subjects
(9) Service charges
(10) Construction of equipment or systems not available off-the-shelf
(11) Reference books and periodicals specifically related to the research product
(12) Tuition remission for graduate students (List here or under "Fringe Benefits.")
(13) **Subcontracts**

(a) Disclose in the proposal.
(b) Give a complete budget in the above format for each subcontract.
(c) List total amount for each subcontract as a line

item under "Other Direct Costs" in the master
budget for the project.
(d) Requires prior written approval unless you have
an OPAS

h. **Indirect costs**

(1) Negotiated between your institution and NSF
(For information, call NSF Cost Analysis Unit, (202)
357–7547.)
(2) Must be computed for your proposal
(3) For details about eligibility, see page 7, col. 2, paragraph 1 in NSF Instructions.

K.   Budget Explanation Page(s) **(Budget Justification)**

1. See item 1d, page 20 in NSF Instructions.
2. Title this section "Budget Explanation Page(s)."

a. Use additional sheets of paper
b. Put your name, social security number and project title
on each sheet.
c. Place the "Budget Explanation Page(s)" immediately
following the Budget pages.

3. Identify each budget explanation by the line item in the
budget.
4. Document and justify amounts requested in each
category.

a. List all senior personnel.
b. Fully justify each requested item of equipment costing
> $1000.
c. Justify all other expenses.

L.   **Current and pending support**

1. Use **Form 1239,** Appendix VI, page 22 of NSF Instructions.
2. List all support from all sources.

a. Current
b. Concurrent
c. Pending
d. Planned for submission

3. Include all projects and proposed projects that require any portion of time of any senior personnel —even if they receive no salary support from the project.
4. For each senior personnel give person-months or % effort to be devoted to the project—regardless of source of support.
5. Give all above information for the immediately antecedent project period, if this project has been previously supported by other than NSF.

M. **Residual funds statement,** if appropriate (see page 3, col. 1, paragraph 2 and page 20, item 2K of NSF instructions).

N. **Appendices**

1. Appended information must not be used to circumvent the page limits of the project description.
2. Extraneous appendices will not be sent to reviewers.
3. **Facilities and Equipment**

a. Available for the project

(1) Describe available facilities and major items of equipment to be used in the research if they are

(a) Of a specialized nature
(b) Essential to the performance of the project

(2) Other Information

(a) Degree of use
(b) Compare capabilities with research needs
(c) Specify manufacturer and model number

b. Requested for the project

(1) Justify purchases of multiple-use equipment.

(a) Discuss degree of utilization.

(b) If there is already that type of item, explain why it can't be used.

(c) If you say you have 5 terminals, but you asked for another in the budget, explain why 5 are not enough—or what is unique and necessary about the new one you will buy.

(2) For equipment to be purchased, modified, or constructed, describe item in sufficient detail to allow comparison of its capabilities to the needs of the proposed activities.

(3) Specify manufacturer and Model number.

c. Discuss your **Organization's contribution to cost** of

(1) Equipment

(2) Construction/renovation of needed facilities

(These may be considered by NSF as an indication of your organization's commitment to the project.)

d. For Equipment proposals, describe maintenance and operation arrangements (see page 8, col. 1 of NSF Instructions).

e. For equipment costing > $10,000, see page 8, col. 1 of NSF Instructions.

4. **Special considerations**

a. Will part of the project be done away from campus or organizational headquarters? If so

(1) By whom? (Document collaborative arrangements with a letter.)

(2) Where?

(3) Why?

b. **Special information and supporting documents required for**

(1) Activities with actual or potential impact on the **environment**

(2) Work in **foreign countries**
(3) Research in the **Antarctic and in Greenland**
(4) Research at a registered historic or cultural site
(5) Research involving use of **recombinant DNA** generated *in vitro*
(6) Research involving

    (a) **Human subjects**
    (b) **Hazardous materials**
    (c) **Vertebrate animals**
    (d) **Endangered species**

(7) Projects that

    (a) Involve technology utilization/transfer activities
    (b) Are complex and require a management plan
    (c) Involve special reports or final products

(8) Field projects that require assurance that data and samples collected are properly inventoried and archived
(9) Unusual circumstances that require **special handling**

    (See page 8, col. 2, paragraph 9–11 in NSF Instructions.)

    (a) Alert NSF about these in the proposal.
    (b) Provide appropriate documents

        (i) Special Permission
        (ii) Clearance
        (iii) Certification

    (c) **Proprietary/privileged information** in a proposal
    (d) Matters affecting **individual privacy**
    (e) Required intergovernmental review for activities that directly affect state or local governments or have possible national **security implications**

III.   **Checklist**

     A.   A Checklist for Proposal submission is provided in Appendix I, page 16 of the NSF Instructions.

     B.   This checklist is **not** part of the application form.

     C.   Use the checklist provided when planning your proposal and before mailing your application.

     D.   You may also find it helpful to consult the checklist provided in Appendix III of this book

IV.   Other information available in the NSF Instructions

     A.   Types of proposals accepted

     B.   Who may submit a proposal

     C.   When to submit

     D.   Where to submit

     E.   Proposal processing and evaluation

     F.   Declinations, returns, and withdrawals

     G.   Special programs

     H.   Award and continued grant support

     I.   Grant administration

Appendix X

Some Strategies for Good Expository Writing

Strategies for Getting Started

Always write for the reader rather than for yourself, the writer. Ask yourself, "What does the reader need and/or want to know about this subject?"

Think about the criteria for the evaluation of the grant proposal. What are the reviewers being asked to assess? Thinking about the evaluation criteria will help to clarify the objectives for you. The more measurable the objectives the easier the evaluation. (Compare having to grade a multiple choice test as opposed to one made up of essay questions.)

Begin to write only after you have made an outline. An outline will save you much time in the long run and will avoid a lot of frustration. Many good writers spend 50 to 60% of their project time making the outline, 10 to 20% of the time writing and 30% of the time revising! Begin to write when you are 99.99% happy with your outline.

To help you make an outline, write down the answers to the questions below for each pertinent section of the grant proposal:

- What is the purpose of this section of the grant proposal?
- What should the scope of this section of the grant proposal be?
- How should I introduce the subject of this section of the grant proposal? (Your first paragraph.)
- What are the main ideas to be included in this section of the grant proposal? (Main topics.)

    - What is the best logical sequence for these main ideas/topics?
    - If subheadings would help the reader, the main topics can be used to create subheadings.

- The main topics should also be used to generate a good informative topic sentence for each paragraph.

  - Tell the reader in the first sentence of each paragraph what you are going to discuss in that paragraph. Readers who skim may never get any further. They will decide whether or not to read the rest of the paragraph based on what you write in your topic sentence.

- What information should go into each paragraph to support the main idea in the paragraph?

  - These will be subtopics for the outline.
  - What is the best logical sequence for these subtopics within the paragraph?
  - Which of the pieces of information requires particular emphasis?

- What illustrations/diagrams/photos are needed, if any, in each paragraph or section?

  - Where should each illustration/diagram/photo be placed for optimal clarity and effectiveness?

- What is an effective closing paragraph for this section of the grant proposal? A conclusion? A summary? A recommendation? A plan for future directions?
- Which of the items that you wrote down are essential and which ones can be omitted because they are irrelevant or just not really very important for this section of the grant proposal?

Strategies for Achieving Clarity and Brevity in Your Writing

DON'T MAKE THE READER DO EXTRA WORK

Readers of expository prose generally want the maximum information in the minimum number of words.

- Don't use long or complex sentences that have to be reread to be understood.
- Tell the reader "up front" what you will discuss in each paragraph.

- Start each paragraph with a good topic sentence.
- A good topic sentence also provides the reader with a context into which s/he can fit details you give subsequently.
- The object of expository writing is to expose; don't turn your writing into a mystery for the reviewer.
- Remember that busy, efficient people who only have time to skim, use the first (topic) sentence of each paragraph to decide whether or not to read the rest of that paragraph.

- Don't use big words that the reader may not understand. (English may not be your reviewer's native language! Never send your reader to the dictionary.)
- Don't use JARGON. (Think about a computer specialist talking to a primary care physician!)
- Avoid use of the words *former* and *latter.*

> *The reader may have to reread what came before to see what was former* and what was *latter.* If the reader is not careful, or has a poor memory, unfortunate errors may occur:

> > Please take care of my son and my cat while I'm away. Be sure the former is in by 11 PM; let the latter stay out all night.

AVOID AMBIGUITY CAUSED BY MISPLACED MODIFIERS AND OTHER "REFERENCE" PROBLEMS

> On Tuesday, a volumetric flask was brought to the glassware washing room by a technician with a broken neck. (Who had the broken neck, the volumetric flask or the technician?)

> After spilling the drink, the photomicrographs were ruined. (How did the photomicrographs manage to spill the drink?)

> The spectrophotometer should be turned off before leaving the laboratory. (Does the spectrophotometer really leave the laboratory?)

> A fasting urine specimen should be collected. (Have you ever seen a urine specimen fasting?)

AVOID AMBIGUITY CAUSED BY UNCOMMITTED PRONOUNS

It has been shown that ... (Who showed ... ?)

Hooper and Cooper (1984) showed that ...

It is well known that ... (By whom?)

A survey has indicated that 57% of faculty members at ABC University know that ...

We noted that most of the rabbits were sick and all the rats had bald spots. This finding ...

(Which one—or both taken together?)

Taken together, the findings that most of the rabbits were sick and all the rats had bald spots indicated that ...

AVOID AMBIGUITY CAUSED BY COMPLEX SENTENCES

• Avoid long convoluted sentences such as:

Looking back on it, it is curious that nobody was heard to ask why, since vitamin A has long been known to be very insoluble in aqueous media in general, scientists did not set about looking for a likely carrier protein that might be responsible for transporting vitamin A to its target tissues.[*]

• Use short direct sentences. (Be sure they can be interpreted in only one way.)

AVOID WORDS THAT MEAN DIFFERENT THINGS TO DIFFERENT PEOPLE

• Replace vague modifiers that state opinions with quantitative information

---

[*] Adapted from a sentence by Russell Baker, *New York Times*, February 1, 1986, page 27. This sentence is fine in a piece of creative writing but not in a grant proposal.

NOT: *most* or *many*

BUT: 68–70%

NOT: This experiment requires *enormous* numbers of test tubes . . .

BUT: This experiment requires *133* test tubes . . .

- Specify time and place rather than using words like *recently* or *here*

  What will the word *recently,* in an article you publish in 1988, mean to someone who reads the article in 1995?

  What will the word *here,* in an article you wrote in Boston, mean to someone who reads your reprint in China?

BE BRIEF

Say it once and say it right. (Don't say the same thing in three different ways out of insecurity.)

ELIMINATE UNNECESSARY WORDS

Extra words waste the reviewer's time—and your space. Save space for more important information—remember the page limitations.

NOT: Reports were lengthy this year because the page limitations were eliminated from the instructions.

BUT: Reports were long this year because there were no page limitations.

NOT: Please find enclosed, herewith, our new catalog which was issued in January of this year.

BUT: Here is our January, 19XX catalog.

When you edit your proposal, ask yourself—*for each word*—Is this word really necessary? Does it add anything to the meaning of the sentence?

MORE EXAMPLES OF UNNECESSARY WORDS

At the present time we are experiencing precipitation.

It is raining.

One of the members of the group said . . .

A group member said . . .

There is a new method that helps . . .

A new method helps . . .

He said *the reason* the grant was late *was* because . . . . .

He said the grant was late because . . . . .

It was suggested by the reviewers that the Principal Investigators include an Appendix to amplify the background section.

The reviewers suggested the Principal Investigators include an Appendix to amplify the background section.

The reason I am worried *is* because *I think* she is writing a very poor grant proposal.

I am worried because she is writing a very poor grant proposal.

The Progress Report report was in need of additional data.

The Progress Report needed more data.

It is imperative that you fill out the personal data sheet.

You must fill out the personal data sheet.

USE SHORT WORDS

Use	instead of	Utilize
Need	instead of	Require
Vanish	instead of	Disappear

INSTEAD OF:	**WRITE:**
in order to	to
for the purpose of	to
have a preference for	prefer
with the exception of	except
in excess of	more than
in the near future	soon
in the not too distant future	soon
in addition to	also
at this point in time	now
at the present time	now
in the event that	if
in the course of	while (during)

(Note: While and Since refer only to time)

in a number of cases	some (several)
in the majority of instances	usually (most of)
in all probability	probably
in the nature of	like (similar to)
in view of	because
in view of the fact that	because

(Don't use the word fact unless it IS a fact)

in the vicinity of	near
it would thus appear that	apparently
it is possible that the cause of	the cause may be
it is imperative that	be sure that
may result in damage	may damage
on a few occasions	occasionally
in the neighborhood of	about
on the other hand	or
on the assumption that	assuming that
it is of interest to note that	note
in the amount of	for
arrived at the conclusion	concluded
make decisions	decide
take action	act
give assistance to	assist, help
last but not least	finally

YOU CAN USUALLY **OMIT:**

Needless to say (Then why bother to say it?)
In summary
In the last analysis
In actual fact (How can a fact not be actual? Is it really a fact?)
The fact of the matter is (Is it really a fact?)
It is apparent that
In my opinion (If you say something, it is usually understood to be your opinion. If you must make clear that something is your opinion, use the shorter expression, "I think* .")

OMIT: *Unnecessary transition words* and phrases such as "In conclusion, . . . "

(But, KEEP transition words that tell the reader that you are "changing direction:" For example, "In contrast, . . . " "Nevertheless, . . . ")

OMIT: *Modifiers that* do not add to the essence of what you want to say (NOT: This *cleverly conceived* experiment . . . BUT: This experiment . . .)

AVOID REDUNDANCY

DON'T WRITE:	**WRITE:**
In this day and age	*Now*
Each and every	*Each or Every (Not both)*
One and only	*One or Only (Not both)*
First and foremost	*First or Foremost (Not both)*

USE ACTIVE VOICE RATHER THAN PASSIVE VOICE WHEN APPROPRIATE

Passive voice contains some form of the verb "TO BE" before the main verb.

---

* I think, I feel, I believe: If your field is psychology it is sometimes appropriate to say, "I feel." If your field is religion, it is sometimes appropriate to say, "I believe." If your field is science, or you are engaged in a research aspect of your profession, it is generally more appropriate to say, "I think."

Therefore, the passive voice form may have extra words.

The active voice is also clearer; it tells you "up front" who (or what) did (or does or will do) the action of the verb. The passive voice evades the issue and does not give this information.

To turn a passive voice sentence to an active voice sentence, answer the question, "Who (or what) is doing the action of the verb?"

It *was suggested* that the laboratory reports *be revised.*

Who did the suggesting?

The head of the department suggested that the laboratory reports *be revised.*

Who will do the revising?

The head of the department suggested that the post-doc revise the laboratory reports.

Note that passive voice occurs in all tenses:

The solutions were mixed. (Active voice: John mixed the solutions.)

The solutions are being mixed. (Active voice: John is mixing the solutions.)

The solutions will be mixed. (Active voice: John will mix the solutions.)

AVOID TURNING VERBS INTO NOUNS

*23 words: Utiliza***tion** of marine plant species for food produc**tion** will bring about a reduc**tion** in food costs and crea**tion** of cheaper sources of calories.

17 words: Utilizing (Using) marine plant species to produce food will reduce food costs and create cheaper sources of calories.

AVOID UNNECESSARY "ING" WORDS

They *were* meet*ing* to . . .

    They met to . . .

He will *be going* to . . .

    He will go to . . .

THINK ABOUT STYLE

- Use simple words. **TRY TO EXPRESS RATHER THAN IMPRESS.**

- Use short direct sentences. Use transition words (e.g., however, nevertheless, in contrast), *in moderation,* to avoid a "choppy" sound.

- Keep paragraphs short and start them with informative topic sentences.

THINK ABOUT EMPHASIS (in the context of the psychology of the reader.)

- In a sentence, start with the clause you want to stress:

   In the previous project period several approaches were developed to solve . . .

   Several approaches were developed in the previous project period to solve . . .

- Don't begin a paragraph with unimportant words. Try to capture the reader's attention with "high-information" words.

TRY NOT TO SPLIT INFINITIVES

NOT: Be sure *TO* quickly *GO* . . .

BUT: Be sure *TO GO* quickly . . .

DON'T OVERSTATE YOUR CASE

• Avoid superlatives: Use *best,* most, etc., only if you are *sure* the superlative is correct:

  NOT: One of the best ways to purify ...
       (There can be only one *best* way)

  BUT: ... is the best way to purify ...

• Avoid useless multiple modifiers:

  "I repeat this experiment every single month." (Are there double months?)

THINK ABOUT TONE

• Attitude and tone are sometimes "contagious."

• Avoid words such as *unfortunately.*

• *Be positive*

  NOT: I won't be able to finish this project by the end of the first year.

  BUT: I will be able to finish this project by March of the second year.

Appendix XI

Resources

All prices given in this appendix are subject to change without notice.

The list of Resources provided in APPENDIX XI is not intended to be comprehensive or exhaustive. It is intended to alert you to items that may be helpful to grant writers/researchers. It is a collection of items that have come to my attention and will, I hope, pave the way for further inquiry by the reader. Suggestions for additions to the list will be received with gratitude by the author, and saved for possible insertion in the list of resources should there be yet another revision of this book. Please send suggestions to TWC/EA, Box 645, Belmont, MA 02178.

Books and articles about getting grants and writing grant proposals

GRANTSMANSHIP: MONEY AND HOW TO GET IT, 2d Ed., Marquis Academic Media, Marquis Who's Who, Chicago 1978.

Henley, C., *PEER REVIEW OF RESEARCH GRANT APPLICATIONS AT NATIONAL INSTITUTES OF HEALTH* Federation Proceedings: *36*, 2066–2068, 2186–2190, 2335–2338, 1977.

Hill, W. J., *SUCCESSFUL GRANTSMANSHIP*, 4th Ed., Grant Development Institute, Steamboat Springs, CO, 1980.

Hogan, A. R., *FEW APPLICANTS APPEAL DENIAL OF GRANTS*, THE SCIENTIST, *1*, # 15, June 15, 1987, page 1.

Kiritz, Norton J., *PROGRAM PLANNING AND PROPOSAL WRITING*, The Grantsmanship Center, Los Angeles, CA, 1978.

An 8-page article about writing proposals. Especially good for writing foundation proposals; includes examples of budgets and budget justifications. Available for $3 from The Grantsmanship Center or Associated Grantmakers of Massachusetts, Inc. (See addresses under Resource Centers.)

Kurzig, C. M., *FOUNDATION FUNDAMENTALS: A GUIDE FOR GRANT SEEKERS*, The Foundation Center, New York, 1981.

Margolin, J. B., *THE INDIVIDUAL'S GUIDE TO GRANTS*, Plenum Press, New York, 1983.

Meader, R., *GUIDELINES FOR PREPARING PROPOSALS,* Lewis Publishers, Chelsea, MI, 1985.

Available from Lewis Publishers, P. O. Drawer 519, Chelsea, MI 48118.

See also review by Harold Waters, Deputy Chief for Referral in the NIH Division of Research Grants (DRG), in *Chemical and Engineering News*, June 3, 1985, page 53.

Good, but some of the information is outdated.

Pearson, G., *RED TAPE AND FEDERAL GRANTS*, Science, <u>239</u>, February 19, 1988, page 859.

PREPARING A RESEARCH GRANT APPLICATION TO THE NATIONAL INSTITUTES OF HEALTH, Selected Articles, May 1987.

A collection of articles on grant proposal writing. Includes the articles by Henley, listed above, and others. Published by the Department of Health and Human Services, National Institutes of Health, Public Health Services.

Available from Division of Research Grants, Office of Grants Inquiries, Westwood Bldg., Room 449, 5333 Westbard Ave., Bethesda, MD 20892.

White, V., *GRANT PROPOSALS THAT SUCCEEDED*, Plenum Press, New York, 1983.

White, V. P., *GRANTS: HOW TO FIND OUT ABOUT THEM AND WHAT TO DO NEXT*, Plenum Press, New York, 1979.

Lots of good information , but some of the agencies listed no longer seem to exist.

Books about Writing

CHICAGO GUIDE TO PREPARING ELECTRONIC MANUSCRIPTS FOR AUTHORS AND PUBLISHERS.

> *University of Chicago Press, Chicago, 1987, 156 Pages, Hardbound $25; Paperbound $9.95.*

Cook, C.K., *LINE BY LINE : How to edit your own writing,* Houghton Mifflin, Boston, 1985.

> 219 pages, indexed. Hardback, $14.95.

Manhard, S. J., *THE GOOF-PROOFER,* Collier Books, Macmillan Publishing Co., New York, 1985.

> An 84-page paperback. Especially useful for those who missed out on learning basic grammar and spelling, $3.95.

Strunk, W., Jr., and E.B.White, *THE ELEMENTS OF STYLE,* 3rd ed. Macmillan, New York, 1979.

> A 92-page, indexed book on English usage. A classic. Paperback, $2.95.

Newsletters and Periodicals

> Some of the commercial publications are expensive. You may prefer to check your library or Office for Sponsored Research (Office for Grants and Contracts).

"THE BLUE SHEET" - Health Policy and Biomedical Research News of the Week

> By subscription ($265/year) from Drug Research Reports, 5550 Friendship Blvd., Suite 1, Chevy Chase, MD 20815.

CONTRIBUTIONS

> Issued 6 times/year. A newsletter for and about non-profit professionals; geared toward development, public relations and communications personnel and executive directors of non-profit

organizations. Available free to staff of non-profit organizations ($18/year for others) from Contributions, 634 Commonwealth Ave., Suite 201, Newton Centre, MA 02159; (617) 964–2688.

FASEB PUBLIC AFFAIRS NEWSLETTER

Issued monthly.

Available free to members of FASEB (Federation of American Societies for Experimental Biology), 9650 Rockville Pike, Bethesda, MD 20814; (301) 530–7075.

FEDERAL GRANTS AND CONTRACTS WEEKLY—Project Opportunities in Research, Training and Service

By subscription ($230/year) from Capitol Publications, 1101 King Street, P. O. Box 1454, Alexandria, VA 22313–2054.

GRANT PROPOSAL NEWS

By subscription ($150/year) from Grants Administration News Company, P.O. Box 964, Berkeley, CA 94701.

GRANTS MAGAZINE

By subscription ($65/year) from Plenum Press, 233 Spring St., New York, NY 10013; (212) 620–8000.

HEALTH GRANTS AND CONTRACTS WEEKLY—Selected Federal Project Opportunities

By subscription ($195/year) from Capitol Publications, 1101 King Street, P. O. Box 1454, Alexandria, VA 22313–2054.

THE HLB NEWSLETTER—Reporting on Heart, Lung and Blood Disease Research Program, Policy Development

By subscription ($97/year) from HLB Newsletter, Suite 306, 1001 3rd Street SW, Washington, D.C. 20024–4408.

NEWS AND FEATURES FROM NIH. See NIH listings.

NIH WEEK. See NIH listings.

NSF BULLETIN. See NSF listings.

SCIENCE AND GOVERNMENT REPORT

Published 20 times a year.

By subscription ($112/year); from SGR, 3736 Kanawha St., NW., Washington, D.C. 20015; (800) 522–1970; (202) 785–5054, 244–4135.

THE SCIENTIST—The Newspaper for the Science Professional

From Institute for Scientific Information (ISI), the publisher of *Current Contents.*
By subscription ($58/year) from The Scientist, P.O. Box 677, Holmes, PA 19043 .

WHOLE NONPROFIT CATALOG

Available free to qualified agencies from The Grantsmanship Center, 650 S. Spring St., Suite 507, P.O. Box 6210, Los Angeles, CA 90014; (800) 421-9512; (213) 689–9222.

National Institutes of Health

To obtain PHS-398 Application Forms

Single copy: Office of Grants Inquiries (PHS 398), Division of Research Grants (DRG), National Institutes of Health (NIH), Westwood Bldg., Rm. 449, Bethesda, MD 20892; (301) 496–7441.

Multiple copies: Office Services Section (PHS 398), Division of Research Grants (DRG), National Institutes of Health (NIH), Westwood Bldg., Rm. 436, Bethesda, MD 20892; (301) 496–9797.

Awards/grants not specifically discussed in this book

NATIONAL INSTITUTES OF HEALTH **"FIRST" (R-29) AWARD**

The first Independent Research and Transition Award (also called "First Award") provides research funding for new investigators and investigators changing to a new field of research. The **"FIRST"** award provides for a maximum of $350,000 for a maximum period of 5 years and permits carry-over of unobligated balances from one budget period to the next.

For information about the "**FIRST**" award see *NIH GUIDE FOR GRANTS AND CONTRACTS 15*, #3, February 28, 1986, *15*, #4, March 28, 1986 and *15*, #6, May 23, 1986. Also contact your NIH Institute.

OTHER *NATIONAL INSTITUTES OF HEALTH* GRANTS

A partial list of other types of NIH awards is given on pages 9–10 of the NIH Instructions reproduced in Appendix I of this book.

Publications

EXTRAMURAL TRENDS: NIH FY 1978–1987

Available from Information Systems Branch, Division of Research Grants, National Institutes of Health, Bethesda, MD 20892.

Data about grant awards organized according to activity, institutes, etc. Includes award rates, priority scores, length of project periods, and so forth.

GRANTS PEER REVIEW

The 3 publications listed below are out of print; check the library.

Grants Peer Review: Report to the Director, NIH: Phase I, December, 1976. U.S. Government Printing Office: 1977 241/161/3032.

Decisions by the Director, NIH, on Recommendations of Grants Peer Review Study Team, February 8, 1978.

Opinions on the NIH grants Peer Review System, Phase II of the Report to the Director, NIH by the NIH Grants Peer Review Study Team, December, 1978. U.S. Government Printing Office: 1979–281–217/3138.

HELPFUL HINTS ON PREPARING A FELLOWSHIP APPLICATION TO THE NATIONAL INSTITUTES OF HEALTH.

August, 1987; a 12-page booklet available from the Office of Grants Inquiries, Division of Research Grants, National Institutes of Health, Bethesda, MD 20892.

[See also *NIH GUIDE FOR GRANTS AND CONTRACTS, 17* #3, January 22, 1988, about letters of reference for Individual Postdoctoral Fellowship (F32) Applications.]

INFORMATION FROM THE NIH ON GRANTS AND CONTRACTS, May, 1986

> Available from Office of Grants Inquiries, Division of Research Grants, National Institutes of Health, Bethesda, MD 20892.

> A list of books, brochures, periodicals, articles, guidelines and application forms (many free); tells you what each publication is about and where to get it.

NEWS AND FEATURES FROM NIH

> Published 6 to 8 times/year.

> Available free (by written request) from NIH News Branch, Bldg. 31, Room 2B-10, 9000 Rockville Pike, Bethesda, MD 20892; (301) 496–2535.

> Articles, in lay-language, about research activities at NIH and at some of its grantee institutions.

NATIONAL INSTITUTES OF HEALTH GRANTS AND AWARDS: NIH FUNDING MECHANISMS

> September, 1987; available free from Office of Grants Inquiries, Division of Research Grants, National Institutes of Health, Bethesda, MD 20892.

> This booklet gives an overview, largely in the form of charts, about the programs available at each of the NIH Institutes.

NIH EXTRAMURAL PROGRAMS: FUNDING FOR RESEARCH AND RE-SEARCH TRAINING

> NIH Publication No. 85–33. Latest issue: January, 1985.

> For sale by Superintendent of Documents, U.S. Government Printing Office, Washington, D.C. 20402.

NIH GUIDE FOR GRANTS AND CONTRACTS

> Published weekly. (See *NIH Guide,* Vol. 18, #20, 6/9/89, p. 4.)

> Available free from NIH Guide Distribution Center, National Institutes of Health, Room B3BE07, Bldg. 31, Bethesda, MD 20892; (301) 496–1789.

NIH PEER REVIEW OF RESEARCH GRANT APPLICATIONS

Revised, February, 1988; available free from Office of Grants Inquiries, Division of Research Grants, National Institutes of Health, Bldg. WW, Room 449, Bethesda, MD 20892.

This booklet is based on a set of slides prepared by the Referral and Review Branch of DRG. It gives a brief overview of the review process.

Contains a list of NIH information sources with names and phone numbers.

Contains a small list of reference articles.

NIH ADVISORY COMMITTEES: AUTHORITY, STRUCTURE, FUNCTION, MEMBERS

NIH Publication No. 87–10

Available free from Division of Research Grants (DRG), National Institutes of Health (NIH), Bethesda, MD 20892.

Updated in October of each year.

Lists members of Study Sections, etc.

NIH WEEK

By subscription ($175/year) from NIH WEEK Limited Partnership, Box 2239, Washington, D.C. 20013.

ORIENTATION HANDBOOK FOR MEMBERS OF SCIENTIFIC REVIEW GROUPS, November, 1983

Available free from NIH.

Has bibliography on Peer Review.

Amended in August, 1987 by the document reproduced in Part I of this book entitled, *Guide for Assigned Reviewers' Preliminary Comments on Research Grant Applications (R01).*

PUBLIC HEALTH SERVICE GRANTS POLICY STATEMENT

Department of Health and Human Services (DHHS) Publication No. (OASH) 82–50,000 (Rev.) December 1, 1982.

Probably available at your institution; can be purchased from Superintendent of Documents, U.S. Government Printing Office, Washington, D.C. 20402.

RESEARCH AWARDS INDEX

Prepared annually in the Division of Research Grants, NIH. A subject guide to research supported by grants and contracts awarded by agencies of DHHS.

Can be purchased from Superintendent of Documents, U.S. Government Printing Office, Washington, D.C. 20402 for approximately $55.

SMALL BUSINESS INNOVATION RESEARCH (SBIR) GRANT APPLICATIONS Department of Health and Human Services

Document PHS 88–2 (U.S. Government Printing Office: 1988–199–953:32372) for Phase I applications.

For information contact: Ms. Lily O. Engstrom, SBIR Program Coordinator, National Institutes of Health, Bldg. 31, Room 1B54, Bethesda, MD 20892; (301) 496–1968.

OTHER NIH PUBLICATIONS

The individual institutes at NIH also have numerous publications about specific programs, grant award mechanisms, program goals, and projects supported by the Institute. For example, two new publications available from the National Eye Institute are:

(1) *1987 UPDATE AND EVALUATION, VISION RESEARCH—A NATIONAL PLAN 1983–1987.* The National Advisory Eye Council's most recent evaluation of the research needs and opportunities in vision research. The 354-page publication is available from Mr. Julian Morris, Associate Director for Planning and Reporting, National Eye Institute, National Institutes of Health, Building, 31, Room 6A27, Bethesda, MD 20892.

(2) *CLINICAL TRIALS SUPPORTED BY THE NATIONAL EYE INSTITUTE: EVALUATING NEW APPROACHES TO THE TREATMENT OF EYE AND VISION DISORDERS.* This 67-page booklet is available from Ms. Judith Stein, Information Officer, National Eye Institute, National Institutes of Health, Building 31, Room 6A32, Bethesda, MD 20892.

Call the corresponding officers at your funding Institute and ask for copies of publications relevant to your needs/interests.

National Science Foundation

> The National Science Foundation (NSF) does not have a general office for grants inquiries. For information about NSF, contact your institution's grants office. If your grants office cannot give you the information you need, ask for the name and telephone number of the NSF Program Director relevant to your research interests and call that person. General questions to NSF should be sent **by mail** to NSF, Division of Grants and Contracts, Room 1140, 1800 G. Street, NW, Washhington, D.C. 20550.

NATIONAL SCIENCE FOUNDATION (NSF) BULLETIN

Issued monthly.

Available free from Public Affairs and Publications Office, National Science Foundation (NSF), Washington, D.C. 20550.

NATIONAL SCIENCE FOUNDATION: *Grant General Conditions*

May be obtained from Forms and Publications, National Science Foundation, Washington, D.C. 20550.

NATIONAL SCIENCE FOUNDATION: *Grant Policy Manual* NSF 77–47 (Revised)

Information about the NSF grant process, proposers, and grantees Updated periodically.

Available from Superintendent of Documents, Government Printing Office, Washington, D.C. 20402. About $13.

NATIONAL SCIENCE FOUNDATION: *Grants For Research and Education in Science and Engineering*

Document NSF 83–57; revised 1/87.
This document contains the application forms and instructions for applying for an NSF grant.

SMALL BUSINESS INNOVATION RESEARCH (SBIR) GRANTS—NSF

Document NSF 88–8 (OMB No. 3145–0058).
For information write: National Science Foundation, 1800 G St., NW, Room 1250, Washington, DC 20550, ATTN: SBIR; (202) 357–9859.

Other Government Agencies

CONTRACT RESEARCH AND TECHNOLOGY PROGRAM, OFFICE OF NAVAL RESEARCH (ONR-1)

Describes grants and contracts available through the Office of Naval Research (ONR).

In addition to other programs, ONR has a Biological Sciences Division with programs in Molecular Biology and Cellular Biology; ONR also has a Psychological Sciences Division.

Available from Office of Naval Research, 800 N. Quincy St., Arlington, VA 22217; (202) 696–4517.

THE DEPARTMENT OF DEFENSE, UNIVERSITY RESEARCH INITIATIVE, RESEARCH PROGRAM SUMMARIES, JUNE,1987

Defense Advanced Research Projects Agency, 1400 Wilson Blvd., Arlington, VA 22209–2308; (202) 694–3035.

Also, Departments of the Army, Navy and Air Force.

UNSOLICITED PROPOSAL GUIDE: AIR FORCE SYSTEMS COMMAND

Write or call Air Force Office of Scientific Research, Bolling Air Force Base, Washington, D. C. 20332; (202) 767–5017.
Scientific programs include Aerospace Medicine and Aerospace Medical Research.

U.S. ARMY RESEARCH OFFICE PROGRAM GUIDE

Write or call Army Research Office , P.O. Box 12211, Research Triangle Park, NC 27709–2211; (919) 549–0641.

Scientific programs include Biosciences.

UNITED STATES DEPARTMENT OF AGRICULTURE, COMPETITIVE RE-SEARCH GRANTS PROGRAM

For information, write or call Grants Administrative Management, Office of Grants and Program Systems (OGPS), West Auditors Bldg., Room 010, U.S. Dept. of Agriculture, Washington, D.C. 20251; (202) 475–5048.

UNITED STATES DEPARTMENT OF ENERGY, OFFICE OF ENERGY RESEARCH, APPLICATION AND GUIDE FOR THE SPECIAL RESEARCH GRANT PROGRAM, 10 CFR, Part 605, October, 1985.

Document DOE/ER-0249; U.S. Government Printing Office: 1987–181–179:50115.

For information, write or call United States Department of Energy, Office of Energy Research, Washington, D.C. 20545; (202) 586–8800.

Scientific programs include

Biological Energy	(301) 353–2873
Chemical Sciences	5804
Ecological Research	4208
Health Effects Research	5468
Human Health and Assessments	5355

For Small Businesses

SMALL BUSINESS INNOVATION RESEARCH (SBIR)

Department of Health and Human Services

For information contact: Ms. Lily O. Engstrom, SBIR Program Coordinator, National Institutes of Health, Bldg. 31, Room 1B54, Bethesda, MD 20892; (301) 496–1968.

For information about the review of PHS/SBIR grant applications, contact: Dr. Jeanne Kettley, Special Review Section, Division of Research Grants, NIH, Westwood Bldg., Room 2A16; (301) 496–7558.

National Science Foundation

For information write: National Science Foundation, 1800 G St., NW, Room 1250, Washington, DC 20550, ATTN: SBIR; (202) 357–9859.

Especially for non-scientists

Kiritz, Norton J., *PROGRAM PLANNING AND PROPOSAL WRITING*, The Grantsmanship Center, Los Angeles, CA, 1978.

An 8-page article about writing proposals; published by The Grantsmanship Center (see Resource Centers).

Especially good for writing foundation proposals; includes examples of budgets and budget justifications.

Available for $3 from The Grantsmanship Center or Associated
Grantmakers of Massachusetts, Inc. (See addresses under Resource Centers.)

Government Agencies that fund programs in non-science areas

Write to the agencies for information about their programs and for
application kits.

U.S. Department of Housing and Urban Development

P.O. Box 280, Germantown, MD. 20874; (800) 245–2691; (301)
251–5154.
or
451 Seventh St. SW, Washington, D.C. 20410.

National Endowment for the Arts

Nancy Hanks Center, 1100 Pennsylvania Ave. NW, Washington,
D.C. 20506; (202) 682–5400 or 5419

Dance	(202) 682–5435
Design Arts	5437
Expansion arts	5443
Folk Arts	5449
Inter-Arts	5444
Literature	5451
Media Arts	5452
Museums	5442
Music	5445
Opera-Musical Theatre	5447
Theater	5425
Visual Arts	5448

National Endowment for the Humanities

Division of Research Programs, Room 319, 1100 Pennsylvania
Ave. NW, Washington, D.C. 20506; (202) 786–0438.

National Foundation for the Improvement of Education

1201 16th St. NW, Washington, D.C. 20036; (202) 822–7840.

U.S. Department of Education (USDE)

Application Control Center, Washington, D.C. 20202; (202)
732–2495.

Writing a Successful Grant Application

Directories of Grant Support

ANNUAL REGISTER OF GRANT SUPPORT

> Academic Media, Orange, NJ.

> Lists both public and private support.

DIRECTORY OF INTERNATIONAL OPPORTUNITIES IN BIOMEDICAL AND BEHAVIORAL SCIENCES

> This is an updated version of a Directory originally published in January, 1984. It contains information about fellowship support in biomedical and behavioral sciences. A limited number of copies of this booklet are available. Send a self-addressed label with your request to International Research and Awards Branch, Building 38A, Room 613, Fogarty International Center, National Institutes of Health, Bethesda, MD 20892.

FEDERAL REGISTER

> Published each weekday. Lists all federal program deadlines, U.S. Government notices, public regulations, etc.

> By subscription ($300/year) from Superintendent of Documents, U.S. Government Printing Office, Washington, D.C. 20402.

FOUNDATION DIRECTORY

> The Foundation Center, 888 7th Ave., New York, NY 10106.

> Lists foundations with assets over $500,000.

SOURCES OF FEDERAL FUNDING FOR BIOLOGICAL RESEARCH,

> P. C. Escherich and R. E. McManus, eds., Association of Systematics Collection, Lawrence, KA, 1983.

> Association of Systematics Collection, 730 11th St. NW, 3d Floor, Washington, D.C. 20001; (202) 347-2850.

Other directories of, or about, available funding (try the library; some are expensive):

> — Catalog of Federal Domestic Assistance (lists government programs)

> The Catholic Guide to Foundations

Encyclopedia of Associations

The Foundation Center Source Book

Foundation Information Services

Foundation News

State Foundation Directories

International Foundation Directory

Foundation directories published in other countries.

Annual Survey of Corporate Contributions

Corporate 500: The Directory of Corporate Philanthropy

Corporate Foundation Profiles

Corporate Fund Raising Directory

Computerized Resources for Funding Information

FEDERAL ASSISTANCE PROGRAM RETRIEVAL SYSTEM (FAPRS)

For locating federal funding sources.

Check with the grants office at your institution.

For information write or call Federal Program Information Branch, Budget Review Division, Office of Management and Budget (OMB), 6001 New Executive Office Bldg., Washington, D.C. 20503; (202) 395–3112 or 395–3000.

GOVERNMENT INFORMATION SERVICES

Maintains a database of both federal and private funding sources. Check with the grants office at your institution.

For information write or call Government Information Services, 1611 North Kent St., Suite 508, Arlington, VA 22209; (703) 528–1082.

SPONSORED PROGRAMS INFORMATION NETWORK (SPIN)

A computerized network for locating external funding sources.

Check with the grants office at your institution; they may subscribe.

For information write or call Sponsored Programs Information Network, Research Foundation of SUNY, P.O. Box 9, Albany, NY, 12201; (518) 434–7150.

Resource Centers for Funding Information

Academic Research Information System, Inc. (ARIS)

> Information about government and other sources of grants and contracts in science, social science, arts and humanities.

> For information and prices, write or call: Academic Research Information System, Inc. (ARIS), Redstone Bldg., 2940 16th St., Suite 314, San Francisco, CA 94103; (415) 558–8133.

Associated Grantmakers of Massachusetts, Inc., 294 Washington Street, Suite 417, Boston, MA 02108; (617) 426–2606.

> A resource center for philanthropy. They have a library and will introduce you to their resources.

The Grantsmanship Center, 650 S. Spring St., Suite 507, P.O. Box 6210, Los Angeles, CA 90014; (800) 421–9512; (213) 689–9222.

> They publish a funding newsletter, the *WHOLE NONPROFIT CATALOG*, available free to qualified agencies.

The Office for Sponsored Research (OSR) (or Office for Grants and Contracts) at your institution.

> For example, Harvard University OSR publishes a monthly *OSR Bulletin*.

> At many institutions the OSR also maintains lists of granting agencies and small grants given by the institution. Check these lists for agencies with interests that match your research interests. To avoid wasting your time, call to see if the agency in question is interested in your proposal before you begin to write.

State Departments of Commerce

> For example, Massachusetts Department of Commerce, 100 Cambridge St., Boston, MA 02202; (617) 727–3218.

The Taft Group

> Public Service Materials Center, 5130 MacArthur Blvd., NW, Washington, DC 20016; (202) 966–7086.

> They publish a catalog of reference works, newsletters and books of interest to grant proposal writers/fund raisers.

Other Resources

Workshops on Proposal Writing

The Grantsmanship Training Program

> 5-day workshops; pre-scheduled series in major cities—or on-site. Tuition $495/person.

> The Grantsmanship Center, 650 S. Spring St., Suite 507, P.O. Box 6210, Los Angeles, CA 90014; (800) 421–9512 (not for CA, HI, or AK) or (312) 689–9222.

Great Plains National (GPN)

> A set of 10 video tapes: *Winning Grants: A Systematic Approach For Higher Education* ($1,995).

> Available from The American Council on Education, Videocassette Services, Box 80669, Lincoln, NE 68501; (800) 228–4630.

Tech-Write Consultants/Erimon Associates

> On site half-day and one-day workshops: How To Write A Good Grant Proposal. Geared to scientists or to a more general audience. Tuition $60/person for half-day workshop (minimum of 25 people) + travel expenses and per diem for speaker. Discounts for groups of over 100 people.

> Workshop will be available on videocassette in the future.

> Tech-Write Consultants/Erimon Associates, Box 645, Belmont, MA 02178; (617) 863–1117.

Services for Scientists

Information Services

> There are numerous information services available (see other listings below).

> One example is ISA Atlas of Science; available in Pharmacology, Biochemistry, Immunology and Animal and Plant Sciences.

> Contains surveys by experts in the field; 4 issues per year. For free sample surveys, subscription rates or additional information write or call Institute for Scientific Information (ISI), 3501 Market St., Philadelphia, PA 19104; (800) 523–1850; (215) 386–0100.

ISI also publishes *Current Contents; Science Citation Index* (Allows you to search forward in time); *The Genuine Article* (Provides tearsheets of articles); *Automatic Subject Citation Alert;* etc.

Laboratory Services

Numerous services are available to help scientists with research needs.

A number of private companies do analyses or prepare sophisticated biologicals to suit the needs of researchers.

Several centers at universities and elsewhere provide materials to which individual researchers may not otherwise have access because of limited facilities in their own laboratories.

One example of an NIH facility is The MIT Cell Culture Center, headed by Dr. Phillip A. Sharp.

The Center is a national resource available for researchers to obtain large quantities of animal cells, cell products, and viruses. It is supported by the Division of Research Resources, NIH. Products are obtained by application, subject to committee approval. Researchers are charged only for the consumable material used on the project plus a small portion of the labor costs. Inquiries and requests for application forms should be addressed to Donald J. Girard, Director, MIT Cell Culture Center, E17–321, Massachusetts Institute of Technology, Cambridge, MA 02139; telephone: (617) 253–6430.

The Center also contains a Cell Sorter Laboratory for flow cytometry and sorting. Users are required to pay a fee to cover part of the operational costs. Inquiries about the cell sorter services should be directed to Mr. Paul Kaye, E17–358, Massachusetts Institute of Technology, Cambridge, MA 02139; telephone (617) 253–6454.

On-line Science/Technology Information Systems

BIBLIOGRAPHIC RETRIEVAL SERVICE (BRS)

Bibliographic citations and abstracts. Full texts available on some databases.

After Dark; Colleague(for physicians); BRS/Search.

Prices vary according to service.

BRS Information Technologies, 1200 Route 7, Latham, NY 12110; (800) 345–4277; (518) 783–1161.

CURRENT CONTENTS SEARCH

The online version of the five scientific editions of Current Contents: Clinical Medicine; Life Sciences; Engineering, Technology & Applied Sciences; Agriculture, Biology & Environmental Sciences; and Physical, Chemical & Earth Sciences.

Institute for Scientific Information, 3501 Market St., Philadelphia, PA 19104; (800) 523–1850; (215) 386–0100.

GENBANK

A genetic sequence data bank with on-line access. Data can also be obtained on floppy disks for IBM and compatibles and on magnetic tape for larger computers.

GenBank is a federally funded central repository of all reported nucleotide sequence data.

GenBank, c/o IntelliGenetics, Inc., 700 East El Camino Real, Mountain View, CA 94040. Distribution Information: (415) 962–7364. Data Submission Information: (505) 665–2177.

Sequences may be entered online via the GenBank online service (415) 962–7364 or through the NIH supported BIONET resource (415) 962–7337.

Author entry software on floppy disks should be available by early 1989. For more information about such access, call (415) 962–7364.

INTERNATIONAL DICTIONARY OF MEDICINE AND BIOLOGY

John Wiley and Sons, Inc., 605 Third Ave., New York, NY, 10158; (212) 850–6000.

JAPAN TECHNOLOGY FILE

DIALOG

English abstracts of about 80,000 Japanese articles on science and technology; research and development.

Japan Technical Information Service, University Microfilms International, 300 North Zeeb Road, Ann Arbor, MI, 48106; (800) 233–6901; (313) 973–9821.

MCGRAW-HILL CD-ROM SCIENCE AND TECHNICAL REFERENCE SET

A combination of the Concise Encyclopedia of Science and Technology and the Dictionary of Scientific and Technical Terms. Lets you look up a term in the dictionary while you are reading an article in the encyclopedia.

McGraw-Hill Book Company, Attn: Ms. Elizabeth Crawford, 11 West 19th St., New York, NY, 10011; (212) 512–2000.

MEDLARS

The National Library of Medicine's computer-based Medical Literature Analysis and Retrieval System. A vast store of biomedical information in a family of databases of which the MEDLINE database is the best known. There are 20 other databases. For information, write to Public Information Office, National Library of Medicine, Bethesda, MD 20894.

MEDLINE

Index to articles in over 3,200 journals. (Essentially an online version of *Index Medicus.*

Check at your institutional library or call BRS/Colleague (212) 247–7770; Cambridge Scientific Abst. (301) 951–1400; DIALOG (415) 858–3742; EBSCO (213) 530–7533; Horizon (213) 479–4966; On-line Research (212) 408–3311; Silver Platter (617) 239–0306.

For information about obtaining matching funds for students and hospital housestaff, call PaperChase, Beth Israel Hospital, Boston; (800) 722–2075.

SciSEARCH

Online version of Science Citation Index.

Institute for Scientific Information, 3501 Market St., Philadelphia, PA 19104; (800) 523–1850; (215) 386–0100.

SUPERINDEX

BRS

Indexes of 2,000 reference books in science, engineering and medicine.

Supersearch, Inc., 2000 Corporate Blvd., NW, Boca Raton, FL 33431; (518) 783–1161.

Other sources of technology search and/or document services

[The information in this sub-section is taken from pages 11-12 of PHS 88–2, *Omnibus Solicitation of the Public Health Service for Small Business Innovation Research (SBIR) Grant Applications,* U.S. Government Printing Office: 1988–199–953: 32372 and pages 12–13 of NSF 88–8, *NSF Program Solicitation, Small Business Innovation.Research (SBIR),* OMB No. 3145-0058.]

Information retrieval services are available via Regional Medical Libraries and academic and health science libraries throughout the United States through a network supported by the National Library of Medicine. A list of Regional Medical Libraries and information about network services may be obtained from the Public Information Office, National Library of Medicine, Bethesda, MD 20894; (301) 496–6308.

Other organizations that provide search and/or document services:

Aerospace Research Applications Center
P.O. Box 647
Indianapolis, IN 46223
(317) 264–4644

Defense Technical Information Center
ATTN: SBIR
Building 5, Cameron Station
Alexandria, VA 22304–6145
(800) 368–5211
(202) 274–6902/03

Kerr Industrial Applications Center.
Southeastern Oklahoma State University
Durant, OK 74701
(405) 924–6822

NASA/Florida State Technology Applications Center
State University System of Florida
500 Weil Hall
Gainesville, FL 32611
(904) 392–6626

NASA Industrial Applications Center
University of Pittsburgh
701 LIS Building
Pittsburgh, PA 15260
(412) 624–5211

NASA Industrial Applications Center
University of Southern California
3716 S. Hope Street, #200
Los Angeles, CA 90007
(213) 743–6132

NASA/UK Technology Applications Programs
University of Kentucky
109 Kinkead Hall
Lexington, KY 40506–0057
(606) 257–6322

National Technical Information Service
5285 Port Royal Road
Springfield, VA 22161
(703) 487–4600

NERAC
Mansfield Professional Park
Storrs, CT 06268
(203) 429–3000

North Carolina Science and Technology Research Center
Post Office Box 12235
Research Triangle Park, NC 27709
(919) 549–0671

NSF Research Reports
Capital Systems Group, Inc
1803 Research Boulevard
Rockville, MD 20850
(301) 762–1200

Software

Watch for software programs—for microcomputers and larger computers—that may be of help in your research, in writing grant proposals and research papers, in managing grant and laboratory budgets and in other research-related needs.

There are many more programs available than those listed here and new programs to meet a variety of specific needs are emerging rapidly. I am not endorsing or recommending the software programs listed below. I am only calling them to your attention should you wish to investigate whether they might be of help to you. The programs listed here are not necessarily the best programs in their category.

Word processing programs, other than those specifically dedicated to scientific writing, are not included; they are too numerous to mention and I assume that by now most readers have access to a general word processor.

Spelling checkers are also too numerous to include in this appendix. Many spelling checkers are included in word processing programs. Spelling checkers for the Apple Macintosh were reviewed in Macworld Magazine, October, 1987. Spelling checkers for the IBM PC were reviewed in PC Magazine, October 13, 1987.

The prices given below, are as of summer, 1987, and are included only as a rough guide. All prices are subject to change without notice. Many software programs can be purchased at substantial discounts from the list price at local stores or mail order houses. Here are a few mail order houses that I have found useful:

Diskette Connection	(800) 451–1849
The Diskette Gazette	(800) 222–6032
In California:	(800) 262–6660
Icon Review	(800) 228–8910
In California:	(800) 824–8175
The Mac Connection	(800) Mac–Lisa

Watch your professional journals for programs that may meet your needs.

You may also want to check your library for a quarterly periodical, *Science Software*, which contains reviews of science-related software. Available from John Wiley and Sons, Subscription Dept. 7–6909, 605 Third Ave., New York, NY 10158–0012; (800) 526–5368; (212) 692–6026.

See also, McKiney, K.M., *Productivity Tools for the Nonprogramming Chemist,* American Laboratory, Vol. 20 #3, 94–99.

ACTA

Outline Processor for the Apple Macintosh (Desk accessory). Convenient and easy to learn.

Symmetry Corp., 761 East University Drive, Mesa, AR 85203; (602) 844–2199.

Under $50.

AUTOBIBLIO

Bibliographic storage and retrieval system for the Apple Macintosh.

Biosoft, P.O. Box 580, Milltown, NJ, 08850; (201) 613–9013.

$199. Demo disk: $20.

CORRECTEXT

Grammar checker for a variety of computers. (CorrecText will be available in mid 1988.) Aimed at writers of business and technical documents. Flags discontinuities, subject-verb disagreement, redundancies, ambiguous words, split infinitives, and incorrect spelling and punctuation.

Houghton Mifflin Business Software Division, 1 Beacon St., Boston, MA; (617) 725–5000.

DOUG CLAPP'S WORDTOOLS

Electronic editor for the Apple Macintosh. Checks punctuation and style, finds long sentences and paragraphs. Catches vague words and clichés. Does character, word, sentence and paragraph count. Tells how many times each word has appeared in your text. Program reads Macwrite, Microsoft Word 1.0 and text files; it does not read Microsoft Word 3.0/3.01 and has a number of other limitations. (See review in Macworld, September, 1987, pages 162–163.)

Aegis Development, 2210 Wilshire Blvd., # 277, Santa Monica, CA 90403; (800) 345–9871; (213) 392–9972.

Under $80.

GRAMMATIK II

Grammar and style checker for the IBM PC.

Reference Software., 330 Townsend St., Suite 123, San Francisco, CA, 94107; (800) 872–9933; (415) 541–0222.

$89.

GRAMMATIK III will be available in August, 1988.

GRANT ACCOUNTANT

Grant-Fund accounting and Ordering.

Software for the IBM PC and compatibles; will be available for Apple Macintosh in 1988.

Research Information Systems, 1991 Village Park Way, Suite 206, Encinitas, CA 92024; (800) 722–1227; (619) 753–3914.

Trial package: $49; can manage 2 grants and limited number of employees and purchase orders, etc.; complete package: $295.

GRANT MANAGER

Grant-Fund accounting and Ordering.

Software for the IBM PC and Apple Macintosh.

Niles and Associates, 1545 Scenic Ave., Berkeley, CA 94708.

$425.

MANUSCRIPT MANAGER

A word-processing program (for the IBM PC and Apple II series) dedicated to scientific manuscript preparation. Program automates insertion of references and citations, footnotes, heading levels, as well as positioning of tables, figures, equations, and the abstract. Available in CBE or APA style.

Available from Pergamon Software, Maxwell House, Fairview Park, Elmsford, NY 10523–9982; (914) 592–7700.

Demo disk: $10; complete package: $175 to $225.

MEDICAL RESEARCH TIME-ORIENTED DATABASE (MR-TOD)

This is a microcomputer adaptation (for the IBM PC and

compatibles) of a mainframe program called CLINFO. It is a database management package for storage, retrieval, and analysis of medical (or other) research data. The program can mathematically manipulate, statistically analyze, and graphically display your data.

Available from Retriever Data Systems, 1102 33rd Ave. South, Seattle WA 98144; (206) 324–2203.

Demo disk available; complete package: $995.

NIH GRANT RO1 APPLICATION PROTOTYPE SOFTWARE PROGRAM

Computer program for Macintosh, IBM and IBM compatibles under development at NIH for computerization of grant application submission. See description in main text of this book, under "Mailing the Application."

Trial floppy disks of the prototype program for IBM or Macintosh are available from Mr. Richard J. Feldmann, DCRT, NIH, Bldg. 12A, Room 2008, Bethesda, MD 20892.

REFBASE

Database program to handle personal reference database needs. For IBM PC; available for Macintosh in 1988. Compatible with popular word processing programs.

DataChip Corporation, 5624 Pierce Street, Omaha, NE 68106; (402) 553–4333.

Demo disk and tutorial: $5; complete program: $150.

REFERENCE MANAGER

Reference management system. Can store up to 2 million references; you can edit, retrieve, format for different journals, etc.

Software for the IBM PC and compatibles; will be available for Apple Macintosh in 1988.

Research Information Systems, 1991 Village Park Way, Suite 206, Encinitas, CA 92024; (800) 722–1227; (619) 753–3914.

Price varies according to capacity.

REFERENCE GATEWAY

Reference management system. Can store references; you can edit, retrieve, format for different journals, etc.

Software for the IBM PC and compatibles; will be available for Apple Macintosh in the future.

G.S. Sales Corporation. P.O. Box 187, Cochituate, MA 01778.

Demo diskette: $18; complete package: $195.

THE REFERENCE SET

Electronic thesaurus for the IBM PC.

Reference Software., 330 Townsend St., Suite 123, San Francisco, CA, 94107; (800) 872–9933; (415) 541–0222.

$89.

REFERENCE UPDATE

Subscribers receive, weekly, a floppy disk containing the tables of contents from current issues of more than 300 major journals of biology and medicine. Allows user to search for any combination of authors, words in titles and/or journal names. Can reprint request cards supplied by RIS. Selected references can be transferred to "Reference Manager" database or transferred into a disk file as a Medline formatted text file. Available for IBM PC and compatibles and for Macintosh.

Research Information Systems, (RIS) 1991 Village Park Way, Suite 205, Encinitas, CA 92024; (800) 722–1227; (619) 753–3914.

The price is approximately $15 per week.

RIGHT WRITER

Grammar and style checker for the IBM PC.

RightSoft, Inc., 2033 Wood St., Suite 218, Sarasota, FL, 33577; (813) 952–9211.

$95.

SMART ALARMS

> Reminder program for the Apple Macintosh (Desk accessory). Will remind you to go check on an experiment while you are writing a grant application—or that it's been 6 weeks since you submitted your proposal and you should have received your Study Section assignment. Stores up to 1600 reminders; can go up to 50 years into the future. Comes with an appointment diary program. Convenient and easy to learn.

> Imagine Software, 19 Bolinas Rd. Fairfax, CA 94930; (415) 453–3944.

> Under $50.

THINKTANK

> Outline processor for the Apple Macintosh and IBM PC.

> Living Videotext, a division of Symantec, 10201 Torre Ave., Cupertino, CA, 95014; (800) 441–7234; (408) 253–9600.

> Under $200.

TOOLS FOR WRITERS

> Electronic editor for the Apple Macintosh. Checks punctuation and style, finds long sentences and paragraphs. Compiles word frequency lists. Catches vague words. Finds all forms of the verb "To be." Reports overused articles. Does character, word, sentence and paragraph count. Program has a number of limitations. (See review in Macworld, September, 1987, pages 162–163.)

> Kinko's Academic Courseware Exchange, 4141 State St., Santa Barbara, CA 93110; (800) 235–6919; In California: (800) 292–6640; (805) 967–0192.

> Under $20.

T^3

> Word processor for technical/multi-lingual writing on the IBM PC, XT, AT or compatibles, or IBM PS/2.

> Handles mathematical equations and complex chemical formulas including multi-ring organic structures.

TCI Software Research, Inc., 1190-B Foster Rd., Las Cruces, NM 88001; (800) 874–2383; (505) 522–4600.

Under $600; Demo disk available for $60.

WORDFINDER

Electronic thesaurus for the Apple Macintosh and IBM PC.

Microlytics, Inc., 300 Main St. East Rochester, NY, 14445; (716) 377–0130.

Under $60.

Groupware

IBM-PC

The program called **For Comment** is geared to "group authoring" and is specifically designed to support the interactions of work groups that write large documents (training grants, etc.) jointly. This program sounds like a very convenient way to get help with your grant proposal or research paper. [I read about this program in *The Scientist* (July 25, 1988, page 22) just as this book was going to press.]

In this program a document has one "author," but can have as many as 15 "reviewers" or collaborators, each of whom can add as many as 26 comments to/about a given line of text in the "author's" original text. Each comment is identified by the reviewer's initials and the date of entry.

The program presents the document on a split screen with the original text in one window and reviewer's comments in the other. A swap feature allows you to substitute a reviewer's comment for a piece of original text. You can revert to the original with a single keystroke.

The program does not include extensive editing features, but works with file formats generated by WordPerfect, MultiMate and WordStar; any ASCII formatted text can also be input into the program.

Broderbund Software, Inc., San Rafael, CA; Floppy disk version: $295; Local Network version: $995

Apple Macintosh

A program for the Apple Macintosh computer similar to **For Comment** is called **Comment.**

Deneba Systems 7855 NW 12th Street. Miami, FL; (305) 594-6965; $99

NOTE: The "hidden text" feature of programs, such as Microsoft Word and WordPerfect, can also be used for reviewer's comments, but is less convenient and doesn't provide the "trail" of edits and date documentation of the more specialized programs.

Notes added in second printing:

A new PHS-398 form (revised 10/88) was released in spring, 1989. Revisions from the 9/86 release are minor. The biggest change is on the Checklist page.

There is a new NIH funding component: The National Institute of Deafness and Other Communication Disorders (NIDCD); As of 6/89, a 2-letter (grant) code for the new institute has not yet been assigned.

NIH has just announced the impending electronic availability of the *NIH Guide for Grants and Contracts via BITNET* (see *NIH Guide for Grants and Contracts*, Vol. 18, No. 20, June 9, 1989, p.4). For information, call Dr. M. Janet Newburgh, (301) 496-5366.

Additional Resources:

Gordon, S.L., NIAMS, Westwood Bldg., Rm. 407, Bethesda, MD 20892. Ingredients of a successful grant application to the National Institutes of Health. *J. Orthop. Res.*, 1989;7:138-141.

Trumbo, B.E., How to get your first research grant. *Statistical Science*, Vol. 4, No. 2, May, 1989.

Hawkins, C. and Sorgi, M., *Research: How to plan, speak and write about it.* 195 pp., Springer-Verlag, 1987. 1-800-777-4643.

SCI/GRANTS Search: Identifies granting agencies that support the purchase of scientific instruments. International Marketing Ventures, Ltd., 7211D Hanover Parkway, Greenbelt, MD 20770; (301) 345-2866.

SCI/GRANTS News: Information about granting agencies and foundations. $195/yr. (11 issues). International Marketing Ventures, Ltd., 7211D Hanover Parkway, Greenbelt, MD 20770; (301) 345-2866.

Guides to Grants: Various fields including Directory of Biomedical and Health Care grants, Directory of Research Grants. Updated annually. ORYX Press, 1-800-457-ORYX.

Annual Register of Grant Support, National Register Publishing Co., Macmillan Directory Division, Box 609, Wilmette, IL 60091; 1-800-323-6772 (in Illinois: 1-312-441-2210).

Directory of Financial Aids for Women, 1987-1988. Dr. Gail Ann Schlachter; 375 pp. Reference Service Press, 10 Twin Dolphin Drive, Suite B-308, Redwood City, CA 94065. $42.

Foundation Directory Supplement, Edition 11, 1988; Foundation Center, 79 Fifth Ave., Department QX, New York, NY 10003; 1-800-424-9836.

The Chronicle of Philanthropy; for non-profit professionals. 1255 23rd St. NW, Washington, DC 20037; (202) 466-1200. $47.50/year for 24 issues.

Publish or Perish. Computer program that stores and organizes up to 1000 references; Park Row Software, San Diego, CA; (619)581-6778. <$50.

Cooperative Human Tissue Network, National Cancer Institute. Provides biomedical researchers with access to human tissues. Regional centers: East: (215) 557-7361; Northwest: (614) 292-0890; Southwest (205) 934-6071.

Taped Technologies. Produce videotapes of scientific procedures for training laboratory personnel. P.O. Box 384, Logan, UT 84321; (801) 753-6911.

Journal of NIH Research. News and information about NIH and intra- and extramural research funded by NIH. For information: 2000 Pennsylvania Avenue, NW, Washington, D.C. 20006; (202) 785-5333 (as of 1989).

DATE DUE

OC 23 '91		
DE 03 '92		
FEB 28 '95		
1/16/97		
DEC 1 8 1998		
JE 30 05		

Demco, Inc. 38-293